Justified and
Philosophy

Popular Culture and Philosophy® Series Editor: George A. Reisch

For full details of all Popular Culture and Philosophy® books, visit www.opencourtbooks.com.

Popular Culture and Philosophy®

Justified and Philosophy

Shoot First, Think Later

EDITED BY

ROD CARVETH and ROBERT ARP

OPEN COURT
Chicago

Volume 88 in the series, Popular Culture and Philosophy®, edited by George A. Reisch

To order books from Open Court, call toll-free 1-800-815-2280, or visit our website at www.opencourtbooks.com.

Open Court Publishing Company is a division of Carus Publishing Company, dba Cricket Media.

Copyright © 2015 by Carus Publishing Company, dba Cricket Media

First printing 2015

Printed and bound in the United States of America.

ISBN: 978-0-8126-9876-3

Library of Congress Control Number: 2014955512

Contents

Contents

Gray Areas in a Gray Area

An FX series based on Elmore Leonard's novels, *Pronto*, and *Riding the Rap*, and his short story "Fire in the Hole," *Justified* might appear to be just another Western set in contemporary times. After all, Raylan Givens in his cattleman's hat is more Western gunfighter than modern law enforcement—he's the type of Eastwoodian anti-hero who *might* ask that you drop your gun, but surely will blow you away if you don't.

"I want you to understand," Raylan tells one criminal who's considering his options, "I don't pull my side arm unless I'm going to shoot to kill. That's its purpose, to kill, so that's how I use it. I want you to think about that before you act and it's too late."

But *Justified* is a much more nuanced, much more complex show than that. Not only are the storylines involving, but the characters also possess motivations that are never simple or what they seem to be. There aren't any characters, for example, who are *purely* evil (even Mags Bennett had some good in her)—some are stupid and some are a bit crazy, for sure. On the other hand, no one's completely good. Even Art has an unpleasant side, as Raylan will attest when Art gives him a black eye. Characters such as Boyd Crowder, Mags Bennett, and Ellstin Limehouse commit vicious crimes, yet often come across as sympathetic and, well, human-ly.

Justified resonates with its audience because, at its core, it's a series about believable human beings, not "black hats" and "white hats." And the issues and topics addressed are too complicated to be considered "black-and-white" too. For example, you may think that the rampant crime in Harlan County is wrong, and you would be right . . . sorta. After all, it's corporate exploitation of the people in Harlan by the coal industry that has bred many of the ills, and you find yourself empathizing not only with the desperation of folks in the fictional scenarios of Harlan, but also with real-life coal mining towns where this kind of exploitation is occurring right now.

The topic of religion and belief in a god are certainly not portrayed as black-and-white areas in the show either. Billy St. Cyr seems at times to be genuinely concerned with the souls of the people of Harlan County, and religion offers a way to reform your life and do some good in the Appalachian mountains, but not everything is as it appears. Perhaps St. Cyr has discovered a heavenly way to exploit folks at the Last Chance Salvation Church by lining his own pockets with their Sunday offerings? We also find out that Boyd claims to be a born-again Christian and self-proclaimed leader of a rival church group not to save his soul from the fires of Hell, but to dupe a group of ex-cons into ridding Harlan of meth labs so that he could ultimately control the business. Or maybe not, as there are certain reflective moments where Boyd does some of his own soul searching. Again, no black-and-white areas here.

And, of course, in the Pilot episode Raylan is kind of baiting and threatening Tommy Bucks by giving him twenty-four hours to get out of town or else he's gonna kill him. And when the twenty-four hours are up, and they're both sitting at the table at that Miami rooftop bar, we might think Tommy deserves being shot and killed because he pulled first—oh, and he's a scumbag to boot. However, even scumbags have basic rights and fundamental dignities. If you stop to think about it, killing Tommy doesn't feel very legal or ethical, and Raylan really should have been at a minimum stripped of his badge for such a move, if not tried and convicted. Raylan gets away with it, and there are many more moments in *Justified* where we wonder if Raylan really is justified in killing folks, or if it's straightforward murder in the guise of "cleaning up Harlan County."

We've mentioned just a few of the issues in ethics and political philosophy that are explored in the show with a fair amount of sophistication. There are other topics in epistemology (the study of knowledge), metaphysics (the study of what exists), and logic (the study of correct reasoning) that the authors in this book draw a bead on.

As you read, remember that none of the issues discussed can be considered totally black-and-white; rather they're oftentimes gray. Possibly as gray as the coal-ridden skies of Lexington and the surrounding areas of Harlan County.

I

Vittles 'n' Such

1
Know Your ABCs (Always Be Cool)

JON COTTON

Consider this scene from Season Two's "Cottonmouth." It's Ava Crowder's living room, and Kyle is nervously explaining to Boyd the plan to rob the payroll money from the trailer at the mine they work. Boyd meditatively flips his phone open and closed while he concentrates on the strategy session. Kyle tells Boyd matter-of-factly that he'll be required to kill the payroll manager, Shelby, and Boyd says politely that if he'd known that beforehand he may not be sitting here now. Kyle says Boyd has killed people before, killing is no big deal, don't pretend it's a big deal to you now.

The kitchen telephone visibly flusters Kyle and disrupts their conversation. We've already learned to feel a sense of danger around Kyle. Boyd, across from Kyle, watches in perfect calm from the cushions of his chair while it rings again.

"Well," Boyd says, "I suppose I should answer that."

Boyd passes to the kitchen as Kyle nods to crony Pruitt to follow and watch. By the time Boyd answers the phone Kyle already issues the order "Let's get going," so Pruitt puts his hand on the receiver to end Boyd's call. "Let's wrap it up Boyd!" he says.

"No," Boyd says calmly into the phone while gesturing to Pruitt to grant him a few seconds. "That's just the TV. I'm here all by myself." As this statement preserves the cover of the robbers, Pruitt is soothed and backs off.

Over the phone line we hear some background static and, then, not Ava's voice, as we expect, but the voices of Kyle and his crony Marcus in the next room. Boyd called the kitchen from his flip phone and left it back in his chair as a bug for impromptu reconnaissance.

Marcus asks if Boyd will be a problem. "When he goes down in the mine, we'll just blow him up," Kyle answers, and the two laugh.

As they laugh, a little smile breaks on Boyd's face as if to say "Oh, you humans are so foolish!" Boyd strolls back carefree, as if he's strolling the beach. And we the viewer feel our anxiety for Boyd diminish in face of the mastery he exudes. We don't know what he'll do, but we feel somehow he may be able to handle this bind. Kyle and company continue to treat him like a clueless dolt, and we feel the danger.

And as they're leaving the house, with Kyle's wolves constantly harassing Boyd about one thing or another, Boyd addresses them as if their mentor. He tells them they're rushing too much, they need to slow down and think. "If you want to make a living in this business," he teaches them, "you got to know your ABCs." And with both hands in pockets he struts to the door and says: "Always Be Cool."

Next scene he switches the cash with the explosives and ends up with the money while Kyle and company blow themselves up trying to kill him.

The name "Boyd" is one letter from "bold." Boyd is bold. And self-controlled, charismatic, decent despite his criminality, and intelligent. He is daring and able to get away with things that most people couldn't get away with. I think we'll agree we can sum up these qualities in one word: "cool."

What Is Coolness?

According to a study called "Coolness: An Empirical Investigation," the concept of coolness involves "a detached, effortless attitude defined in part by emotional control and a certain unflappable confidence." But coolness is hard to define. Although it involves some qualities we might agree on, people have different models in mind. We may differ on who we think is the coolest, and through history the images of coolness change somewhat as culture changes.

Also, coolness may include other qualities we can add to the list. For example, being wily, a trickster, a fox, having the ability to gain advantages or information in surreptitious ways, and also the ability to read people. Boyd is wily in the above example. He outwits the bad guys through in-house telephone reconnaissance. He does a similar thing in the episode "This Bird Has Flown." Cassie St. Cyr comes in to Shelby Parlow's office and Shelby asks her if she has anything on Boyd that he can use to bust him.

Cassie was the sister of that preacher guy who died when Boyd challenged him to permit a random snake from the pit to bite him instead of one that Cassie had taken the venom out of. When Cassie gives some dirt on Boyd, Shelby presses her farther, asking if there's anything else. She leaves, and we learn that Boyd has actually listened secretly to this whole conversation by speaker phone.

Shelby tells Boyd that this is his final favor to him, but we feel that Boyd probably used his favor wisely, because we the viewer, I think, really trust Boyd's strategy intelligence. And in general Boyd is really good at reading people; he has social intelligence; he can't be outfoxed.

I think coolness also includes unconventionality. This is probably one of the more obvious features, so it's less controversial as we try to find defining features. If you pick any example of a cool person, it's probably the most common thing for such a person to do things at odds with what is normally expected. But he *gets away with it!* Not only does the cool person "get away with it," but in fact if the new behavior is sanctioned by a cool person, then it may actually become the new fashion. The conventions of yesterday are changed by the cool. Coolness is therefore fashionable. Always.

Definitions in General

Sometimes it's hard to define a word because there's an array of different features that make up the quality the word refers to. People have different conceptions, even though the word itself has a legitimate role in the language and has a real meaning. Even though words have a real meaning, a real use, they sometimes can't be defined by only a single feature.

The Austrian-English philosopher Ludwig Wittgenstein had a way of dealing with this problem. He compared it to a family. A family might show a resemblance among its members so that you can recognize any one of them, but every member has a feature or two that some other members of the family do not have. That's how human qualities like coolness often work. Coolness is a quality of character that involves a bunch of other qualities of character, just as the word "athletic" can include many different abilities. Since there are a number of qualities that make up coolness, you can be cool and lack a few. So someone else might be cool too but not in the same way as you.

Wittgenstein's "family resemblance" model works like this. What does it mean to look like, say, a member of the *Crowder* family? To make an adjective out of this, on analogy with "cool," we'll ask "What does it mean to look *Crowdery*?" Analysis: The Crowder family might have ten members, and eight of them have a similar nose, seven have similar eyes, nine have similar hair color, and so on. So we'll pick only the qualities that enough people have to make it count. If only one member of the Crowder family has a particular quality, we won't include it in our definition of "Crowdery." An artist could then take the list of qualities that defines Crowdery and draw a composite person with only those features, the "ideal Crowder." That would be the definition of "Crowderness."

What's interesting is you have the *actual* Crowder family, and then you have an "ideal" Crowder as an artificial construct, which doesn't exist, but it's *more* Crowdery than any of the actual Crowders. That's what happens when you envision ways to solve problems of definition. You go beyond the actual in order to make sense of the actual. Likewise, there may be no person who is perfectly cool. It may even be that some features of cool conflict with other features of it, so that no one person can have those two together. We can see this in the idea of "athletic." If the athletic person is very strong, for example, then she may not also be very fast. Her body is adapted to her function, which means she can't be ideal for another function that conflicts with it. It may also be the case that the definition of cool does *not* include such internal tensions.

I like to explore the definition of coolness because it's an exciting quality in a person, and because I think the more we explore it the more we see that it's a *good* thing to have. Deep coolness isn't an indifferent quality of character, like liking to watch basketball. It goes deep, and makes a person remarkable—and may be something people should strive for.

So coolness is probably a reality that requires this kind of "family resemblance" type of definition where a cluster of features make up our understanding of the word instead of a precise definition triangulating on just a single quality that can tell us for every case whether a thing counts or not as having that quality. In other words, family-resemblance terms entail vague examples. Not that all examples are vague. Just that with a singular definition there can be no vague examples, but with a family resemblance definition they're unavoidable. When it comes to some of the most important human qualities, like virtues of character, it's impossible to define them rigorously.

In other cases the definition of a term is so precise that for every case we can say whether it fits or not. "Triangle" is an example, and math is a huge relief to some people because there's a paradise of unambiguous definitions. A triangle is three line segments that enclose a space and form three corners where the lines meet each other. With this definition you can take anything whatsoever and rule out anything that's not a triangle and rule in anything which is.

There's another kind of interesting definitional situation where everyone agrees on the examples, so there's no confusion about what a given word applies to, yet it's hard to agree on how to find a precise definition. For example "human." We all agree on who's human and who isn't. But to find a rigorous definition of "human" that is as good as the definition of

7

"triangle" may be impossible. It's not that we can't identify humans. But it's probably impossible to find a definition of "human" as precise as the definitions we find in math and logic.

The definition of coolness is not like the definition of "human" because people disagree on cases. It's more like "intelligence." Everyone agrees there's such a thing, and we can even agree on a general characterization of features. But when we try to get more precise we disagree, and we pick different cases. For example, someone passionately insisted to me that Hitler was "a genius." I had to figure out what the person meant because to me "genius" meant "intelligence, and "intelligence" meant the ability to probe one's assumptions and be able to question them and continually achieve better knowledge through constant intellectual self-criticism. That could be called "philosophical intelligence," and Hitler didn't show this kind.

He didn't critically examine his beliefs and ask if they were true. But the person had a point because Hitler was good at some things. So it made me realize at least that my own operating definition of "intelligence" was not the same as for other people. And maybe by "genius" the person didn't want to imply "intelligence." But then again, we're going to have the same kind of problem with "genius." And so with "coolness." We start to some degree with different conceptions.

"Intelligence" might be easier to define than "coolness" because we might agree on cases better. We all agree that Einstein and Newton were intelligent. And then we can try to figure out what they were like and what other intelligent people are like. But with coolness there might be disagreement both about definition and also about who's cool. In other words agreement on definition doesn't guarantee agreement about cases, or the other way around. But it doesn't follow that coolness doesn't exist. Sometimes a word has meaning and application even when it has a vague core of meaning.

Situations like this bring us back to family resemblance. We try to collect both examples and conceptions and collate them all and hope to patch together a loose picture of the common usage or usages that give the word its power. One thing we can say for example is that Dewey Crowe is obviously *not* cool.

The Uncool

If Boyd is a clear example of the cool, Dewey is a clear example of the uncool. Boyd often makes bold moves and we worry he will fail through unforeseeable consequences. When Dewey makes a bold move—when he *attempts* a bold move—we only smile with pity, and wonder in which particular way he might fail. He has no mastery, can't schmooze anyone, can't conceive future consequences, and is impulsive. So we might deduce that the opposites of these qualities are in the cool bag.

In "The I of the Storm" Dewey can't resist Ellen May when she comes on to him at the bar, and in general, as that episode illustrates, Dewey has no concept of consequences, no concept of other people's motives, or their intelligence, or their abilities. He's lost in the storm. Boyd is the opposite. He may create a storm for others, but he generally knows where the horizons are and sees the storm as a passing phase.

In "I of the Storm" Boyd even offers Dewey money to pay for Ellen just to keep Dewey distracted from getting into bigger trouble. Boyd sees what's on the horizon for Dewey, though Dewey doesn't see it himself.

Later that episode, Boyd becomes so concerned about Dewey's stupid actions he actually calls Raylan because Raylan might be the only one able to save him from himself. This is the opposite of cool. And despite problems of definition, here are examples both of "cool" and "not cool" that we'll agree on.

James Dean is supposed to be cool, and Fonzie, and Don Draper. One thing that definitely characterizes all of them is they stand out for not following along and blindly doing what everyone else does. Some even say Jesus is cool, and Socrates. They might be controversial cases. At any rate Jesus and Socrates were both killed for nonconformity.

Perhaps it's for that reason that we might consider them as cases.

In one of Plato's presentations of Socrates (*The Symposium*), Socrates stays up all night drinking and discussing the meaning of "love" with a group of young people. By morning no one is able to stay awake anymore, but Socrates walks away from the table to start his day unaffected by a night of drinking and no sleep. When I read that, I thought "Hmm, Plato is trying to make his teacher Socrates out to be like the Fonz. He can out-talk everyone, hold his liquor, and has superior stamina."

Socrates used to sit around defining ethical concepts like love, and various ethical qualities of character like piety, justice, and courage. Socrates stuck to ethical qualities, but today we've branched off in our definitional escapades to a much wider array of terms. Today for example we have a whole study called *psychology*, which tries to explore hundreds of features of personality that play a role in everyday life. And there's an official book used as the standard called the *Diagnostic and Statistical Manual of Mental Disorders*. The DSM lists a few hundred definitions of mental disorders.

Coolness as an Ethical Virtue

While Socrates focused only on the greatest and most glittering possibilities of human personhood, modern science has focused rather exclusively on the maladies. A movement has sprung up in recent decades called "positive psychology," which focuses instead on qualities that make a person function optimally instead of maladaptively. You have no doubt heard, for example, of the concept of "flow."

When people are happy with what they're doing and lose themselves in concentrated absorption, that's called "flow" because time seems to flow and they forget where they are for hours on end. In a sense, therefore, positive psychologists are getting back to the tradition of Socrates by providing guidance to people looking for advice on how to be their best. That's how I see the task of defining coolness.

The idea of being the best person we can be, taken in the broadest sense, is the idea of ethics. Ethics is the investigation of what it means to be a good person, or the best kind of person. What are we "meant" to be? Traditionally ethics was embedded in religion, so people who relinquish their childhood faith often think that ethics has become irrelevant, that discussion of values is now rendered philosophically fraudulent. "It's all relative," they say. "If there is no God," Dostoevsky said, "then everything is permitted." This belief was held also by many of the ancients. No gods, no ethics.

Religion Isn't Required for Ethics

I disagree with this. I think ethics can be scientific and not religious. Rather than being based in the will of God, it can be based on things like brain science. For example, Buddhists focus on the virtue of compassion, and studies of their brains reveal various healthy effects. Such investigation can give us insights into our evolutionary past by helping us understand in the present what makes our brain function optimally. In other words ethics fits into the whole picture of science, just as every other legitimate pursuit of knowledge also fits snug into the whole. As the religious domination over science continues to recede, I see this as no problem for ethics.

That's a deep concern for many people. Another concern I have is that coolness is not normally construed as an *ethical* quality. But, as our conception of *virtue* is no longer about obedience to God, it makes sense that it could become more about what makes us function most optimally. And, if you scrutinize the cluster of qualities that make up coolness, we find that some of them are classical virtues themselves, and others are common-sense necessities for thriving in life as a human organism.

Too Cool for School

Sometimes people complain that they learn irrelevant material in school. In recent years it seems to have become accepted that social intelligence is the most important factor for success in life. If you are socially intelligent, you're able to find a good job, find a mate, and work through all the problems of life. If you've gotten a lot of A's in classes, this is not the only indicator of success in life. School should presumably help us succeed in life. So if school's important, then so is social intelligence, which seems to be at the base of the definition of coolness. Coolness means success. I could be wrong about this. I'm only exploring the idea, and I hope you like it.

The word Socrates used for "virtue" is translated as "excellence." For something to be "excellent" means for it to fulfill the purpose of its basic design. By "design" I don't mean conscious or intelligent design. If you're a knife, your virtue is hardness and sharpness. The virtues of a computer are all the specs everyone keeps trying to improve: large storage space, fast speed, good graphics, and so on The chief virtue of a person is to have whatever it takes to function optimally.

Many of the classic religious virtues are still good, but they just don't need God. Take the classic religious anti-virtue ("vice") of *sloth*. Sloth is one of the "deadly sins." Sloth means incorrigible laziness, refusal to make an effort toward your duties or responsibilities. You don't have to be religious to feel that someone who refuses to work and seeks only to collect from the government and sit before the television and doesn't seek to improve his mind or abilities in any way might not be an optimally functioning person. Just as an animal in the forest has certain virtues that define its function and make it "well ordered" and happy, so also do we. It's not only religious people who smile indulgently at Dewey for being an idiot. It's just a fact of our psychology and even our biology.

Know Thyself

When I talk about religion being unnecessary for knowledge, I don't mean necessarily that there is no God. I mean that we don't have to refer to a God when we do our physics or try to figure out the workings of a car, because that doesn't help our understanding of the thing. If I want to know who ate the last cupcake, I investigate. I don't look in the Bible. If I want to know what material the sun is made from, I get a telescope and use all the powers of modern science. I don't consult God. Likewise, if I want to know how I function, I meditate and pay attention to myself and learn what I can through empirical investigation. Call it an atheism of method, not of belief, though there is some tendency for them to go together. I'm not saying I do believe in God either. I'm talking about the logic of the situation.

If Boyd's Alone in the Forest, Is He Still Cool?

Coolness might not be definable apart from other things. "Up" can't be defined without a "down." "Father" can't be defined without "child." "Leadership ability" can't be defined without reference to a few other people. "Love" may not be definable without something or someone to love.

By contrast, "strong" might be definable without reference to other people. But even then someone might ask "Strong compared to what?" The easiest things to characterize without reference to other things are numerical qualities. "Alone." Or "as tall as himself." Every person is as tall as himself no matter who else exists or not. And "alone" is a good example of an adjective that applies to something even though other things are not there. Colors have some independence. Something may be white even if it's "alone in the forest."

But if you consider the definition of coolness you see that it's filled with qualities that require other people. It's a social quality. It's relational. In philosophy qualities that can stand alone are called "intrinsic properties" and ones that require two or more entities in relation are called "relations." Maybe coolness has some intrinsic properties that make it up, but it seems to have a relational aspect. If Boyd is in a forest with no one to hear him, can he still be cool? I guess not. (By the way, the old question about the "tree in the forest" making a sound is asking whether sound is itself relational or intrinsic).

Virtue, then, is no longer what God approves, but what makes the organism healthy and makes it thrive *as that type of organism*. Humans are meant to be cool, at least to some extent. Being cool is what makes us thrive. We're meant to be confident, clever, creative, and courageous. This is what makes us proud and feel good. And that feeling is an indication of health and that we're achieving what we're meant to, so to speak. Just as our hearts are "meant to" beat in a regular rhythm, and our lungs are "meant to" enrich our blood with oxygen, so our characters are meant to be competent and proud. This is a nonreligious view of virtue and ethics.

The Features of Cool

In addition to having a relational aspect, coolness also has a *compound* aspect. It's not just one thing but it's a collection of other qualities. It's defined by a family resemblance type, in which there's no single quality which alone defines it but rather a group of qualities that make it up. If a person is functioning optimally, it will be not only his heart that works right, but also his lungs, his liver, and his other organs. Likewise, if a person's character is in good order, it will not be only one quality, but others as well which are working properly.

Suppose the perfect person. Is there a name for that one quality, the quality of being right overall? Plato seems to explore something like this idea in the *Republic*. The word he used for this is translated as "just." "Just" is similar to "right." So for Plato the perfect person is basically "right." For Plato this quality consisted of being well ordered internally. Today we might use terms like "balanced" or "well adjusted" to get at the same thing. When we think a person is just "right" overall, we also might say he is a "really good person." My point is that coolness involves balance.

Maybe if someone is really, really "right" in the head in every way, then he'll be cool. He'll be independent enough not to be draining and difficult, always seeking approval from others. He'll be competent and confident in his abilities, so I can benefit from his ideas and advice.

All in the Family

Even using Wittgenstein's "family resemblance" model of definition, I'm not sure I'm really nailing the definition of coolness. I'm only exploring the issue, and I know you may notice things I've missed. But another quality I believe enhances coolness is intelligence. To be cool must require some minimum of intelligence. Dewey is pretty unintelligent, and comes out, partly for that reason, as uncool. I think it's deliberate that the writers show Boyd reading the literary classic *Of Human Bondage* by W. Somerset Maugham in Season Two ("For Blood or Money") and knowing various concepts of law and literature. In fact, you never quite know what kind of knowledge will suddenly come out of Boyd's mouth.

Intelligence as a Feature of Coolness

I think too that sometimes really smart characters like scientific nerds come off as a little bit cool because they know what's going on when the others are panicking or confused. I think of Jeff Goldblum like this in *Jurassic Park*. Within the family-resemblance cluster of qualities that make up coolness, intelligence seems able to carry off a bit of coolness almost on its own. Maybe that's because it lends itself to some of the other concepts in the cluster, like competence and a certain kind of confidence and independence of thought, and these lend themselves to composure.

Dewey is transparent, not clever or smart. We can predict his trajectory better than he can himself. Boyd, by contrast, as Walter Goggins put it in an interview for the *New York Times*, "keeps people guessing, because that's when Boyd is strongest, when he keeps people in Harlan guessing." When asked to compare Boyd with the role he played previously on "The Shield," Goggins said that Shane's actions "are reactive, not proactive. Boyd is the antithesis of all of that. He's a guy who more often than not is ahead of the curve." We saw that quality displayed when Boyd outsmarts Kyle. Whereas Dewey is blind to his own trajectory, Boyd actively chooses his.

Goggins says further that Boyd "has to believe fervently in something in order for the universe to make sense," which seems to imply a sort of philosophical orientation (which for me equates to intelligence). In "The Man Behind the Curtain," Boyd makes a reference to his own intelligence. Robert Quarles thinks Raylan works for Boyd, Raylan thinks Boyd propagated this impression, and Boyd says "You think that idea came from me? This is our home, Raylan. I start to turn on my own people, no matter how contentious at times our relationship may be, that's a world that becomes so muddy even I can't fathom it." And he's right. I mean Boyd really does see deeply through situations, their interconnectedness, their consequences.

In "Loose Ends" Boyd's clever enough to get himself out of jail by giving Raylan information about the relationship between Tanner Dodd and Quarles. In "The Gunfighter," Boyd's clever enough to get himself *into* jail (by picking a fight with Raylan) in order to try to kill Dickie Bennett.

And check out this dialogue from "Decoy":

AUGUSTINE: I got to ask. Where'd you get all those teeth?

BOYD: Courtesy of the American taxpayer while serving our great nation in Desert Storm.

AUGUSTINE: Man, I love the way you talk . . . using forty words where four will do. I'm curious. What would you say if I was about to put forty bullets through that beautiful vest of yours?

BOYD: What're you waiting for? [*This line ends on a rising tone.*]

AUGUSTINE: Oh, you're cool, huh?

BOYD: I tried to keep it to four words. You'll allow the contraction as one.

AUGUSTINE: [*nodding to Yolo*] Yolo. [*Yolo hits him and knocks him to the floor.*]

These examples indicate that Boyd is smart in a cool way, and that, therefore, intelligence can contribute to coolness.

Likability as a Feature of Coolness

One final quality of coolness: likability. To be cool you have to be likable. Or at least people have to want to be like you. That seems close enough. They like who you are enough to want to be like you so that they will like themselves better. We like ourselves if we think we're cool.

I Rest My Case (on Boyd)

I hope I've made you open to the possibility that coolness involves a "family-resemblance" collection of qualities like composure, dignity, control, wily cleverness, unconventionality, courage, and social intelligence. The qualities which make up coolness are also qualities which make a person good and "right" as a person. I take Boyd's character as an example that proves my case.

2
Can Proactive Policing Be Justified?

JOHN R. FITZPATRICK

The journalist Radley Balko has for years now been covering the consequences of the War on Drugs and the subsequent changes in what are considered acceptable police tactics. An early example comes to us from January 1992. A team of narcotics officers in Gregg County, Texas, conducted a no-knock raid on the home of Annie Rae Dixon at 2:00 A.M. An informant, according to the officer's account of events, had purchased crack cocaine from Dixon's granddaughter.

At the time of the raid, Dixon was suffering from pneumonia, and as we would expect was asleep in her bed. According to Officer Frank Baggett, Jr. as he kicked open the door to Dixon's bedroom, he lost his balance, and this caused the accidental discharge of his weapon. As a result, a bullet was fired directly into Dixon's chest. She was dead almost instantaneously. The police found no illegal drugs in her home, no guns, and no evidence of any illegal activity. It also turns out that the narcotics team was performing a raid out of its jurisdiction. Dixon's home was not in Gregg County but in neighboring Smith County.

Annie Rae Dixon was eighty-four and a paraplegic.

A Damn Shame

An inquest was held. As is often the case in these incidents the police officer, Baggett, was white, the victim, Dixon, was black. The inquest divided along racial lines. A subsequent grand jury declined to press Baggett with any criminal charges. One black county commissioner expressed the frustration of his community to the *New York Times* as follows: "People can't accept the idea that an eighty-four-year-old grandmother gets shot in her bed and it's not even worth a negligence charge." he said. Balko reports:

> Once again, an innocent person died in a drug raid that turned up no drugs, weapons, or criminal charges. Once again, no one was held accountable, and no policies were changed. And so once again, the inevitable message sent to Annie Rae Dixon's friends, relatives, and community is that dead innocent 84-year-old women are a regrettable but inevitable—and therefore acceptable—occasional outcome in the war on drugs. Annie Rae Dixon was more collateral damage.

The killing of Annie Rae Dixon was justified. Or so the defenders of the no-knock raids would argue. After all, Baggett was just following procedure, and accidents happen.

Time's Up

As the TV series *Justified* opens, we find our central protagonist, US Marshall Raylan Givens, searching the patio of a swank, sunny motel. He sees a man sitting at a table. This is the man Raylan has been looking for, so he approaches the man, sits down, and says, "The airport is a good forty-five from here, but I figure you'll be alright if you leave in the next two minutes." It turns out that Raylan has given the man twenty-four hours to leave town, and that the twenty-four hours is about up.

The man tells Raylan how much he loves Miami, and how he is loath to leave. He suggests he and Raylan share a meal, and how good the crab cakes are. Raylan's response: "One minute." The man seems bewildered. How can Raylan, a law enforcement officer, give him twenty-four hours to leave town or he will be shot on sight? When he tells this to his friends, they suggest Raylan must be joking. Raylan responds: "You tell them about the man you killed, or the way you did it? 'Cause I found nothing funny in that."

The man asks for some slack. After all, he once was in a position to kill Raylan and he didn't; does he not deserve some credit? Raylan agrees, which is why he is still allowed to leave: "Thirty seconds." The man asks how this is supposed to work. Will Raylan gun down an unarmed man? In front of all these people? Raylan scoffs at the idea that he is un-armed, and says: "Twenty seconds." The man is still puzzled, and Raylan says: "Ten." As time expires the man pulls his piece, and is outdrawn by Raylan who calmly shoots him three times in the chest, pausing slightly between each shot until the man drops his gun. We later discover that the man is dead.

And the killing is deemed justified. After all, a man sus-pected of being both a killer and high-ranking member of a drug cartel drew his weapon first. And yet, as with the case of Annie Rae Dixon, but for the use of aggressive police tac-tics, it is not clear that anyone would have had to die.

Proactive Policing

David Packman has defined proactive policing as follows:

> The use of nearly autonomous elite police units that are trained to be more aggressive than regular officers as a response to gang and drug related violence by targeting people they suspect of being criminals before they commit crimes. These units are encouraged to use whatever tactics they can get away with in order to get re-sults, those results being a high arrest rate.

The use of these units and their aggressive tactics is on the increase. And as Radley Balko has argued this cuts against many important American values. Most importantly, many Americans have long supported what is known as the "Castle Doctrine," the idea that your home is your castle and that you have the right to lawful self-defense against those who would intrude upon it. But as Balko notes, in an age of aggressive police tactics this right may be highly diminished. In the last twenty-five years, there has been a growing militarization of all branches of law enforcement, along with what Balko calls "a dramatic and unsettling rise in the use of paramilitary police units (most commonly called Special Weapons and Tactics, or SWAT) for routine police work."

It's becoming increasingly common for these SWAT units to serve warrants against suspected drug dealers and users even when the warrant does not suggest that these individuals are suspected of violent crimes. And these units' usual tactics include forced, no-knock entry into homes in the middle of the night. One estimate suggests that these kinds of raids are becoming increasingly frequent, and now number over forty thousand.

Balko maintains that these tactics are unnecessary with most nonviolent drug offenders, dangerous to bystanders, and often wrongly subject individuals to the extreme fear—can we say terror?—involved in having teams of what do not appear to be normal police but rather heavily armed paramilitary units invading their homes in the middle of the night. After all, many nonviolent drug offenses are only misdemeanors.

Even worse, these raids can target innocents when police are mistaken as in the case of Annie Rae Dixon. And the costs of the unintended consequences of these raids can be enormous and lead to needless deaths and injuries. Once again, most drug offenders are not violent criminals. But in a country with as many guns as ours, entering other people's castles is dangerous business, and the resulting gunfire will be dangerous not merely to drug offenders, but also to their children and other bystanders, and even to the police.

The problem is that these aggressive tactics may work well in theory, but in practice they can go horribly wrong. In the opening scene of *Justified* Raylan's tactics seems to work. He has provoked the man he knows to be a killer and a drug dealer into drawing first, and this killer and drug dealer's death seems justified. But we can imagine this scene going horribly wrong. In the scene our villain draws his gun, but is shot before he can fire it. But we can imagine a scenario where our villain fires off a few rounds, and Raylan misses once or twice before dispatching our villain. Now we have a situation where a gun battle has taken place in an urban, target rich environment. And if one misplaced round can kill Annie Rae Dixon in her home, so could several have injured or killed one or more of the many innocent civilians around the hotel's pool.

But even as Season One of *Justified* plays out, Raylan's aggressive tactics have unintended consequences. The head of the cartel finds Raylan's cold-blooded execution of his lieutenant requires a response. After all, if the police play aggressive one can expect tit for tat from the bad guys. This leads to the gun battle that ends Season One. And this leads Raylan to another aggressive tactic as a response. He kidnaps the cartel head's wounded niece, hijacks a plane, and flies her to Miami to bargain with her uncle. Only on TV could this work out for the best.

Suspiciously

But the second part of David Packman's concern is also represented in Raylan's behavior in *Justified*. Raylan is often pursuing groups of individuals who have not been charged with crimes, but whom he has suspicions or reasons to believe may be engaged in ongoing criminal enterprises. As usual, those concerned about civil liberties will be concerned about police targeting the eccentric because they act "suspiciously."

There are many reported cases of police targeting minority youth because they fall under an overly broad profile. One example involved police placing Asian female high-school honor students on a list of potential gang members. Why? Because their baggy jeans and tight tops were purportedly popular with supposed Asian female gang bangers. The largely white and middle-aged gang unit didn't consider that they might be completely clueless about what teenage Asian girls in general find attractive; this example does give new meaning to the term "fashion police."

There are several examples of Raylan prejudging groups in the series, but his treatment of the Bennett clan in Season Two is informative. Since he's right about the Bennetts, his aggressive tactics, once again, seem justified. But it is often the case that Raylan directly or indirectly gets people killed. And there's an important moral question here. Do we really want to support police targeting and tactics that lead to the deaths of individuals when there is little possibility of the individuals being sentenced to death in a court of law? Do we want our Raylan Givenses and our SWAT teams to be judge, jury, and executioner?

Ricochet

In the final episode of Season Two Raylan finds himself concerned about Loretta. She seems to have a gun, and is headed to the Bennett compound to confront Mags about her father. To gain access to the Bennett compound Raylan kidnaps Dickie Bennett and has Dickie drive him there. On arrival, Raylan confronts Doyle Bennett at the gate, and threatens to blow Dickie's brains out unless he's admitted.

A tense Mexican standoff then ensues; Raylan points his pistol at the back of Dickie's head, and a dozen members of the Bennett crew point rifles and shotguns at Raylan. This ends when one of the Bennett crew, in what appears to be a nervous accident, fires several rounds into Raylan's car. A ricochet catches Raylan in the abdomen; he falls to the ground and loses his weapon. Doyle cocks and points his pistol at the now unarmed Raylan, and suggests he is about to do what he should have done twenty years earlier. As he is about to fire, a bullet hole magically appears in Doyle's forehead. He appears to have been shot by a sniper. The explanation ensues when a large number of US marshalls emerge from the woods with SWAT-team armament. What is left of the Bennett crew surrenders. Later, when Mags learns of Doyle's death she commits suicide.

In retrospect, Raylan appears to be the beneficiary of a highly unlikely outcome. If the nervous shooter had shot differently he would be dead. Ditto the marshall's service not showing up, or not showing up in time to place a sniper. But the real piece of luck was the stunned response of the Bennett crew to uniformly fail to fire into the woods after Doyle's death. One nervous round from the Bennett crew, or for that matter one nervous round from the marshalls, would have led to a blood bath.

Means and Ends

We live in a society that seems to glorify proactive policing and aggressive police tactics. And while these tactics can often be "justified," as Raylan Givens's shootings are on *Justified*, lots of people will be troubled with this the-ends-justifies-the-means approach. Many of the actions that Raylan performs are clearly illegal. But we can further ask: are these actions wrong?

David M. Kennedy is a professor of criminal justice, and an opponent of many of the usual aggressive police tactics. In a discussion of street stops he notes that the law regarding search and seizure is crystal clear: when the police stop somebody on the street they are allowed to pat someone down as a check for weapons. This is justified by appeals to officer safety. But that's it! To go further requires probable cause. But in many crime-ridden inner city neighborhoods, police procedure is to routinely violate the rights of minority young men. This is so common that Kennedy reports officers routinely empty the suspects' pockets, look through their socks, check their mouths for contraband, and none of this is legal. It's so routine that Kennedy reports watching an episode of the TV show *Cops* showing a police officer searching for someone who had stolen some lawn furniture. While searching for the lawn furniture thief the officer runs across a young man he knows, stops him, and goes through his pockets. Not only "totally illegal," but so routine that the officer will do it: "on TV."

Someone might want to argue that given the crime rates in these communities the search and seizure law is too restrictive, and prevents effective policing. Perhaps these laws should be changed. But the current law is the current law! Can the police really be justified in breaking it? Do the ends justify the means?

Ethics basically gives us two approaches to answering a question like this: the *deontological* approach, which requires us to follow rules of conduct that conform to duty, obligations, and rights, and the *consequentialist* approach which looks at the desirable or undesirable consequences of our actions.

According to deontological ethics, stopping the young man who is clearly not the lawn furniture thief, let alone turning out his pockets, is just wrong. If the police don't have a moral duty to respect the law, follow its obligations, and respect the rights of citizens, then it would be hard to argue that anyone should. Under this ethical approach Raylan's playing fast and loose with the law can't be justified, regardless of any important ends that he might achieve.

Applying consequentialist ethics requires us to perform those actions that will produce the best consequences when the interests of all relevant parties are considered. Under this ethical approach we can at least ask whether kidnapping individuals and holding them at gunpoint is okay, as long as these terroristic threats lead to good results.

The problem for Raylan is that even many who follow consequentialist ethics will wonder, when the police abandon the law so flagrantly, whether they are causing more harm than they are preventing. Raylan Givens leaves in his wake a large number of body bags. Did all of these people need to die? And if not, should we prefer a less proactive style of policing?

According to David Kennedy, much of proactive policing is deontologically wrong, and even from a consequentialist perspective it has not worked. Proactive policing has put a lot of people in prison. A recent Human Rights Watch report tells us that since 1980 the federal prison population has increased over 700 percent and in the last twenty-nine years the state prison population has increased 240 percent. For every 100,000 black men in the country 3,023 are currently in prison. (The number for white females is 51.)

While the murder rate has fallen dramatically for the country as a whole in the last twenty years, in the neighborhoods where proactive policing occurs the murder rates have in many cases gone through the roof. As Kennedy reports, at its height the murder rate for the nation was roughly ten per 100,000, and it is now about half that. But nobody lives in the country as a whole; we all live in specific neighborhoods. So, it turns out that the murder rates for many young black men in the worst neighborhoods have never been higher. In a recent year the murder rate for young black men in one high-crime Rochester, New York, neighborhood was 520 per 100,000. If this is proactive policing working, we can only wonder what its failure would look like.

3
The Crimes of Old King Coal

CLINT JONES

Ain't a whole lot of legal opportunity outside of a coal mine.

—BOYD CROWDER, "The Life Inside"

Appalachia has become the mercurial epicenter of the criminal underworld replacing the dense urban centers of the twentieth century—New York, Cleveland, Chicago, Boston—as the enterprising Appalachian hillbilly archetype—embodied by Boyd Crowder—replaces the twentieth-century big-city gangster.

Between the profitability of marijuana due to its current prohibition, the thriving trade in prescription pills, the rising popularity of methamphetamines among drug users, and the lucrative trade in both traditional drugs and illicit activities, Harlan County can represent the seedy underbelly of a world increasingly dominated by a destructive dichotomy. Like the gangsters and gun thugs represented in Harlan County the mob networks that developed in the early twentieth century were incubated in a social milieu of disease, bigotry, desperation, and extreme want. That these conditions persist in Appalachia only serves to underscore the nature of an environment that produces a steady stream of ne'er-do-well characters to carry on the criminal enterprises of Harlan County.

The depiction of Harlan County in *Justified* is one of a community divided between the two possibilities of a meager impoverished existence or a meager impoverished existence with the impoverishment slightly alleviated by a life of crime. Harlan is portrayed as a hotbed for criminal activity with a wide assortment of criminal endeavors ranging from petty crimes to drug running to bank robbery to murder.

While it's easy to imagine that all of these things do happen in Harlan, just as they do everywhere else, the real Harlan has a dynamic that is much more difficult to discern in the way Harlan is depicted in *Justified*: coal.

Justified only directly tackles the problems of coal culture briefly in Season Two, and then only to highlight the aggressive nature of the coal industry's rough-shodding of the citizenry embodied by the fictional Black Pike Mining Co., using the company to explore the exploitation and devastation that is attendant upon mountaintop removal.

Welcome to Harlan

There is much to be said about the insidious nature of the coal industry, and saying those things can make you quite unpopular in Eastern Kentucky, especially since "to think about the commons"—or the people that depend on them—"under patriarchy and capitalism is to utter ideas that we have been conditioned to find dangerous," as Herbert Reid and Betsy Taylor say in their 2010 book, *Recovering the Commons*.

And yet, it is nevertheless true that coal is the driving force behind the impoverishment of Harlan specifically, and Appalachia generally, and coal is what makes it possible to believe that Harlan is a place of continual, and often extreme, criminal activity and violence. Harlan is a place of leveled mountains, abandoned deep pit mines, lung disease, low pay, and dwindling jobs, thoroughly insulated from outsiders—a condition necessary to coal's continued dominance of Appalachia and a principle Boyd Crowder is keen to impress upon those who would exploit Boyd's fellow Harlan Countians. The sentiment is best summed up by Mags Bennett right before she murders Loretta's father saying, as he dies of poison, "You never go outside, Walt. You know that."

While recalling the Appalachia of his youth during his keynote address at the 2013 Annual Meeting of Kentuckians for the Commonwealth, Wendell Berry speaks directly to the problems of Appalachia that make a crime-plagued Harlan believable. In reference to the modern history of Eastern Kentucky, which he describes as "deplorable," Berry claims that at mid-century,

> every town was a thriving economic and social center. Now all of them are either dying or dead. . . . The people in these towns and their tributary landscapes once were supported by their usefulness to one another. Now that mutual usefulness has been removed and the people relate to one another increasingly as random particles.

The thriving economies and social centers Berry refers to were based on social ties that were bound up with ties to the land. Every person was well off even if every person wasn't well-to-do. One didn't need to be rich to be wealthy in Appalachia, but as coal began to choke off other opportunities, decimate the land, and displace the citizenry it became much more important to have money because the support systems that were once the backbone of Appalachia were gone. The fragmentation of Appalachian communities and the dependence upon the coal industry for survival makes a less-than-legal life a viable option.

Coal Culture, or Why Crime Pays

Many of the relationships and several of the criminal capers that take place throughout the storylines of *Justified* center on the relationship between Harlan County citizens and coal companies. We are reminded several times by Boyd that he and Raylan "used to mine coal together" and though Raylan maintains that he and Boyd "are not exactly buddies" the tenuous bond that binds the two together, like most of the relationships that form in the coal dust of Appalachia, was forged in the darkness of Eastern Kentucky pit mines.

Raylan's father, Arlo, it is claimed several times throughout the show, got his start in crime exchanging stolen mining equipment for cocaine. Arlo's connections to Bo Crowder, and the first generation of criminals to cut a swath through Harlan County, are rooted deeply in their shared beginnings in the coalfields. Learning how to apply the techniques necessary for a successful criminal enterprise were learned in the bosom of the coal industry itself.

The coal industry's reign of terror in Eastern Kentucky has a long and bloody history. Harlan County earned the moniker "Bloody Harlan County" in the 1930s when, according to Erik Reece in his 2006 book titled *Lost Mountain*, the "powerful Harlan County Coal Operators Association hired Chicago gangsters and local felons to terrorize miners who were suspected of joining the United Mine Workers of America. The sheriff, his deputies, mayors, even then Kentucky governor Flem Sampson all did the coal company's bloody bidding," which included everything from bullying to murder.

Things got so bad for the miners of Harlan County that years later historian John W. Hevener would be forced to conclude that after a particularly devastating defeat of union activities "the miners were being starved back into the pits." In Season Two Boyd is enlisted by a group of enterprising young thieves to assist in robbing Black Pike of their payroll thus making the coal industry not only a target for their shady business practices and environmental destruction, but also a victim of the very criminal activity their dominance in the region has spawned.

Many of the bonds that tie the community of Harlan together in the show are knotted up in the identity of the area with coal companies. Coal companies have dominated the area and created a culture of dependence that has stifled economic growth and industrial development making the fictive Harlan County believable because when coal is not an option there aren't really any others—as Boyd says, there just aren't that many opportunities outside of mining coal.

This becomes clear in Season Five when Boyd is arranging for the assassination of acting Sheriff Mooney while attempting to clear Ava's name and free her from prison. Sitting on a rural bridge Boyd's would-be assassin confides that he has black lung disease—which he never expected to get at such a young age—which is why he is considering Boyd's offer. Boyd replies, "That's why I left the mines and went to Iraq." Apparently it's safer to fight door-to-door down the streets of Fallujah than to work a coal mine for any length of time.

Where such logic is at work it's easier to see why breaking the law is so appealing even beyond the lucrative nature of the various criminal endeavors—going to prison, or on the lam, or winding up shot, are all much better alternatives than slaving away in a coal mine for poverty wages and black lung—at least crime offers an opportunity to make enough money to support your family in the interim.

Hegel's Rabble and the Creation of Boyd Crowder

Just as the manufacturing industries of the late nineteenth and early twentieth centuries produced the conditions that created a class of people that would voluntarily turn toward a life of crime, coal has had a devastating effect on the lives of the Appalachian populace. The creation of an expendable group of people creates what Georg Hegel refers to as a "rabble," which is the class of people most likely to resort to a life of crime. This is because the generation of wealth necessarily generates poverty and impoverishment for most people, meaning an inability to meet even the basic needs of survival.

Hegel argues in his 1820 work, *Elements of the Philosophy of Right*: "despite an *excess of wealth*, civil society is *not wealthy enough* . . . to prevent an excess of poverty and the formation of a rabble." A rabble is created "when a large mass of people sinks below the level of a certain standard of living

... that feeling of right, integrity, and honor which comes from supporting oneself by one's own activity and work is lost."

Hegel is targeting a capitalist society, or at least a notion of an advanced industrial civil society, whose primary industrial focus is the production of capital. Capitalism requires classes—those who own the means of production, those who manage production, and those who produce—and the class system means there must be a lowest class—Hegel's rabble. Herbert Marcuse argues in 1967 his article, "Liberation from the Affluent Society" that we need to sometimes be reminded of this fact because capitalist societies are societies where

> the material as well as cultural needs of the underlying population are satisfied on a scale larger than ever before—but they are satisfied in line with the requirements and interests of the apparatus and of the powers which control the apparatus. And it is a society growing on the condition of accelerating waste, planned obsolescence, and destruction, while the substratum of the population continues to live in poverty and misery.

So thorough is the individual devastation when social forces reduce a person to the level of the rabble that, according to Hegel, even religion cannot offer consolation. We see this in Boyd Crowder, whose own faith is completely rattled by the realities of his existence in Harlan County. Boyd's machinations are a rebellion against the forces pushing him and his fellow Harlan Countians down to the lowest level of society. Coal companies, as representative of the capitalist apparatus—from their company towns with company scrip, their own bloody history in the region, their exploitation of the people and the land, and their relentless devastation of the area—make Boyd Crowder possible.

Boyd Crowder, Crime Lord

Boyd Crowder's rise to the top of the criminal underworld in Harlan is tumultuous to say the least. But it is through this journey that we are best able to become acquainted with the problems that beset the communities of Appalachia. Boyd begins his career as a small time extremist robbing banks and trifling with outside drug traders from Lexington. Eventually gunned down Boyd recovers from his wounds and seeks a life of faith.

Boyd's life of faith is as transitory as it is itinerant but through his attempts to salvage Harlan from the clutches of evil we are able to see how deeply the problems of Appalachia run. Drug abuse, extortion, corruption and a host of other activities find expression in the depressing environment presented by life in Harlan, and Boyd's life of faith is meant to try to help the lost souls of Harlan find meaning outside of a good buzz or illicit activities.

Once Boyd loses his faith and begins to reclaim his birthright—his father's criminal empire—Boyd's approach to expanding his nefarious business endeavors trades on the notion of no alternative. Boyd becomes a crime lord because working in the mines is his only option and that really isn't an option for Boyd anymore—and not just because he participated in the hijacking of Black Pike's payroll.

Boyd manages to stay ahead of his outsider competitors, be it the Dixie Mafia represented by Wynn Duffy or the Detroit Mob embodied by Robert Quarles. At every turn Boyd is quick to point out that Harlan Countians are self-sufficient, capable, and loyal to one another. This motif is clearly expressed when Boyd pays the entirety of the three-hundred grand to Sheriff Mooney's assassin leaving Lee Paxton's widow, Mara, with nothing but the chance to return back to her home country, and again when Boyd's cousin Johnny complains of Boyd's plans to buy a house in Clover Hill.

Boyd's criminal determination is rooted in his desire to right the wrongs he imagines he has suffered. His willingness to do whatever it takes to bring about justice as he apprehends it transcends the typical understanding most people have of criminal behavior. In fact, when Boyd is dealing with the upper echelon powers-that-be in Harlan County—all of whom have that status because of their affiliation with coal companies—Boyd tells them they may be criminals but he is an outlaw. Outlawry is categorically different than merely breaking the law; it is establishing a different set of codes and laws that will govern the comings and goings of those involved. And so, when Raylan and David Vasquez are discussing Boyd, Vasquez refers to him as a crime lord and Raylan condescendingly asks "You think Boyd Crowder is a crime lord?" to which Vasquez replies, "I can't believe you don't."

It may be difficult for Raylan to appreciate Boyd's crime lord status because, on the one hand, Raylan has, throughout his career, worked against cartels and the Mafia both of which are outlaw organizations or, on the other hand, because having grown up in Appalachia with Boyd, Boyd's activities seem like business as usual. Either way, Raylan fails to understand the dynamics at work in an environment that can produce a man like Boyd Crowder. That is, when Arlo was selling mining equipment for cocaine he was nothing more than a criminal along the same lines that Boyd accuses the Harlan County bigwigs of being, but Boyd is a different breed altogether—one that defies the stereotypes others—outsiders like Nicky Augustine—want to apply to the people of Harlan County, especially the criminal element.

Toeing the Line with Raylan

It seems as though everyone in Harlan has a bone to pick with coal—either from personal experience or through their family history. But if Wendell Berry is to be believed the people in Appalachia live lives that are permanently scarred, not only on the outside, but on the inside as well. Raylan Givens is just such a person as he is continually struggling with his Harlan County heritage. His determination to reject that heritage—as he emphatically claims to Boyd in season one, "Do you understand how I see your people?"—is what ultimately leads Arlo to reject Raylan—but there is something deeper than just a rejection of his lineage at play in the character of Raylan Givens.

That Boyd is a product of his environment is beyond question, but Raylan wants to believe he is not as shaped by his Harlan County upbringing. Yet, Raylan's descent from quick-shooting marshal in Season One to rogue agent in Season Four is obvious as he enforces the law in Harlan. In his 1989 piece titled "Landscape and Narrative," Barry Lopez argues that our "interior landscape responds to the character and subtlety of an exterior landscape," and Raylan's interior is as twisted as the Harlan County he hails from whether he wants to own up to it or not. That Raylan is so well suited to deal with the criminal element in Harlan may in fact stem directly from his interior landscape having been shaped by coal culture throughout his childhood.

Raylan Givens is exactly the kind of marshal one would expect in the twenty-first-century wild west of Eastern Kentucky. He possesses the exact mix of lawman and lawbreaker that so many of the legends of the west embodied. But Raylan's position is an exception that proves the rule. Though he is willing to bend the rules very near to breaking them, his transgressions are shallow compared to the local law enforcement in Harlan. 'Corrupt' somehow fails to capture the level of criminality running through the local law enforcement—a long time problem in coal country. As such, the dichotomy between coal and crime is made even more evident since to make an honest living as a law-enforcement officer, a potential alternative to coal mines and crime, a person has to leave Harlan.

Leaving Harlan is exactly what Hegel would argue is necessary in order to escape the ravages of life in the rabble. The ethical life that Hegel advocates is insufficient to solve the problems generated by the accumulation of wealth and the creation of the rabble. Hegel claims that "the important question of how poverty can be remedied is one which agitates and torments modern societies especially." The solution, it turns out, is emigration. That is, once the state apparatus has reduced a certain population to a rabble the only way to overcome that is to leave, which many people in Appalachia have done. But, while leaving may solve the problems for any particular individual, it also allows the apparatus to perpetuate the situation to its own benefit which is why, we might safely claim, Appalachians have such a hard time fighting against the coal industry to be treated fairly—or even minimally like human beings.

What's more, the fragmentation of Appalachian communities due to emigration from the consequences of coal culture combined with the coal industry's stranglehold on the region, makes many in the region fiercely loyal to coal—a near-inexplicable phenomenon. Yet, Herbert Marcuse argues that domination of such magnitude inflicted on people results in "a mutilated, crippled, and frustrated human existence: a human existence that violently defends its own servitude."

You'll Never Leave Harlan Alive

Harlan County, like many places in Appalachia, is economically depressed, populated by under-educated citizens, and a convenient conduit for a number of underworld goods and services to move between the south (Florida) and points north (Detroit) even as it is also a place where many of those goods and services can be unloaded to willing consumers.

There may be no better way to describe the difficult relationship between coal and Appalachia than the statement Constable Bob makes as he explains to Chief Deputy Art Mullen how he figured out how to get Drew Thompson out of Harlan. Bob says, "Everyone thinks you have to take a plane or a car to get out of Harlan, but that's not the only way: coal train." But the coal train doesn't get you out of Harlan it just gets the coal out. What it doesn't get out of Harlan is the devastation of leveled mountains, ruined communities, and broken families.

As Wendell Berry says,

Local economies, local communities, even local families, in which people lived and worked as members, have been broken. The people who once were members of mutually supportive memberships are now 'human resources' in the 'labor force,' whose fate . . . is either to be 'exploited' by an employer or 'discarded' by an employer when the economy falters or as soon as a machine or a chemical can perform their 'job'.

4
Justified's Message of White Superiority

ROD CARVETH

Being set in Harlan, Kentucky, it's not surprising that *Justified* would be dominated by white characters. The African-American population in the real-life county seat of Harlan is just seven percent, while the population in the county itself is just over two percent.

Rarely Seen

African Americans are rarely seen on the show, and when they are seen, they're depicted as criminals or involved in criminal activity. In Season One's "The Fixer" Raylan is introduced to Arnold Pinter, a bookie and con artist from Brooklyn who, like Raylan, longs to get out of Eastern Kentucky. Towards that end, Pinter informs on criminals for the marshals' office. Art tasks Raylan with trying to give Pinter a $20,000 reward for information that Pinter provided. Pinter hired Curtis Mims, an African-American enforcer from Detroit, to collect gambling debts from customers. Pinter sends Mims to collect a debt from Travis Travers. When Mims goes to collect, Travers talks him into double-crossing Pinter. While Mims and Travers try to get Pinter to divulge where he is keeping his "nest egg," Raylan arrives to see if Pinter is around to give him his reward money. Mims meets with Raylan and says he will pass the money on to Pinter when he sees him. When Raylan leaves to get the reward money, Mims plots to kill Raylan when Raylan returns. Mims is instead killed by Travers, who sees an opportunity to get both Pinter's nest egg and reward money. Unfortunately for Travers, he meets his match with Raylan.

Another African-American character featured in Season Four is Jody Adair, a bail jumper wanted for the murder of two heroin dealers. Raylan takes a side job from his bondsperson Sharon Edmunds to capture him. Raylan finds Adair attempting to visit his estranged wife. She refuses to let him in the house, so he goes back to his car and grabs a gun. Before Adair can get out of the car, Raylan intervenes. Adair declares "You ain't gonna shoot me." Adair is correct— Raylan shoots the steering wheel, instead, exploding the air bag. Raylan takes Adair into custody, and eventually turns him over to Sharon.

While Sharon and her partner, Mitch, are taking Adair back to the authorities, the van blows a tire. A driver, Kenneth Flix, comes across the van and offers to help. Mitch tells him that they don't need help, and then checks on Jody. Flix jumps Mitch and strangles him. Adair then grabs Mitch's gun and shoots Sharon in the neck, killing her. Flix and Adair then drive off. Raylan will later track down Adair, killing him in a gunfight.

With the exception of Rachel, the African-American characters are linked to criminal behavior. While there are many white characters who are involved in criminal enterprises, the representatives of social control—law enforcement—are dominated by white characters. In other words, in *Justified* whites are seen as keeping African Americans in line.

Critical Race Theory

Critical Race Theory arose out of a movement of legal scholars who focused on race and racism as it applied to the law. The essential founder of Critical Race Theory was Harvard law professor Derrick Bell. Bell and other legal scholars argued that while traditional anti-discrimination law assumed racism was an individual and aberrant act, they proposed that racism is pervasive and normal.

Critical Race Theory insists upon race-consciousness in making legal decisions (such as college admissions or voting rights cases) in order to level the playing field between whites and people of color. The notion of being neutral or "color blind" merely supports the status quo of white supremacy instead of eliminating racial inequality. In an effort to focus on outcomes, critical race theorists have shifted their attention from a civil "rights" discourse, which is almost always procedural (to achieve a "fair" process) to one focusing on structural inequalities. The ideas that Bell helped to develop and nurture in legal theory inspired scholars in education, history, social sciences and even literature to re-examine traditional interpretations of race and racism.

There are also a number of ethnic sub-disciplines of Critical Race Theory, each emphasizing different issues. As an example, Latino Criticism, or "LatCrit," scholars often discuss immigration and language rights; Asian-American critical race theorists deal with issues such as the "model minority" myth; and Native American scholars explore aspects of indigenous rights and sovereignty. These perspectives complement Critical Race Theory's critique of the dominant civil rights paradigm—a discussion often framed in terms of "black" and "white."

Principles of Critical Race Theory

There are several central principles that characterize the thinking of much Critical Race Theorty scholarship. The first principle is that racism is a normal part of American society. This principle of the ordinariness of racism—that racism is not an aberrant type of behavior—means that racism is difficult to cure or address. For example, popular images and stereotypes of various minority groups shift over time. In one era, African Americans may be depicted as happy-go-lucky, simpleminded, and content to serve white folks. A little later, when conditions change, that very same group may appear in cartoons, movies, and other cultural scripts as menacing, brutish, and out of control, requiring close monitoring and repression.

Although many more minority group members participate in collegiate and professional sports, studies of sports and media show that overt and covert forms of racism persist. As a result, civil rights legislation and affirmative action laws that promote formal equality may remedy the most egregious and blatant expressions of racism (such as housing discrimination or denial of voting rights), but have little effect on subtle, business-as-usual forms of racism that people of color experience as go about their everyday lives, leaving racism's structural core untouched.

The second feature is called "interest convergence" (or, sometimes, material determinism). Because racism advances the interests of both white elites (materially) and working-class people (psychically), large segments of society have little incentive to eradicate it. Thus, when social changes occur to at least appear to benefit people of color, it is only because the interests of the dominant white society and the subordinate people of color in society have temporarily converged. Ultimately, though, any social change that benefits people of color actually has greater benefits for whites.

Bell argued that the Supreme Court decision in *Brown v. Board of Education*—a landmark case in civil rights litigation—may have come about more from the self-interest of elite whites than a desire to help blacks. Bell proposed that after World War II, the United States had become the primary world power. In order to maintain that position, however, the US government needed to expand its influence over developing nations. One barrier to achieving this influence was the symbolism of legally mandated segregation that existed in the US. So, while *Brown v. Board of Education* got rid of the "separate but equal" doctrine that prevented African Americans from having equal access to a quality education, it also helped the white power structure by elevating its prominence in global affairs. In addition, the inclusion of the statement that the provisions of *Brown* needed to be accomplished with "all deliberate speed" meant that racial progress would occur at a comfortable enough speed to not disrupt the social system.

A third theme of Critical Race Theory, the "social construction" thesis, holds that race and races are products of social thought and relations. The argument here is that "races" are categories that society invents, not biological or genetic realities. While it is true that people with common origins often share certain physical traits such as skin color, physique, and hair texture, these characteristics are dwarfed by that which we have in common. These physical similarities also have little or nothing to do with higher-order traits, such as personality, intelligence, and moral behavior. That society frequently chooses to ignore these scientific facts, and endows these socially constructed races with pseudo-permanent characteristics is of great interest to critical race theorists.

Thus, race is a social construction defined by the dominant culture at a historical moment in time. In the United States, this historically has meant that whites are accorded benefits and non-whites are disadvantaged due to their position in the social structure. Being white (or possessing whiteness) makes one part of the most powerful in-group in society. This in-group defines who is non-white (which includes African Americans, Latinos, Asian Americans and Native Americans) and then denigrates the out-group.

Differential Racialization

Another, somewhat more recent, development concerns what is referred to as "differential racialization" and its many consequences. This concept refers to the tendency for the dominant parts of society "racializing" different minority groups at different times. Historically, by 1940, the Japanese had achieved general acceptance into US culture, at least on the two coasts. Yet, with the attack on Pearl Harbor, these same Japanese were removed to war relocation camps, while African Americans were recruited for the war effort—either as troops (albeit in segregated units) or for jobs in war industry. Additionally, fifty years ago, the dominant economic class in the United States had a great need for Latino workers in the agricultural industry. Now that the US economy is suffering through a prolonged slump, these agricultural workers are illegal (and often "dangerous") immigrants.

For example, the portrayal of African Americans on *Mad Men* illustrates differential racialization. Black characters are there to support white characters, not to challenge their privileged positions. For example, in the episode, "Six Month Leave," the Drapers' African-American maid, Carla, begins to offer marital advice to her employer, Betty. Betty will have none of it—"This is not a conversation I am going to have with you." In other words, stay in your place; you are black and thereby subordinate to me in terms of societal power.

Later, African-American elevator operator, Hollis, laments the death of Marilyn Monroe to passengers Don and Peggy: "You hear about Marilyn? Poor thing." Hollis not only knows that Don and Peggy are part of the dominant white culture that has lost one of its icons, but also relates to Marilyn being a victim of the male power structure of Hollywood. Peggy then observes, "You just don't imagine her ever being alone. She was so famous." Hollis replies, "Some people just hide in plain sight."

Hollis should know—he's been hiding in plain sight to the people of Sterling Cooper for a number of years. Yet, while Hollis can talk to his white riders about the death of Marilyn Monroe, he is silent when black civil rights icon Medgar Evers is assassinated. Maybe Hollis knows that his riders will be uninterested, or even offended, if he mentions Evers's passing. Overall, then, the picture of race as seen through the lens of *Mad Men* is one where oppressed blacks are there to serve the dominant white power structure.

African Americans on TV

Research reveals that African Americans portrayed on television are generally depicted in service or blue-collar occupations, such as a servant, cook, entertainer, musician, or athlete. African Americans are seldom depicted as having a professional or supervisory position in comparison to white television characters.

Many African Americans have negative personality characteristics; they're portrayed as being disrespectful, violent, greedy, ignorant, and power-driven. Research also indicates that African Americans have lower socio-economic status roles on television than whites, as well as possessing lower educational levels. Most importantly, African Americans are over-represented as criminals on television compared to white characters.

Ellstin Limehouse

Ellstin Limehouse is the most prominent African-American character on the show. Limehouse is a butcher and runs a diner in Noble's Holler, where the residents frequently eat. He is first shown at the end of the Season Three episode "Cut Ties." While butchering a pig carcass in his shed, Limehouse reprimands his assistant Bernard for sleeping on lookout duty. He tells Bernard a story about arguing with Bernard's father regarding training dogs. Limehouse tells Bernard that some dogs can learn obedience without being punished, but that others take lenience as weakness and will thereafter disobey you. Those dogs will never behave again if they are shown lenience and have to be killed.

Limehouse suggests that if Bernard can remember and learn from this warning, he will never make another mistake. On the other hand, if Bernard does make another mistake, Limehouse will have no choice but to kill him. Limehouse offers Bernard a choice: he can be punished by having his hand dipped in lye, or he can promise that he will never fail Limehouse again. Shaking, Bernard promises that he will never fail Limehouse. Bernard is then led out of the shed by Errol, who has had his hand mutilated for previously failing Limehouse.

Despite being off in Noble's Holler, Ellstin Limehouse is well-known in the area. He had a past (unspecified) relationship with Mags Bennett, who trusted him enough to leave him the three million dollars she received from selling her land to the Black Pike coal company. Mags instructed Limehouse to give the money to Loretta, a teenage girl she took in after she murdered her father. Limehouse also provided a place for women to hide from abusive husbands. Ava Crowder used to take refuge in the Holler when her husband Bo beat her. Raylan's mother Frances also once hid out from Raylan's father Arlo when he got out of control.

Aside from being a butcher and running a BBQ restaurant, Limehouse is a drug trafficker. In addition, there are at least several folks in the area who "bank" with Limehouse, depositing money and getting information. In the episode "Get Drew," Limehouse attempts to extort a total of $600,000 for the return of Drew Thompson and Ellen May—another criminal enterprise the audience sees Limehouse engaging in. Yet, in "Slaughterhouse," Limehouse has hundreds of thousands of dollars stacked in a pig carcass.

Tight Ship

Limehouse runs the Holler like a tight ship. Decades before, white supremacists tried to drive the African Americans out of the area. Since that time, residents of the Holler have kept a low profile. When Errol wants to take over the drug operations of Boyd Crowder and Robert Quarles, Limehouse objects vehemently, warning Errol that encroaching on territory outside their tight community could bring back the same type of horror from whites as before.

Limehouse not only likes to control business operations in the holler, he also likes to control information. When Boyd Crowder wants to do business with Limehouse, Boyd asks why Limehouse knows so much about him, but he knows nothing about Limehouse. Limehouse replies that it is in his community's best interest to know what is going on outside of his community. That way Limehouse knows what is coming.

Despite his criminal activity, Limehouse has managed to avoid prison. Limehouse is indeed brutal, but he is also cunning. The death of Errol in the episode "Slaughterhouse" serves as an object lesson for those who would cross Limehouse.

Influencing Perceptions

In and of itself, the portrayal of Ellstin Limehouse is not a major issue. Research suggests, though, that the cumulative portrayals of African Americans on television have an influence on viewers and their perceptions about African Americans in general. These negative portrayals often lead to the continuation of stereotypes of African Americans in general. Research further suggests that when there is no first-hand knowledge of African Americans, television images have a significant effect on viewers' perceptions.

Not all of the African-American characters on *Justified* are involved in criminal enterprises. Deputy US Marshal Rachel Brooks is African American, and while her character is essentially a positive portrayal of race, the character is also a bit of a mystery. Over the course of the series, viewers find out information about Rachel in bits and pieces. She apparently spent her childhood in Hendersonville, Tennessee, and was raised by a single mother. Her family later moved to Lexington, Kentucky. While her mother was out working, Rachel was a surrogate parent for her younger sister. Once she finished high school, Rachel went to the University of Mississippi, and later joined the Marshal's Service as a Deputy US Marshal. A car accident took the life of her sister, and though her brother-in-law survived, Rachel took custody of her nephew, raising him with the help of her mother. When office director Art Mullen is shot in Season Five, Rachel is named Interim Director.

We can see that *Justified* is quite similar to other prime-time television series in its depiction of African Americans. From the perspective of Critical Race Theory, *Justified* is yet another media vehicle that, through its depictions of race, reinforces the superiority of "white" over "nonwhite."

When the dominant paradigm of corporate exploitation is the bottom line, there can be no alternative other than the creation of a violent rabble seeking to balance the scales of justice by tipping those scales completely over.

5
Justified True Belief

CYNTHIA JONES

In the first episode of *Justified* Deputy Marshal Raylan Givens is reassigned to Kentucky after he shoots Miami mobster Tommy Bucks. Following his exile to the Lexington, Kentucky office, Raylan tells Chief Deputy US Marshal Art Mullen that the shooting in Miami, for which he is in a bit of hot water, was a "justified" shooting.

Raylan is referring to a kind of ethical, or maybe even a legal, justification. His argument is that Bucks drew on him first and so he was well within his duty as a US Marshal to shoot him. And there's no sense in shooting to wound—if you're going to draw your gun on a criminal, you shoot to kill.

Philosophers have been much concerned with justification. *Justified* is about whether it's justified to shoot someone. Philosophy has mainly been concerned with something that may seem very different—whether it's justified to believe something.

What Plato Knew

Plato was the first to go on record as claiming that knowledge is "justified true belief" in his dialogue called *Meno*. But what does it mean to say that knowledge is justified true belief?

Some kinds of knowledge don't necessarily involve any belief. Knowing how to ride a bike, for instance, isn't a matter of what you believe but whether you have learned a certain skill. We can take it that Raylan knows how to draw his gun and pull the trigger—this is a skill he has learned, not a belief he accepts. Another kind of knowledge is knowledge by acquaintance. You may know a certain person or a certain city.

The kind of knowledge that Plato thought is 'justified true belief' is knowledge of the truth of factual claims. We can talk about whether Raylan Givens, Boyd Crowder, and Ava Crowder know things like: "The working girls at Audrey's need to be watched over to keep them and their customers out of trouble," or "Ava shot her husband Bowden over dinner one night with a shotgun." According to Plato, to know such things is to believe something that is true and to be justified in believing it.

To know some factual claim, you do have to believe it. You can't *know* that "Boyd Crowder believes in God between the time he is shot by Raylan and the time his father Bo Crowder kills all of Boyd's followers at their encampment" unless you believe that statement. Yet merely believing something doesn't make it true. Just because, for some bizarre reason, you believe a statement like "Robert Quarles is a really good person at heart," doesn't mean you *know* it, mostly because it's just not true. So you can only know something if you first believe it, you can't know it if you don't believe it, and just because you believe it, doesn't mean you know it.

It's the Truth!

We can't know something if it's false. I can't *know* "The Earth is flat" even if I really and truly believe it, because it is false—the Earth is not flat. Notice that this is different from being able to *determine* whether a statement is true or false. It's notoriously difficult to ascertain the truth of some kinds of statements, like "God exists", although we can have evidence for the truth of a claim like "Boyd Crowder believes God exists during most of the first season of *Justified*." The evidence for the truth of this latter statement, does not require evidence for the existence of God as this statement is about what Boyd believes regarding the existence of God and not about the actual existence or nonexistence of God. So Plato tells us we can't *know* a false statement because knowing requires that the known statement be in fact true.

But believing something and that something being true aren't enough to know it. For example, I can't *know* "Raylan will die in the final season of *Justified*" unless I have good reasons to believe this is the case. And I don't. Let's say I do in fact believe Raylan will die in the final season and it turns out that Raylan *does* die in the final season—does that mean that I *knew* it when I first asserted it? No. Even if I believed that Raylan would die in the final season and it turned out that he does die in the final season, I didn't really know it. My belief would have to be justified. How can it be justified? Most philosophers would say it can be justified only by good evidence.

What if my friend, Linda, a die-hard *Justified* fan, tells me she believes that Raylan will die in the final season, and she produces some interesting evidence for her belief, including consulting her Ouija board and Tarot cards. Linda's belief would not amount to knowledge, because not just any sort of evidence will do for justifying beliefs, only good evidence.

People often claim to know things because they have a "gut feeling" about them or because of intuition or faith or some other form of "knowing." None of these forms of "knowing" really count as knowledge. There is, perhaps, a possible exception in the case of intuition or "gut feelings" about something, although it's controversial. Sometimes we feel we know something based on intuitions or gut feelings whereas we actually have decent evidence that we either cannot recall or don't exactly know that we have.

Let's say, for example, after Ellen May witnesses her boss and pimp, Delroy Baker, killing her friend following the botched armed robbery of a check cashing store ("Loose Ends"), she honestly doesn't remember seeing the incident because of post-traumatic stress. But for some reasons that she simply can't articulate, Ellen May is just sure that Delroy is responsible. Can she be said to *know* "Delroy killed my friend"?

Some would say she *knows* that Delroy killed her friend because she is justified in believing it, even though the evidence is buried somewhere in her mind, but others might contend that she doesn't know Delroy killed her friend, as she really lacks the evidence. If we assume that her gut feelings or intuitions count as reliable evidence, then she does know it. But the problem is that gut feelings and intuitions are not reliable or verifiable kinds of evidence. Even though she saw Delroy murder her friend, she couldn't be said to *know* that he did.

What Plato Didn't Know

For over two thousand years most philosophers bought into the idea that knowledge is justified true belief. But in 1963, a very short article by Edmund Gettier questioned the justified true belief account tradition by providing apparent counter-examples.

Gettier's article, "Is Justified True Belief Knowledge?", argued that we can have a justified true belief that probably doesn't count as knowledge (or that most people wouldn't agree amounts to knowledge). Gettier claimed, and most philosophers who have thought about this now agree with him, to have demonstrated that justified true belief is not sufficient for knowledge.

Here's a variation of the Gettier example.

Suppose Boyd Crowder is told by a very reliable source that Raylan is under investigation by the FBI for a recent shooting and is about to be arrested. Boyd then confides to Ava Crowder that "A Deputy US Marshal from the Lexington office is going to be arrested today for shooting someone." Unbeknownst to Boyd or Boyd's source, Deputy US Marshal Rachel Brooks has been under investigation for a different shooting and she is arrested that same day, but, it turns out, Raylan is not.

Did Boyd know that a Deputy US Marshall from the Lexington office would be arrested that day for shooting someone? Most people would say no, because Boyd thought, and had good evidence for, Raylan's impending arrest, not Rachel's.

And yet the claim that a Deputy US Marshall would be arrested that day for shooting someone is indeed true, Boyd believes it, and he is justified in believing it because he was given good evidence for the claim. Boyd's belief thus seems to satisfy the justified true belief criteria for counting as knowledge, although we wouldn't think that Boyd can actually be said to *know* it.

Since Gettier's 1963 article, many philosophers have produced similar, Gettier-type counterexamples to the definition of knowledge as justified true belief. Some have taken the route of the skeptic and argue we can't really *know* anything, while others have tried to rescue the justified true belief theory.

The two main ways offered to rescue the justified true belief theory involve either adding a further criterion or re-describing the justification bit in a way that can handle Gettier-type counterexamples. My personal favorites from these theories come from Alvin Goldman and Gilbert Harman, who adopt the path of adding to justified true belief a further condition requiring either the correct causal connection (on Goldman's analysis) between the belief that turns out to be true and some other true claim (so knowledge cannot be derived from a false claim) or adding 'inference to the best explanation' as a fourth criterion (on Harman's analysis).

So, in order for me to know something, I have to believe it, it has to be true, I have to have justification for my belief, *and* the belief either has to follow causally from a true claim (Goldman) or the belief has to be the best explanation for the evidence at hand (Harman).

What Raylan Knows

One of Raylan's strong points as a lawman is his ability to figure out what's going on in a situation—he's really good at understanding how the bad guys work. In many instances, he's pretty sure that someone is involved in a crime, but can he be said to *know* that a particular bad guy is involved if he isn't one hundred percent positive or if he lacks any real evidence that he can articulate? Let's look at a situation where Raylan seems to know what's going on and evaluate his belief via the justified-true-belief-with-something-added theories of knowledge.

In "Over the Mountain" Raylan is pretty damned sure that the Crowe clan is responsible for the death of Wade Messer and not, as Assistant US Attorney David Vasquez believes, that Boyd Crowder is responsible for the death of Messer. Does Raylan *know* this? Raylan clearly believes the Crowes are responsible, it is true that the Crowes are responsible, and he seems to have some good reasons for believing it, but are these reasons enough for us to conclude that he *knows* that the Crowes, and not Boyd, killed Messer?

According to the justified-true-belief-with-something-added theory, in order for Raylan to *know* that the Crowes killed Messer, his belief either has to be causally connected to the evidence or the belief has to be the best explanation for the facts of the case. It seems that the latter condition is satisfied here. After David Vasquez tells Raylan that Messer, who manages Audrey's, was an informant for the US Attorney's office, alerting them to criminal activities of Boyd Crowder, Raylan tells Mullen and Vasquez that Messer is a crappy choice for an informant.

Raylan has a pretty good handle on what Boyd is capable of and assumes, correctly, that Boyd and Messer are playing Vasquez and making a profit from it. Raylan's evidence is the lack of credible evidence that has followed from Messer's "informing" on Boyd. Raylan suspects that Messer is loyal to Boyd and not his new employer, Dewey Crowe, who now owns Audrey's. Raylan thus correctly concludes that the Crowes had more to gain from eliminating Messer than Boyd had to gain—indeed, Messer's death wasn't good for Boyd so he wouldn't have killed him.

In this situation, Raylan is making numerous assumptions, based upon his understanding of the people and the relationships between the people in his hometown. Raylan points to the evidence that Messer has given the US Attorney's office no real evidence to use against Boyd Crowder, along with his understanding of Boyd himself, to draw the most plausible conclusion, or to make the inference to the best explanation, that Boyd is not responsible for the disappearance and the resultant killing of Wade Messer.

So it's reasonable to conclude that Raylan *knows* that Boyd didn't kill Messer. His further belief that the Crowes are responsible is based upon the evidence that they were likely the ones who had been or could be harmed by Messer's loyalty to Boyd. Again, while it's always possible that some hit man from Detroit killed someone in Harlan County, the best explanation for the facts surrounding the death of Wade Messer is that the Crowes were responsible.

Raylan needs more than that for an actual conviction, given the legal requirements for "beyond a reasonable doubt", but he still can be said to know it on the justified-true-belief-with-something-added theory, even if he can't prove it.

Unfortunately, for Raylan, his insights regarding the women he dates do not match his insights into the psyches of the criminal element in Harlan County.

What Boyd Knows and What Chief Mullen Knows

Boyd Crowder has a religious or mystical experience of sorts after he faces death at Raylan's hands. Raylan shoots Boyd in the chest and Boyd finds God. Does Boyd *know* that God exists? As we saw, this one is too much to tackle here because determining whether Boyd *knows* this requires that we ascertain the truth of the statement that God exists, which turns out to be a topic of much dispute throughout human existence. But let's look at another belief asserted by Boyd Crowder.

Boyd, like Raylan, is very good at reading people and he rightly assumes that a fair number of people are completely self-interested and willing to sell him out to the highest bidder. Time and time again, Boyd gets the upper hand on other members of the criminal population, as well as law-abiding citizens, as he always seems to have a backup plan (or at least he always seems to have a few more armed thugs at his disposal). Let's look at two things Boyd seems to know in relation to his encounters with the St. Cyrs in Season Four.

A former religious leader of sorts himself, Boyd finds that the newcomers, Preacher Billy and Cassie St. Cyr, are cutting into the profit margin of Boyd's business ventures (drugs and prostitution) and vows to put an end to their "interference" ("Truth and Consequences"). After Cassie demands far more than Boyd is willing to pay to get her brother to move on to a different town, Boyd sends two henchmen, Colton and Jimmy, to shake down the St. Cyrs. Jimmy is bitten numerous times by the rattlesnakes in Preacher Billy's tent, including on the right cheek, and Colton and Jimmy escape with a dead snake still attached to Jimmy's face.

Miraculously, Jimmy doesn't die from the bites, which makes Boyd suspicious. Boyd suspects that Billy's sister, Cassie, who seems to Boyd to be far more practical than her preacher brother Billy, has been milking the venom out of the rattlesnakes so her brother doesn't die a horrible death from a rattlesnake bite the way their father died. At the end of "Truth and Consequences" Boyd walks into the revival tent and confronts Billy St. Cyr, bringing along a freshly-caught rattlesnake that he taunts Billy into handling, knowing that his sister Cassie will intervene to stop him and confess to milking the venom from the snakes. The two things Boyd seems to know in this situation are "Cassie St. Cyr milks the venom from the rattlesnakes used in the revival meetings" and "Cassie St. Cyr will confess to milking the rattlesnakes, discrediting her brother, to prevent him from handling the new poisonous snake I brought to the revival tent." Both of these statements turn out to be true, Boyd seems to believe them both, and he seems to be justified in both his beliefs. Let's look at the evidence he has for these beliefs.

His evidence for believing Cassie milks the venom from the snakes is a straightforward example of inference to the best explanation. Jimmy didn't die, despite numerous snake bites, and the best explanation for this is that there was very little venom in the snakes. Since Boyd strongly suspects that Billy St. Cyr is a true believer, he rules out his participation in the milking and rightly concludes Cassie was responsible. There are other possible explanations, like the rattlesnakes in question had bit so many things recently that they were all low on venom or that they were members of a mutated strain of rattlesnakes that produce non-lethal venom or divine intervention, but Boyd's belief is by far the best explanation of the available evidence. We can conclude that he knows that Cassie is responsible.

Boyd's belief that Cassie will intervene when he brings a fresh rattlesnake into the revival tent is a bit more contentious, as it relies on someone he doesn't know well (Cassie) reacting in a certain way in the contrived situation. But Boyd's general knowledge of people and their motivations is perhaps the strongest evidence he has for his second belief that Cassie will intervene, which turns out to be true.

Did Boyd *know* she would intervene? Boyd had good evidence for this belief as well, coupled with his talent at swaying people with his convictions, his knowledge of scriptures, and his local charm. It is, however, much harder to say that he *knows* this second claim and I would argue that even though the belief turned out to be true, there were too many possible confusing variables in this situation to say Boyd *knew* Cassie would intervene.

Chief Mullen often gives Raylan a sort of sideways look, seemingly indicating that he knows something about Raylan's shenanigans. There are two different points where the audience is led to believe that Chief Mullen may know that Raylan is involved in illegal activities: the theft of the missing money from the evidence locker ("Blaze of Glory" and "Save My Love") and the murder of Nick Augustine at an airfield in Kentucky ("Ghosts"). Does Chief Mullen *know* that Raylan and his ex-wife Winona were involved in the first disappearance of the money from the evidence room? Does Chief Mullen *know* that Raylan is the insider who was present on the tarmac when Nick Augustine was killed?

In the case of Nick Augustine's killing, Mullen suspects the truth, but he doesn't seem to be sure, at least not until Raylan confesses to it. In this instance, Mullen doesn't actually completely believe Raylan is involved and so he can't be said to *know* it until after Raylan confesses ("Shot All to Hell"). After Raylan confesses, he *knows* it because he believes it, it is true, he is justified in believing it, and it is the best explanation for the facts.

In the case of the disappearance of the money from the evidence room, it is clear that Deputy US Marshall Charlie Weaver is the "real" thief in the end, as we see him driving his new red Mustang into Mexico ("When the Guns Come Out"), but at the end of "Save My Love" Mullen runs into Raylan and Winona exiting the evidence room and seems to suspect something is awry. Perhaps because he just doesn't want to believe that Raylan is involved in something directly illegal he doesn't truly believe Raylan is involved, although he has suspicions. It doesn't seem then that he *knows* Raylan is involved, as again, he doesn't completely believe it.

Do Any of Us Really Know Anything?

And so in the end, what can we conclude about knowledge and can we know anything? Skeptics about knowledge claim that *knowledge* is an illusion and that we can't really *know* anything. Although there are several varieties of skepticism regarding knowledge, they all can be said to share the notion that knowledge, as it has traditionally been conceived, just isn't possible.

Skepticism, like the justified true belief theory, traces its roots to ancient Greek philosophy, although David Hume (1711–1776), a Scottish philosopher, is perhaps the best-known, or at least the most infamous, philosophical skeptic. Hume's skepticism encompasses many areas, but in relation to knowledge, his skepticism typically took the form of doubting whether we can be absolutely sure of any of our beliefs.

Hume's most famous form of skepticism concerns cause and effect, which is relevant to his skepticism regarding knowledge. He argues that the evidence we have for causation is causation, thus yielding a circular and unacceptable proof. Generations of philosophy students have been enlightened or frustrated by skeptics like Hume.

There are many responses that can be given to skepticism about knowledge, but the strongest seems to be the appeal to probabilities and what we have already discussed *as inference to the best explanation*. Absolute knowledge may be reserved for mathematical proofs but inductive knowledge, which is found in scientific explanation as well as the inferences made by detectives and investigators like Deputy US Marshal Raylan Givens, still counts as knowledge.

In other words, Raylan doesn't need absolute, indisputable proof in order to *know* which bad guy committed a particular crime. Indeed, absolute, indisputable proof is rarely found in the real world and it is usually reserved for mathematics. But this doesn't mean we can't *know* things, it just means that we should believe what we have the best evidence to believe (inference to the best explanation) and if our beliefs turn out to be true, and they are based on reliable evidence, then we have knowledge, and Raylan can be said to know a few things—excluding anything connected with the women he's dating.

II

Signs from God

6
Was Boyd Truly Born Again?

MICHAEL D. JAWORSKI

In Season One of *Justified* the shady character Boyd Crowder suffers a potentially fatal gunshot wound and interprets his survival as a sign from God that he must change his ways. This sets Boyd on a journey in which he feels he has been born again to a life of service to God.

The idea that certain happenings in our lives are part of a larger, divine plan is a familiar one. So too is the idea that a particular event might be a sign from God, calling a person who has strayed to reform and be born again to a life of righteousness. Many religious people see key moments in their lives in just the way that Boyd sees his brush with death.

Atheists, of course, don't believe that there's a God, and so they don't believe that any event is a sign from God. Atheist philosophers often counter the idea that an event must be a sign from God by arguing that there's a simpler explanation for the event in question, one that does not appeal to supernatural forces. The basic idea is that simpler explanations are to be preferred over more complex ones, and since we all agree that the natural world exists, an explanation that sticks to only natural occurrences avoids unnecessarily complicating things by bringing in the supernatural. Wherever a purely naturalistic explanation can be given, it is to be preferred, and according to the atheist philosophers, a purely naturalistic explanation of any event is always out there, waiting to be discovered. Boyd Crowder's survival was not a sign from God, but merely the result of the bullet missing his vital organs.

Some religious philosophers have countered this line of reasoning by finding fault with the standard the atheists use to judge that an event isn't a sign from God. The atheist treats the existence of a purely naturalistic explanation for an event as decisive in favor of the judgment that the event isn't a sign from God. Religious philosophers can respond by asking us to suppose for the sake of argument that God did create the world. As part of the creative process, God would have chosen all the laws of nature for His world. And of course He would have chosen laws that allowed His will to be done in His world. But then it would be no surprise to find naturalistic explanations available for most events in God's world. God's will would normally be carried out through the laws of nature themselves; miraculous interventions would be few and far between. So, even if Boyd's wound could be explained in a purely naturalistic way, it might have been a divine act, nonetheless.

Bearing the Fruits of Faith

Rejecting the atheist's standard of judgment for whether or not an event is a sign from God is one thing; finding a suitable replacement for it is another. Surely, there have been people who believed falsely that events in their lives were signs from God, when in fact the events were simply coincidences, and the beliefs brought on by wishful thinking or self-delusion. How can we distinguish a genuine sign from God from a mere delusion of grandeur?

William James, the great philosopher and psychologist of the late nineteenth and early twentieth centuries, provides an alternative standard, one that judges whether an event is a sign from God by considering its impact on the event's subject: does the subject's life bear the fruits of faith? But this approach, promising though it may be, isn't without its difficulties. Some transformations are more complete and permanent than others, so how can we draw a line between the real thing and mere illusion? Boyd Crowder's transformation is messy and impermanent. Boyd's life following his wounding thus provides an interesting case study to illustrate the debate about whether an event is a sign from God, and illuminate the challenges one faces when one attempts to apply William James's standard to get an answer.

When we first meet Boyd in the series premiere, he bears the hardened heart of a man so accustomed to crime that it no longer fazes him. He casually discusses plans to blow up a building, determines that the available weaponry won't suffice for the task, and launches a rocket into a church as Plan B. He then shoots his accomplice in the back of the head simply because he doesn't fully trust the man, despite the fact that the results of a background check are mere moments away.

Boyd's plans go awry when his old coal-digging buddy Raylan Givens returns to town as a federal marshal. Though the two men share a bond from their days working the mines, Boyd recognizes that Raylan is likely to interfere with Boyd's shady operations, and plots to eliminate him. Boyd sends his overmatched underlings to ambush the marshals, and sets up a confrontation with Raylan that ends with Raylan shooting Boyd in the chest. The bullet just misses Boyd's heart, and he suffers a serious but non-lethal injury as a result.

When Raylan stops by Boyd's hospital room to check on his recovery, Boyd asks him whether the shot was intended to be fatal. Though Raylan claims that he aimed to kill and simply missed his mark, Boyd has already decided that Raylan's miss was intentional. Boyd recounts a time in his recovery in which he felt terrible pain, not only in his wound, but in his soul. Boyd claims that he knew in that moment that God had acted through Raylan, guiding Raylan's spirit to deliver a wound that would just miss being fatal. Boyd interprets both the wound and his survival of it as a sign from God that his life has been spared so that he may be born again as a changed man.

Boyd's sincerity isn't beyond question. The audience has already seen him control a cult-like group of neo-Nazis by reciting Bible interpretation so ridiculous that Raylan immediately recognizes that Boyd cannot possibly believe it. But put aside for now any questions of Boyd's intent in telling Raylan that he will reform, and suppose that Boyd genuinely believes that God acted through Raylan in order to transform Boyd's life. Certainly, Boyd isn't the only person, fictional or otherwise, who has ever felt the firm conviction that an event in his life was guided by God in order to deliver a divine message. Throughout history and across cultures, many have attested to receiving such "signs from God."

Even among those whose reports are sincere, it would be surprising to find that all of them were correct. Surely, many desperate souls, in their darkest hour, have latched onto the idea that a divine calling has been issued to them. The emotional instability of human beings in conditions such as Boyd's could easily combine with the comfort and inspiration offered by the idea that one has been chosen by God for a special revelation to give them the false but unshakable impression that God has acted in their lives.

A Sign from God?

What method could we use to distinguish genuine divine revelations from potent but delusive emotional crutches? And can we apply our method to Boyd and his gunshot wound? Should it be considered a sign from God?

Atheists, of course, think there's no wheat here, only chaff. God does not exist, so no event is a sign from God. In defense of this position, atheist philosophers can invoke the history of human attempts to explain events in the natural world. Ancient explanations for the changing of the seasons, the cycle of night and day, and natural disasters, cited the actions of various gods and goddesses. These ancient accounts were replaced by worldviews in which such events were attributed to a single deity, and these in turn were replaced by scientific explanations that made no reference to the supernatural at all. This history suggests that a purely naturalistic explanation could be given for any event, including those that people such as Boyd believe to be guided by God's unseen hand. The atheist will remind us of principles like Ockham's Razor, which advises us to keep our explanation of any event as simple as possible. If Boyd's wound, survival, and psychological reaction can all be explained in terms of natural causes, treating the event as the work of God would introduce unnecessary complication to the explanation.

So, in response to our question, "How can we distinguish genuine divine revelations from false ones?" the atheist's response is that a genuine revelation would have to be inexplicable in purely natural terms, a miracle in the strictest sense. And the atheist rejects the existence of miracles. But is the atheist's standard of judgment fair? Some religious philosophers have thought that it is fair, and sought to show that miraculous interventions into the natural order do occur. But there are at least two problems with the atheist's standard. First, it creates a methodological blind spot in which God, even if real, couldn't be discovered. For the atheist will always assume that there's a naturalistic explanation for any event. Presented with an apparent miracle, the atheist will always insist that we simply have not yet figured out the purely natural explanation for it. The second problem is that the atheist's standard treats facts that are actually *neutral* to the debate as if they are evidence *against* divine activity. This problem will lead us to consider a different kind of standard altogether.

Suppose that an all-knowing and all-powerful God went about creating a universe, choosing its fundamental particles, its laws of nature, and so on, with a long-term plan in mind for its development. Would it make sense for God to set things up so that He could never interact with His world, *except by violating the very laws of nature He so carefully chose for it*? Surely, it would be more reasonable to believe that God would set up a world in which He could give people revelatory experiences *within* the system of laws He created, rather than by violating those laws. And if that's the case, then many divine revelations would occur through everyday events—the very type of events we usually can explain without invoking divine activity. And that reveals the flaw in the atheist's standard. The hypothesis that an event is a sign from God and the hypothesis that the event isn't a sign from God *both* predict that we could give a purely naturalistic explanation for the event. That means that the existence of such an explanation is useless as evidence against the claim that the event was a sign from God. Suppose Boyd Crowder's wound, survival, and psychological reaction can all be explained in terms of natural causes; that might simply show us what a good job God did in setting up the laws of nature so that His will could be done through them!

Mystical Experiences

This last point motivates us to seek a different kind of standard entirely, one that does not appeal to the existence of naturalistic explanations. An alternative standard is provided by William James. In his discussion of mystical experiences, James faces an issue similar to ours. Mystical experiences take place in states of consciousness very different from those we know from everyday experience. The abnormal nature of mystical awareness raises the question: how can we distinguish between genuine mystical encounters with the divine on the one hand, and extremely potent hallucinations brought on by abnormal brain function, on the other?

James considers a complaint against the authenticity of mystical experiences much like the one we have raised on behalf of the atheist against the reality of signs from God: abnormal brain processes, such as those brought on by hallucinogenic drugs, can create experiences similar to those reported by mystics. So, the best explanation for mystics' experiences is that they suffered from a bout of neural dysfunction, and not that they received special revelation from God.

Because the complaint against the legitimacy of the mystics' experiences parallels the complaint about signs from God, a similar kind of response can be made on the mystics' behalf. The brain and nervous system are the source of human experiences. If these were designed by a God who wanted to be able to give people special revelatory experiences, surely that God would include within the design a capacity for the type of brain processes that would give rise to those special experiences. The fact that other, non-divine sources can trigger the same processes, and thus simulate the experiences, is no evidence against the idea that some experiences of that kind might be authentically revelatory.

But if we're not to judge mystical experiences or signs from God based on whether or not there's a purely naturalistic explanation for them, what standard can we use instead? James suggests a standard typical of his school of philosophy, pragmatism: we should judge these events by looking at their practical impact on the lives of those who have experienced them, to see whether and how those lives have been changed. Borrowing imagery from the New Testament, we can look to see *what fruit their lives bear* as a result of the experience.

Paul's epistle to the Galatians contains detailed lists of the fruits of the flesh and the fruits of the Spirit. The former list includes idolatry, enmity, strife, envy, and fits of anger. The latter list comprises love, joy, peace, forbearance, kindness, goodness, faithfulness, gentleness, and self-control. In order to apply James's standard to a person such as Boyd Crowder, we could compare Boyd's ways before and after the event he claims is a sign from the Christian God with these lists from the holy book of Christianity.

Saving Souls

Let's look again at the Boyd we meet in the series premiere. He is sorely lacking in the fruits of the Spirit. He's a downcast, unhappy man who lives strategically rather than compassionately. He's unwilling to tolerate anyone or anything that comes between himself and the goals he has set, regardless of how brutal he must be to eliminate them. He longs for his late brother's widow, he lusts after power, and he resorts to violence at the slightest provocation. Boyd's life of crime makes enmity a constant companion; law enforcement agencies and rival criminal operations are enemies that he must scheme to overcome. In order to feel confident that Boyd was truly changed by a sign from God, we would want to see a radical departure from this way of being. We would want to see a marked change in his overall emotional state and patterns of behavior that matches the spirit of his hospital bed conversation with Raylan.

When we meet Boyd again, he's in prison. He has been spending his time trying to save the souls of other inmates. In a conversation with Raylan, Boyd's primary focus is to get Raylan to partake in self-evaluation. Raylan has come seeking information on his own father's illicit activities. Raylan isn't simply doing his job as a lawman; he's motivated by spite for a man who abused him in his younger years. Boyd turns the conversation to the number of men Raylan has killed, and how Raylan views his own standing in God's eyes. The conversation ends with Raylan admitting uncertainty as to his own righteousness. When Raylan returns some time later, Boyd is pleased to hear that Raylan is no longer actively pursuing information about his father, and will instead try to let go of his anger. Boyd seems to be genuinely pleased, and conveys to Raylan a piece of Christian wisdom: only by forgiving can we be forgiven.

All of that is quite promising from the perspective of the Biblical account of the fruits of the Spirit. Peace, gentleness, and self-control are evident in Boyd in a way we had not seen before. Not only has his own anger subsided, but he attempts to lead others to change their ways, as well. Boyd's outlook and goals seem to be consistent with true faith. His response to challenges and threats isn't to fight, but to convey that human threats no longer matter much to him. All will be well for him in the end, because God is now with him. He's more interested in saving other souls than he is in the human affairs that would otherwise make men his enemies. In one instance, he is lured into a fight with other inmates. But even this violence is a last resort: his Bible has been knocked from his hand, his preaching has been ignored and mocked, and he literally has been backed against a wall. Boyd handles these situations with the patience and self-assurance of a man who understands that the only state of affairs worth fearing is distance from God.

Boyd carries on in his new ways when he is granted early release from prison. Boyd also attributes this occurrence to God, saying that his ministry had gone as far as it could in prison, and now God wants him to continue His work in the outside world. If the story ended there, Boyd's actions would probably be judged to have met James's standard. We would have good reason to treat Boyd's "sign from God" as authentic.

Something's Lacking

Though events sometimes wrap up that neatly in stories, in real life they rarely do. And Boyd's story follows a more realistic path: his transformation appears to be lacking in both its totality and its permanence. For one thing, despite the indications that Boyd has truly changed, others are not fully convinced. Boyd's cousin Johnny expresses uncertainty about Boyd's sincerity, citing the many similarities between Boyd's new pursuit of a congregation and his old scheme to attract a Bible-based white supremacist cult. Boyd's associate Dewey Crowe echoes these sentiments: "For a guy who's supposedly changed, you sound an awful lot like you always did."

Furthermore, Boyd's actions after his release are not always peaceful. He shows a willingness to resort to violence against those who he perceives as poisoning the spirit of the local people. This includes organizing a deadly assault on a meth lab. Boyd cites the story of Jesus turning the money changers' tables as justification for such aggressive practices in God's name. During the investigation of these events, Raylan is asked whether Boyd is "completely full of shit" about having found God. Raylan replies that Boyd is indeed full of it—though Raylan isn't sure whether Boyd knows that or not.

These doubts about Boyd's transformation reveal some difficulties for the defender of James's standard. The language of being "born again" tends to obscure the fact that, in many ways, Boyd is still the same old Boyd. He still has a sharp wit and somewhat ironic tone of voice; he still displays the mannerisms of a smooth-talking criminal working an audience. This points to a general problem for those who wish to apply James's criterion: it is unreasonable to expect a completely different personality to emerge from a revelatory experience. Though the tree bears different fruit, it is the same tree. It grew from the same seed, in the same soil.

No matter how dramatic a person's experience of being born again, there will be a great deal of continuity with the person's former life. Experiences, memories, innate tendencies and personality traits—so much of what makes Boyd or anyone else who he is—remain a part of the person even after a transformative event. Family and acquaintances will look at the person and see that continuity between the old and the new. To apply James's standard, we must sort through what has changed and what remains, and try to distinguish between traits that are evidence of a failure to transform from flesh to Spirit, and traits that are simply a product of the person's history and situation.

In Boyd's case, this task is complicated because of how thoroughly immersed in criminal ways he had always been. Boyd comes from a family of criminals, and he has spent his life learning their ways. We must bear that in mind when we judge his actions involving the meth lab. It's easy to look at that situation as evidence that Boyd hasn't truly accepted a new way of being. An average person who plotted to blow up a trailer with a meth cooker inside would certainly be judged to be lacking in fruits of the Spirit. But an average person has not lived Boyd's life. Violent activities are just part of the normal happenings of everyday life for a person with Boyd's background. For Boyd, such actions probably don't seem out of the ordinary. His idea of "normal" is different from ours. We should consider the possibility that his heart has indeed changed. But it is a changed heart paired with a mind that continues to know its way around the shady dealings of the Harlan underworld very intimately.

Jesus Is *the* Man

Another complicating factor is the Christian doctrine that no person—except Jesus—is fully righteous. Even the person who has turned away from the life of the flesh will stumble at times. Those who consider themselves to be on the path to salvation struggle at times with temptation, with their faith, and to accept difficult events in the world and in their own lives. They continue to have imperfect personalities that include traits that can lead them to bear bad fruit from time to time. If these features are present in everyone, saved or not, what distinguishes the saved from the lost? To answer this question, let's return to Boyd as an example.

I believe that Boyd Crowder did indeed change as a result of his experience. I believe this despite the fact that Boyd wavers in his faith, wondering aloud whether he has just been talking to himself in his prayers. I believe this despite the fact that Boyd eventually embraces an identity as a man who is meant to work in organized crime. I believe this despite the fact that Boyd eventually renounces his faith, having decided that he was fooling himself all along. And I believe this despite the fact that the main characteristic that convinces me that Boyd has changed involves the absence of one of Paul's fruits of the Spirit, peace. Given all of these reasons against taking Boyd's transformation seriously, why do I say he was genuinely changed?

Old Boyd and New Boyd

The difference between the old Boyd and the new Boyd is found in struggle. The old Boyd was cold-hearted and unconcerned with any aspect of his actions except strategic payoff. Even the fanatical Boyd of the meth lab incident shows an emotional detachment from his actions. And though the new Boyd does not leave the ways of the criminal behind completely, the more he wrestles with his faith, the more he refuses to use his street smarts with malicious intent. Even as he sinks back into the world of crime he inhabited before, he becomes less hardened. By the time Boyd renounces his new faith, he has come much closer to genuinely exemplifying the compassion and good will that form its foundation. The old Boyd Crowder and new Boyd Crowder both wield weapons and commit crimes, but the unconcerned sociopath has been replaced by a man with a heart. And it is only upon seeing Boyd genuinely struggling that Raylan finally concedes that Boyd really has changed. Like Jacob in the Old Testament, Boyd has become Israel, he who struggles with God.

The biggest reason to doubt this assessment is Boyd's eventual abandonment of his faith. For Boyd, the key test of faith occurs when his father murders Boyd's entire congregation. Boyd fails to bear this loss with the patience of Job. Instead, he gives in to the thought that everything he has been doing has turned out to be meaningless, decides he has been fooling himself into thinking God had chosen him, and begins to sink back into his life of crime. Eventually, we find him once again thinking in purely strategic terms about the situations he is in. His motives have improved—rather than wanting to control criminal activities for the sake of the money and power involved, he now wants to be able to retire and raise a family outside of the world of crime. But he has returned to his old willingness to sacrifice others for the sake of his goals. For example, he has no qualms about attempting to kill Ellen May, a prostitute whose main flaw from Boyd's point of view is simply that she has information that could damage Boyd and can't be trusted to keep her mouth shut.

A Lasting Effect

One might well wonder whether a genuine sign from God would have had a more lasting effect. Paul didn't go back to being Saul the persecutor, after all. In response to this, I want to point out two things. First, even after his abandonment of his faith is complete, he still seems to be a softer Boyd. He can put aside empathy for the sake of business, but he is no longer simply cold and unfeeling. Secondly, and more importantly: just because a person eventually loses their faith, that doesn't mean they never had it in the first place. The language of being "born again" is problematic in this way as well, for it suggests that from the moment of transformation, the person's status as saved is secure. In actuality, faith must be maintained. Faith is a journey, not a destination, and anyone who fails to be vigilant in cultivating it may become lost again. I believe that is what happens to Boyd as the series progresses.

Ultimately, I believe Boyd passes William James's test. The fact that his transformation is incomplete and impermanent does not show that he was still the same old Boyd all along. It just shows that he's human. He has given us reasons to treat his sign from God as legitimate. Granted, the mixed results we get from Boyd reveal some limitations of James's method to give us precise and definite answers. But pragmatists love to turn questions around on their readers. And James would surely want each of us to consider what we reveal about our own characters by the judgments we pass on Boyd. When we consider people like Boyd, shouldn't we keep our hearts and minds open to the possibility that they truly have changed, rather than dwelling on the things that seem the same? Isn't the best policy a guarded form of hope, a hope that communes with the born-again person's spirit of overcoming dark pasts and finding a better way?

7
Handling Snakes with Fear and Trembling

ROBERTO SIRVENT AND CALEB ACTON

Billy St. Cyr should be a top contender for the prestigious Darwin Awards, joining such ranks as "Low Flying Drunks," "Crutch, meet crotch," and "Firecracker Chainsaw Massacre." These winners, by their called vocations, are "improving the human genome" as they "accidentally remove themselves from it."

Coming from a lineage of street corner, snake, and salvation-slinging preachers, Billy distinguishes himself as preacher of the Last Chance Salvation Church. His charisma draws a crowd of drug addicts, prostitutes, and other spirit-seeking townsfolk who flock to the backwoods tent to see a show that defies reason and hear a message that does the same.

Is Billy crazy to allow poisonous snakes to slither up and down his arms while preaching about freedom from oppression? Does he preach to a particular client base because he hopes to save them, or does he choose this specific audience because he trusts their gullibility?

When Billy's conversion of Harlan County starts cutting into Boyd Crowder's Oxycontin sales, Billy and Boyd face off in a match of wits. Unbeknownst to them, they're not fighting in the same ring. Though Billy and Boyd lock eyes and (seemingly) speak the same language, they exist in different realms. One speaks in a way that makes sense and the other seems certifiably crazy.

With the help of Danish philosopher Søren Kierkegaard (1813–1855) we're going to try to make sense of what doesn't seem to make that much sense. We want to see if it's even possible to understand Billy's crazed faith, or whether he's completely out of line.

Best Leave This One Alone

In the episode "Hole in the Wall," we find Billy St. Cyr brandishing a rattlesnake above his head as he begins his nightly ministry. Loud guitars, banging tambourines, and stomping feet set the stage as he walks among the people, preaching and blessing with a certainty that is almost eerie. His confidence in his own actions and words derive from his relationship to the divine, but it's a relationship that can't be questioned by others because it's entirely subjective. It's all a matter of faith—a faith that has been passed down from his grandfather, to his father, and now to him. Billy's faith-initiated, subjective certainty leaves Boyd Crowder with too many questions and not enough answers. But should we call Billy crazy just because he can't provide adequate reasons for his actions?

Perhaps a little philosophy could shed some light on why Boyd Crowder (and maybe you, too) thinks that Billy's faith makes him plumb crazy. Of course, the type of philosophy that might help us out in this instance would be a systematic, rational philosophy, like the kind used by German philosopher Georg Hegel (1770–1831).

Hegel recognized that faith existed as a part of human experience, but he suggested that there came a point that people should *go further* than faith. Hegel acknowledged that faith *could* provide Billy with a way to have a relationship with God, but if this faith were genuine, it would have to be tested against some objective principles of knowledge. For faith to be true, it could not contradict reasonable experience, and if it did, then faith must be abandoned for a reasonable, objective certainty. By Boyd's assessment, "there are some men who choose to stay in the dark, but there are some men who choose to come out into the light" ("Truth and Consequences"). Boyd made his own move past faith to an objective, rational certainty, because in his past preaching experience, his congregation's "faith was not rewarded and his was shattered."

But who needs objective certainty when you *just know*? Billy sees no need to prove his faith through reasonable tests because he doesn't think that faith needs to give way to reason. Believing this, he's in good company with Søren Kierkegaard. Kierkegaard departed from Hegel's view of philosophy as systematic, rational thought that united all ideas into an ultimate truth. Instead, he approached philosophy as an exploration that began with the individual—the beginnings of *existentialism*—a philosophical approach that is much more comfortable with the paradoxes, tensions, and mystery of human existence.

According to Kierkegaard, Hegel's understanding of philosophy can only take us so far. Reason reaches its limits when it approaches the matter of faith. In *Fear and Trembling*, Kierkegaard maintained that reason "should understand itself and know just what it has indeed to offer." But in recognizing itself, it should recognize its boundaries. Faith can't be reflected upon through rationalization; it can only be understood when jumped into with passion. To borrow a phrase from Boyd Crowder, when dealing with matters of faith, reason had best leave this one alone.

As with many of his works, Kierkegaard wrote *Fear and Trembling* under a false name so that he could later critique or offer contrasting perspectives to his own ideas. In *Fear and Trembling* the supposed author, Johannes de Silentio (John of Silence) attempts to paint a picture of what faith looks like in the modern world, and it is *almost* successful. However, since de Silentio insists that words cannot be used to accurately describe faith, *Fear and Trembling* uses the biblical story of Abraham and Isaac to give the closest approximation to what faith is. In the Bible, God tells Abraham to travel to Mount Moriah and sacrifice his son. Abraham, unquestioningly, ties down Isaac and is about to kill him when God halts the execution and provides a ram to be killed instead.

De Silentio uses this story to critique Hegel's concept of the *ethical as the universal*, and he uses Hegelian categories to force the reader to answer questions about Abraham and faith. Ultimately, the reader has to choose between understanding Abraham as a crazy, illogical murderer, or as a loving, faithful father. Either faith exists in a different realm than ethics and reason, or faith needs to know its place when it's time for reason to take over. We must choose!

Speaking the Same Tongue?

It's obvious why Boyd Crowder becomes maddeningly frustrated when trying to deal with Billy. Boyd wants to bargain with someone who's reasonable, but he finds no one like that at home in Billy. He tries to bribe Billy and his sister Cassie to leave town, but money isn't enough to dismantle their ministry. Referring to the failed bribe, Boyd saunters up Billy's aisle and says to the congregation, "It turns out he's a true believer." But after paying Cassie a visit, Boyd comes to the refreshing realization that she is the 'brains' behind the operation.

Boyd's interactions with the siblings have shown him that they don't really share the same world. To use de Silentio's terms, Billy exists in the religious realm and his sister in the ethical. He knows Cassie can be bought with the right price, and tells her it's "good to know we both speak the same tongue." But Billy is another story, and this drives Boyd nuts. He can't comprehend why someone could refuse a free ticket out of town with a generous severance package. It doesn't make sense.

Boyd's offer doesn't appeal to Billy because he speaks a different language. *Fear and Trembling* shows how difficult it is to explain faith because of the subjective nature of a relationship with God. The person of faith exists in a realm that de Silentio calls the *religious*, and in this realm normal language rules don't apply because they are part of the rational, *ethical* realm. In the non-rational, *religious* realm where Billy exists, faith can only be expressed as a tension. This tension exists because faith is an interaction between a finite creature and an infinite God.

For Kierkegaard, faith exists not inside the rational realm but in the paradoxical realms of "eternal happiness by suffering, the certitude of faith by uncertainty, easiness by difficulty, truth by absurdity." It simply doesn't make rational sense. But the difficulty in talking about faith doesn't stop de Silentio from at least *trying* to give us a snapshot of the life of faith.

Faith is absurd. At least, that's how de Silentio describes the internal, contradictory, movement of faith. Abraham believes with certainty that God demands Isaac's life, but *at the very same time*, he believes that God will spare his life. Abraham's internal action is a "double movement" because he first *gives up Isaac* then he takes a leap of faith to *get Isaac back*. It's an internal, paradoxical movement—one that doesn't make sense—a movement that is absurd. To accomplish this movement of faith, Abraham had to submit himself to God's demand, even though by doing so he gave up his son Isaac—the most important thing in his life.

Billy's insanity—or fearlessness—might make a little bit more sense if we look at it in light of Abraham's movements of faith. Billy dangles snakes because he has fully resigned himself to giving up his own life. Even though he's ready to have venom coursing through his veins, he believes *at the very same time*, that his life will not be taken from him. His outward expression of fearlessness comes from this paradoxical absurdity. But this fearlessness doesn't make sense to Boyd. It doesn't logically make sense to believe at the same time that you can die and not die.

Hegel approached faith as a matter that needed to be reflected upon through disinterested, intellectual, rationalization. True faith for Hegel involved believing in a logical system, a system with facts and information piled up to the point where faith just happens as a matter of course. Faith is just belief in accumulated knowledge. Kierkegaard disagreed strongly with this Hegelian approach to faith, which was shared by many Christian philosophers, theologians, and pastors of his day.

For Kierkegaard, it was silly to try to *prove* Christianity's claim about Jesus: "Can any more foolish contradiction be imagined than this, to want to *demonstrate* . . . that an individual human being is God?" Faith is not knowledge. Faith is *passion*. To experience it you must passionately, wholeheartedly fling oneself upon it. You cannot, according to Kierkegaard, wait until it 'makes sense'. Even more, the person of faith cannot expect that the movement of faith will be a one-time event, a one-time leap; rather, it will be lifelong task.

Temptation to Do What's 'Right'

It's one thing for faith to not make rational sense, but Billy's behavior brings up even more questions about the relationship between faith and moral responsibilities. Billy seems to have no regard for his own life, and in a more extreme scenario, Abraham is willing to risk his own son's life. Both men's actions show little to no concern for their communities' social morality. Such an approach to ethics chafed Hegel, who insisted on a universal, objective morality that existed within social institutions. This ethical structure was the highest that people could appeal to when deciding between right and wrong, and reaching this universal, ethical realm was considered the goal for all humanity. Hegel's ethical system did not have room for exceptions that could justify Billy and Abraham's actions.

Billy acknowledges that he has a calling to a higher power or duty. In "Hole in the Wall," he claims that "it was the Lord who saw fit to have me continue my ministry" after surviving two previous snakebites. Billy understands his survival to be a confirmation that God approves of his ministry. It's because of this duty to God that Billy chooses to make unethical decisions that do not serve his best, personal interest. His passionate duty to God allows him to forego safety in exchange for recklessness. Preserving and caring for one's life would be the "ethical" thing to do. However, for Billy, the preservation of his life takes a back seat to his snake-handling calling.

Abraham has a similar experience when he chooses obedience to God over the ethical decision of not killing his son. De Silentio forces the reader to make a decision: if you try to understand Abraham in Hegelian categories and judge him against an objective, ethical standard, then you will have to conclude that Abraham is a crazy murderer. However, de Silentio strongly suggests that Abraham is not a murderer, but is a respectable man of faith because of his obedience to God. But why isn't Abraham considered a murderer? What makes Abraham different from some crazy dude who just plans to murder his child? Did "wrong" become "right," just because God requested Abraham to do this task? Was morality thrown out the window? Not exactly. De Silentio suggests that there was a *teleological suspension of the ethical*. In this suspension, the most important concern for the person of faith is not the end result of an ethical decision. Rather, it's your obedience to the higher power that trumps your ethical goal.

Because the person of faith still exists in an earthly community, she is aware of and pressured by the ethical mandates of her world. However, because she has a duty to something higher than the ethical realm, she is tempted to make the ethical choice if it conflicts with the duty to a higher calling. Abraham's temptation was to do the ethical choice of not sacrificing his son. Billy is likewise tempted to make the rational, ethical choice by skipping town and saying goodbye to his snakes.

Part of the private, subjective experience of faith exists in the hidden realm of the temptation to do what is ethical. Abraham can't tell anyone about his temptation to spare Isaac. He must keep that as a private matter between himself and God, for by disclosing it to other people, he would move from the religious to the ethical—he would move it from a private matter between himself and God to a matter that involved a whole community.

De Silentio insists that keeping mum about Abraham's decision to sacrifice Isaac makes him great, but it's extremely difficult to do. Does Billy also feel pressure to keep quiet about his own temptation to stop handling snakes and take better care of his life? Maybe this is why we're told in the episode "Truth and Consequences" that his sister must "sing hymns over him until his brain's quiet enough to rest." If he were to disclose his temptation to stop cheating death with snakes, would his ministry be discredited? Would his faith be genuine?

Game On

Regardless of the similarities that we've seen between Abraham and Billy, at the end of the day Billy doesn't share the same stage as Abraham as a father of faith because he departs from Abraham's example in some significant ways. If Billy's recklessness and Abraham's premeditated murder can be justified by faith, can *everything* be justified by faith? Are religious extremists who justify their actions by claiming a personal, subjective vision from God in the same category as these two? Might someone, following in the footsteps of Abraham, murder his child and somehow be exonerated on some level (or in some realm) because he claims it was in obedience to God or a duty to a higher power?

In "Truth and Consequences" Boyd Crowder shows up for a final showdown with Billy. He comes armed with a snake and the always-reliable weapon of *truth*. Since his appeal to a *reasonable* buyout backfired, his new plan is directed toward the congregation as a "gift that ain't money, it's knowledge." Upon discovering that Billy's snakes are milked of their venom, Boyd decides to undermine Billy's ministry by exposing his faith and certainty as a farce.

Boyd's counting on Billy to choose the rational option—preserve his life by admitting that he doesn't have the faith to hold an un-milked rattlesnake—but he once again underestimates the radical nature of Billy's faith, and he is genuinely shocked when Billy calls his bluff. In a last ditch effort to convince him to admit defeat Boyd says, "You know what, son? I once stood where you're standing now, mistaking my own hubris for God's touch. That ain't religion, son. That's called self-glorification. Best you'd leave this one alone."

Billy's response to Boyd's challenge makes a striking departure from the person of faith described in *Fear and Trembling*. De Silentio insists that humility is required to demand God's help through the movements of faith, and this can only happen when an absolute trust in God comes from an absolute devotion to God, not out of some fatalistic tendency, or self-centered motive. The pseudonymous author even warns against the narcissism that accompanies a false faith. How arrogant it is, de Silentio writes, to be "convinced that God troubles himself about the smallest thing"?

Kierkegaard doesn't necessarily believe that God actually spoke directly to Abraham in the way depicted in *Fear and Trembling*. In fact, Kierkegaard would be pretty skeptical of anyone who claimed to have a direct line to God. *Fear and Trembling* is not meant to provide a *historical* account of Abraham's confrontation with God, but a picture of the life of faith. So, does the Billy St. Cyr storyline provide a similarly accurate picture?

In the eyes of his congregation, and in a crisis of questioning his own faith in God's protective powers, Billy says, "Alright, Mr. Crowder, I will indulge in your sideshow. For it is not with words that I preach, but with a demonstration of the spirit's power. You may have started this game, but you do not get to say when it is over." Boyd's diagnosis of Billy's hubris proves to be accurate. When challenged, we see that Billy's demand for God's protection doesn't come from a humble, absolute devotion to God. What may have began as an expression of faith has now turned into a game he must win. The sprit of hubris, not God, now possesses Billy.

So Billy is not Abraham. But what about those crazy cult leaders who organize mass suicides? De Silentio anticipates an objection to religious extremism based on someone who would read the story of Abraham and "go off the rails and do likewise." He compares the motives of those who would commit murder on the pretense of having faith, and those who *actually* have faith. Three main differences stand out between a person of faith and a radical extremist. First, true faith requires love, humility, and selfless obedience in fear and trembling, things you don't find in violent extremists.

Abraham expressed all three of these aspects in his relationship with Isaac and with God. In a radical way, Abraham "must love Isaac with his whole soul," and "since God claims Isaac, he must, if possible, love him even more, and only then can he sacrifice him." A violent fanatic has no love in his heart, only hatred. A second difference is that the violent extremist tries to advocate or impose a cause or lesson upon others. The person of faith, on the other hand, "feels the pain of being unable to make himself understandable to others," but at the same time "has no vain desire to instruct others." Abraham's difference from the violent extremist is quite drastic in that he has no desire for others to emulate him. Finally, in the second half of the double movement of faith, we notice that Abraham's desire is that Isaac will be fully restored and returned to him in *this* world, but a fanatic has no hope of worldly restoration, only destruction.

Tread Lightly

For Kierkegaard, reason plays a role in life, but its scope is limited. It's not that facts don't play a role in faith. And it's not that faith and reason are opposed to each other. They're not enemies. Faith and reason are just different. According to Kierkegaard, faith doesn't make sense not because it's *against* reason, but because it doesn't *have* to make sense. And because it *can't*. When it comes to faith, we cannot *reason* our way there. "This, then, is the paradox of thought," Kierkegaard writes, "to want to discover something that thinking itself cannot think."

It's only outside the realm of reason that faith is able to exist—in a place removed from the thinkable, the ordinary, and even the certain. Faith kicks in at this point, and a collision ensues between reason and faith: between the known and unknown, between the probable and the improbable, and between the possible and the impossible.

We may never be able to make sense of Billy's actions. If Kierkegaard's right, then faith should not have to surrender to the category of reason. Billy's demise doesn't require us to take a Hegelian approach and "transpose the whole content of faith into conceptual form." But neither should we uncritically accept a finite human being's claim to have encountered the divine.

If anything, Billy's case makes us pause to reflect on the motives of a person who lives his life in a constant, subjective experience of faith. Our attempts to understand this person will be shaky at best. But regardless of how or when faith kicks in, in our own lives or in others, it'd be wise to proceed with fear and trembling.

III

Right and
Wrong in
Harlan County

8
I Did What I Had to Do

CHRISTIAN COTTON AND ANTHONY PALAZZO

We may feel a certain sense of satisfaction, even pride, in one of the show's unusually strong female characters, Ava Crowder, for putting a bullet in her bitterly abusive husband, Bowman, while he sat down to supper. After Ava explains her life with Bowman to Raylan—how he blamed her for his failures and then took out his anger and frustration with himself on her, even causing her to miscarry (which he also blamed on her)—she says to Raylan:

> I got up off that floor knowin' that he was never gonna hit me again. Next night? He came in. I had his favorite supper on the table. Ham and yams and cream-style corn and leftover okra fixed with tomatoes? I waited till he was shovin' food in his face. Then I got his deer rifle from the kitchen closet, and I went in there, and I did what I had to do.

It gets us to thinking: Could it ever be morally justified to take the law into your own hands and enforce a little "extra-legal" justice? Many of us might say (if only to ourselves and even then under our breath) that Bowman had it coming to him or that he got what he deserved. But, getting what you deserve is one thing; having it handed to you from the barrel of a gun is another.

Domestic violence—and its often tragic consequences—is a difficult topic. To help me sort it all out, I, Christian, called on a therapist friend of mine, Anthony, hoping he could give me some insight into the nature of abusive relationships and maybe even my own reaction to this particular incident. We had met as undergrads in college. We were suite mates. We were both into Black Sabbath and religion. He became a professional therapist, and I became a professional philosopher. We've kept up a pretty lively intellectual relationship over the years, and I hoped this would be no exception. So, we sat down one day at a local pub, The Misty Thicket, to dialogue about it.

Pub-lic Discussion

The Misty Thicket seemed an appropriate name for the spot we'd chosen to discuss the psychological and philosophical dimensions of domestic violence. Plus, they have fine food and even better brew. The dying light and chill of the late-winter evening hinted at the coming sunset. I arrived first and settled into a booth tucked away from the growing crowd of patrons. It wasn't long before he made the scene, a black wool coat and muted, multi-color scarf slung across his arm.

"Cotton." That's what he's always called me, as far back as I can remember.

"Tony. Thanks for meeting with me."

"It's not a problem, old friend. This little . . . incident . . . it has you pretty worked up, does it?"

"You watched the episode. Didn't you want to give a little 'cha-ching'"—I motioned with my fist—"when she told Raylan about it? We already knew she'd killed him; but, when she described her life with him and then laid out how it went down? I mean, how common is it for a victim of domestic violence to stand up for themselves like that?"

"It's *not* common for long-term abused women to lash out lethally, but it happens often enough for it to be an issue. Sad to say, the system still punishes those women pretty heavily, even with the presence of mitigating circumstances. Of course, Ava didn't present the most sympathetic of cases: A day after she shot a man through the heart with a rifle, she was ready to nail our hero when he came to her door, and she was vivacious, happy, and seemed very unconcerned over her deed. A case could be made that Bowman 'got what was coming to him'. No doubt there; but the issue that arises here is more complex."

I raised an eyebrow in uncertainty. He continued.

"Bowman was often gone from their home. They had no children. She had ample opportunity to leave him. There are major difficulties that many abused women have with leaving an abusive system. But, she didn't come off as the 'defeated' type; she came off defiant, empowered. He wasn't holding her hostage. He was killed while eating—a meal she knew to be his favorite—not while he was threatening her or abusing her. The fact that she made his favorite meal could be seen to imply a certain foreknowledge of what she was planning to do. She did plead to manslaughter, but it didn't seem like manslaughter. It seemed a planned killing."

"No doubt. She even tells Raylan, 'I got up off that floor knowin' he was never gonna hit me again.' Then she tells him, 'I did what I had to do.' That tells me that she either felt like she had no other options—that it was the only way she saw to stop the abuse—or that she was giving him what he deserved—a just punishment for his transgressions."

"No one could blame an abused woman who was under an immediate threat—as opposed to the diffuse but still dangerous threat abused women constantly live under—

for shooting her husband. But if he wasn't being aggressive, and he was just home from work, and she had total freedom of movement—not injured or incapacitated in some way—that's a less sympathetic case. If she had the spunk to kill a guy at supper, then surely she had the energy to get in a car and leave, go to a protected location, file for divorce, and seek shelter in other ways."

"Obviously *she* didn't feel that way. The fact that she says she did what she had to do suggests that she felt these other options were not feasible for her. Maybe fixing him his favorite supper was a way to get him into as vulnerable a spot as she could, to make him as defenseless as possible. That way, she stood a better chance of 'taking care of business' before business took care of her.'"

"Well, statistics are on her side: Abusive men do tend to kill their partners eventually. But, it takes more than just statistics to justify a pre-emptive killing. Long-term abuse may lead to these sorts of wife-killing-husband situations; but, it's still killing, and before we're justified in killing people, we have to meet certain conditions, and a history of abuse just isn't enough. I mean, it counts in the sense that it lends support to her actions and helps us understand motive. It may even be something we agree with, at the emotional level. The world hates a bully, after all. But, legally speaking, none of this excuses the killing without the situation being legitimate self-defense."

"Set to the side the question of the legal system for just a minute. Not that it's not important; but I'm really here to discuss the extra-legal dimensions of this."

Bullies Might Be Assholes

"Cotton, if you're planning to ask me if I think she was morally justified in taking the law into her own hands and killing him—"

"That's precisely what I want to ask," I interrupted. "But not just that—"

"—I have to say no. She was certainly morally justified to work against his social and legal interests; to part ways with him; to return abuse for abuse physically if she could get away with it, though clearly she couldn't (as most women can't); and to kill him in immediate self-defense. But, as atrocious as beating women and forcing them to live in a state of fear is, I don't believe that a death sentence—legal or extra-legal—is justified. Death's a big deal, a penalty we reserve only for those who have knowingly and willingly taken life in unjustifiable circumstances. Bullies might be assholes, but I don't think we should just kill them."

"Even if the threat of abuse is ever-present and could in any instance—and statistically will, eventually—result in death itself? Even if the victim of abuse feels the weight of necessity upon them, that they have no other viable option to stop the violence?"

"Death's a pretty high-level penalty, and I don't know that abuse should call for it, any more than rape calls for death anywhere in our laws. This isn't to say that abuse and rape aren't egregiously bad things; there's just a social consciousness here that doesn't connect rape or abuse with the need for death. So, I'm suggesting that, morally speaking, taking a life when one wasn't taken, or wasn't about to be taken, isn't quite congruent. And I think that society largely agrees. The harm of rape or abuse—with therapy, healing, and support—can be ameliorated, undone to a large extent. Ain't no undoing death, and we shouldn't be ripping the branches off of trees if we can't put them back on."

"Okay Tony, but let's think about it from Ava's perspective. Why should she—the victim—be the one who's forced to leave? That does nothing to redress the abuse she has suffered. In other words, there's no *justice* for her in leaving him. She may be safer if she left him—the threat on her life if she tried to leave notwithstanding—but, Bowman essentially gets away with it. I'm a solid proponent of the notion that justice in cases of moral wrongdoing requires a retributive response: You have to pay for your sins, as it were. So, in the end, I'm left wondering, 'Where's the justice in all this?'"

Homeostasis

"Okay. Thinking about it from her perspective means digging into the nature of the abusive relationship. And, in abusive systems—in any system, really—there is a component called homeostasis."

"Homeostasis? Like a thermostat that controls the temperature of a room?"

"That's right. Homeostasis is a basic property of systems that keeps internal conditions relatively stable in response to changes in external conditions. The temperature goes up, and the air conditioning kicks on until the room reaches a set temperature. Then, it kicks off. The term was coined in 1932 by physiologist Walter Bradford Cannon—who, incidentally, also coined the phrase 'fight or flight' to describe an animal's response to threats."

"Interesting. I always wondered where 'fight or flight' came from. It seems to fit in here pretty nicely, don't you think? Ava was certainly under a real threat from Bowman, and she could have chosen fight or flight, right? First, she did choose flight; we learn in a later episode ("Blind Spot") that she left Bowman and moved to Lexington to escape. But, eventually she came back to him. So, you're saying that an abusive relationship can be understood as a homeostatic system?"

"Yes. Systems theory itself was born from the insight that organic systems—like the abusive relationship between

Bowman and Ava—appear to work by the same rules as non-organic systems—like the thermostat. Similar mechanisms behave similarly in both. It also recognized early on that small systems are just tiny reflections of much larger ones. In this case, individual abusive relationships reflect larger sets of relationships that are abusive, such as in the family or in larger social systems, like patriarchy. What's unique here is the particular content of the system."

"Right. So, abusive systems exhibit certain features that make them 'abusive.'"

"Exactly. And the first feature is *helplessness*. Women (and people generally) homeostatically frozen in an abusive system are typically subjected to overpowering feelings of helplessness—the sense that they cannot escape or change the system. Abused women have an extra helping of helplessness tossed in on top of that because of the traditional patriarchal domination of, and condescension to, women. For the longest time, beating your wife was perfectly legal. For an even longer time—before laws were even drawn up to address the issue—abuse may have been frowned upon, but it was nonetheless isolated by the legal system as a 'family matter' that was nobody else's business, and the law would seldom intervene. As far as women have come, there remains the inertia of centuries of their plight being ignored by the community and the system. To this day, it still happens.

"Abusive systems always contain these self-esteem destroying features. I don't know that it could be 'abuse' if it didn't. Abuse is directed harm, and it can take many forms; but it always discomforts a person, may harm them physically, psychologically stresses them, and makes them feel of lesser status—weak, pounded down, inferior, even deserving of the abuse. They lose the natural esteem they have for their own well-being and begin to consider the abuse natural, normal, even deserved. As ugly as this may sound, even our minds can betray us. In an attempt to spare ourselves the awful truth of our situation—that injustice is heaped on us by another person who has no moral right to do so—our minds may normalize the abuse in an attempt to 'fit it in' to daily experience, to make it somehow less of a psychological burden. It's like a chronic illness: you suffer because of it, but you accept it, eventually. It might even kill you; but, after enough time, it's just 'the way things are' for you.

"In abused women, that normalization—nearly always, in my experience—is connected to a second feature: a false sense of hope—a kind of denial of the reality of the situation—that they can change their abuser for the better, or that if they are conciliatory and obedient enough, then they can allay the abuser's wrath and spare themselves abuse in the future. Again, women's traditional role of being passive and compliant creates a form of unconscious inertia in many women, typically conditioned into them by their families and the modeling of their own mothers or female relatives. So, instead of reacting with alarm, anger, and the energy to fight the threat, they do the exact opposite. That's why it's no surprise that abused mothers often have daughters who get caught in abusive relationships. It's another terrible layer of the whole puzzle. Plus, daughters look to the father figures around them to see how men are supposed to treat women, and even a young girl can learn to accept the abuse of her mother if it's all she knows and if her mother fails—or refuses—to teach her that it's wrong. This is one example of how smaller systems are really reflections of larger ones."

Breaking the Cycle

"Wouldn't Ava's leaving Bowman only to return to the abusive system be part of the homeostasis of their relationship? All that history, the inertia, that the system created? Maybe even real feelings of love she felt for him?

And only after continued abuse did she finally choose to fight?"

"That may well be. We know Ava's history with Bowman—from the young, energetic, idealistic kid who was going to make it big in sports to the disappointed and frustrated man who began taking his frustrations out on her. She became his only avenue of stress-relief, the scapegoat for his woes, the tourniquet for his bleeding dreams. And she suffered greatly for it. But, unlike most women—stuck in that cycle of helplessness and denial—something in Ava finally stirred and broke to the surface, a great energy of rebellion that she embraced. Ava's what most of us wish these abused women would become—energetically devoted to breaking the shackles of oppression, to the point that they'll stand up for themselves in a really hardcore way."

"That's it! That's exactly how I felt after we learn 'the rest of the story.'"

"To even dream of killing a husband flies in the face not only of our basic human conditioning which leads us to intuitively shy away from killing, but also of our conservative social conditioning which deifies husbands. So, it's rare. Having said that, I haven't seen the recent statistics on how often abused women kill their husbands; but as I said, it happens enough to put it on the map. It's far more common for the husband to kill them or harm them badly enough to compel the system (and usually her family) to step in and separate them. These days the system has very broad power to charge an abusive husband with everything under the sun, even if his wife refuses to. And that's good. It should."

"But, in this case, that system failed. And I think that's important. But, go ahead."

"Ava's story's a pretty optimistic one, stating out loud that the human spirit—in women or men—isn't always so easily subdued, even in situations of long-term abuse with all the fear and paralysis it brings. Like a wild tiger that might suddenly strike out at the man who keeps it caged and beaten, and luck up and bite out his throat, there's something—deep down—in abused people that never really accepts it and remains a lurking threat."

"The nugget of your therapeutic analysis, for me, is that Ava's what we wish abused women would become, that person devoted to breaking the cycle and standing up for themselves in a really hardcore way. The 'wild tiger' image really pulls it together: caged and beaten, but not broken, with something deep down that remains a lurking threat. But, why is it that we feel compelled to root for the underdog in the first place? I would argue it's just that deep seated sense of fairness, desert, justice, whatever term you want to use. There's a wrong that needs to be made right, a balance upset that needs to be restored."

"I guess it goes without saying that you think it's morally justifiable for a person to take the law into their own hands if the system fails them?"

"I think so, yes. But . . ." I paused. "Maybe it isn't . . . that's why I'm here! I can't help but feel that what Ava did wasn't just excusable; it was the *right* thing to do. And I'm interested in exploring why I have that feeling."

"Let me say this then." He shuffled in his seat awkwardly. "I have a feeling that, if I was really wronged in some epic way, and the system failed me, that I would seek redress in extra-legal ways. I am just emotional enough to get sucked into that; but, I have a pretty idiosyncratic view of honor and right and wrong. So I might; probably would."

"So, I'm not crazy? You just admitted that you would pursue extra-legal means!"

"Having said that, though, I think that my personal emotional urge to do so really has no place, no recognition in our system, which is designed to dis-empower the individuals wronged, and allow a more dispassionate system to handle it, to make sure that people don't fly off the handle and kill the wrong person when they believe that they or their loved ones have been wronged. The individual person doesn't matter as much to our system as the general public. And you can debate the merits of that all night. On the one hand, it seems dehumanizing, like the human person to whom a debt is owed in the face of injustice is passed over, while the offender 'pays his debt to society'—to society, as though he wronged the collective, and not the individual."

"And that's just how the system fails Ava."

"On the other hand, I think that I'm not the only emotional loose cannon out there. And if we didn't have a dispassionate system, then we'd have a lot more 'street justice,' and that's not really a better option."

"See, I don't think it's being an emotional 'loose cannon.' I think it digs into what we truly feel is the 'fitness' of things. That's why we like it so much when we see it acted out on screen. What goes around comes around; you'll get yours. That evinces a deep set of values. Children understand that kind of fairness. Besides, we're only talking about using extra-legal means because that system you mentioned—the dis-empowering, dispassionate legal system—fails sometimes to deliver the goods. When it works, it may work fine; but it doesn't always work. Like you said, this particular issue is still treated, in many cases and in many places, as a 'family matter' that's nobody else's business. So, when the system that's designed to be blind turns that blind eye to the victim, what recourse does the victim have except taking the law into their own hands?"

Anger Is a Gift

"I will tell you this: One of the chief therapeutic tactics for downtrodden clients is to provoke a reaction in them playing on the hope for justice that they may feel deep down. With sexually abused females, for instance, there's usually a long period of inertia for them after the abuse ends because most victims have gotten used to the abuse over the years. The inertia keeps them in that normalized state. Eventually, they go through a 'sleep stage', in which they're ravaged by the various other problems the abuse causes; but a point may come when they become angry over what happened to them, and they seek justice. They learn that the person who did this was never right and it was never normal."

"It's interesting that you mention anger. I've done some philosophical work on anger, and what we see is that anger is arguably the most common response to perceived wrongdoing. In cases of abuse, of course, the wrongdoing is more than just perceived; it's actually wrong. But, even in cases where no wrong has been done, the perception of a wrong tends to provoke an angry response."

"Cotton, it may shock you, but many victims of sexual abuse aren't angry, or angry *enough*, at what happened to them. Most of them blame themselves, and rather than anger, they feel guilt or shame. Just their mind playing tricks on them, in an effort to cope with the circumstances. Usually, they're overwhelmed by the enormity of the wrong. They can't connect that enormity with the contrary feelings of love or acceptance they might have for the abuser—such as if he was a father or a husband. But once they can acknowledge their anger, therapeutic transformation can really happen."

"I think that's what happened with Ava; but I also think it's what happens with *us* as viewers, too. We hear Ava's story, and it makes us angry. We want her to stand up for herself. Where it gets tricky, philosophically, is when we ask if Ava is acting *on* that anger in order to placate it, or if she is acting *from* that anger to bring about justice. It may seem like splitting hairs, but the distinction is important: to act *on* anger is to seek to satisfy the feeling itself rather than to see justice done; to act *from* anger is to be moved to action by it for some other end besides satisfying the feeling."

"Anger in this case is a bridge to therapeutic change, a pool of energy victims of abuse can use to summon long-lost self-esteem and seek reparation. For the first time, they can be honest with themselves about what happened, they can confront their abuser, and they can begin to own the situation. Before they access that anger, they aren't really capable of these things."

"That's acting *from* anger. So, anger is a gift, a gift that motivates us to seek justice."

"That depends on what you mean by 'justice'."

"*Retribution.*"

"You mean vengeance? Payback?"

"That depends on what you mean by 'payback'."

Getting Your Just Deserts

"The core of retribution, or retributive justice, is the notion of *desert:* People ought to get what they deserve. That's simple fairness. It's only fair that people who work hard and do good should reap the fruits of their labor, while those who break the rules should pay for it. Moreover, people deserve to be treated the way they choose to treat others. So, if we behave well, then we are entitled to fair and decent treatment from others; but, if we behave poorly, then we deserve punishment in return. We call this 'getting your just deserts'.

"The German philosopher Immanuel Kant uses the metaphor of debt to discuss just desert. He says that citizens in a society enjoy the benefits provided by the rule of law. So, we're indebted to society and its laws, and we pay that debt by 'respecting' the law—doing our part in a system of reciprocal restraint, where we all agree to abide by the same set of rules. An individual who tries to benefit from that system without actually following, or respecting, the rules or laws is called a 'free rider.' They have helped themselves to undeserved advantages, and created an imbalance that is unfair and therefore unjust. So, the state intervenes to punish the offender and to restore the balance.

"In cases of wrongdoing, someone's been harmed at the expense of someone else being benefited, someone who doesn't deserve those benefits. Punishment removes the undeserved benefit by imposing a penalty, or a harm, to balance the harm inflicted by the offense. It's suffered as a debt that the wrongdoer owes her fellow citizens. Retributive justice aims to restore both victim and offender to their appropriate positions relative to each other. So, it's essentially backward-looking. Punishment's a response to a past act of injustice or wrongdoing. Whatever we do moving forward, whether it's stricter laws and penalties for deterrence or programs designed to rehabilitate offenders, or even therapeutic attempts to provide healing for victims, retribution serves to reinforce rules that have been broken and balance the scales of justice. But, what do you do when that system of laws fails to benefit you?"

"Okay, and so, having brought us to that one sharp point, it appears that you think Bowman could owe his life because of his wrongdoing, and that because the legal system has failed Ava on this matter, that she's justified in dispensing the just punishment instead." He paused. "That's hard core, man. I mean, this puts you out of step with the entirety of our legal system."

"'Legality alone cannot be the talisman of moral people.'"

"What's that supposed to mean?"

"It's Walter Williams, libertarian economist and academic. The full quote is something like: 'How does something immoral, when done privately, become moral when it's done collectively? Furthermore, does legality establish morality? Slavery was legal; apartheid was legal; Stalinist, Nazi, and Maoist purges were legal. Clearly the fact of legality does not justify these crimes. Legality alone cannot be the talisman of moral people.' It means the law isn't some magical device that moral people can rely on to protect them from harm and bring them good fortune. That's why I keep saying it's not about the law; it's about justice . . . specifically, enforcing justice by extra-legal means, if need be. You yourself mentioned earlier that wife-beating was once legal."

"Yeah, but in most people's minds, morality and the law are inseparable. I mean, we want to believe that our laws and the penalties attached to breaking them are grounded in morality, that rules and punishments have some kind of moral justification."

"True. But, everyone also believes that laws can be unjust—you just implied that they do when you said, 'We *want* to believe our laws are grounded in morality'—and so, everyone also believes that the law and morality are both separate and distinct. But, in this case, the issue is that the law has failed Ava. It has failed to protect her from Bowman, and it has failed to punish Bowman for the harm that he has unjustly inflicted on her. Ava was wronged, and she needs to be made whole again. . . . plain and simple."

"Yes, but are we really going to advance the idea that killing Bowman was a way to be made whole? I agree that Ava needed justice, and that she needed healing and reparation and support. And trust me, if a case was really convincingly made to me that killing him would accelerate those things in her, I'd be all for it."

"The presumption here is that being 'made whole' involves healing. But, maybe all it means from the moral —and not merely the psychological—point of view is that justice has been done and balance in the moral sense has been restored. 'Healing' is something else and only comes with time and effort on Ava's part, and maybe then only *after* justice has been done. The sense of closure that justice provides opens up the way to healing."

"This is hard because few people are willing to boldly stride over the social shunning that we all have for the naked reality of death and announce that someone just needs to die in a case like this. Death is that super-packed moral quandary; no one wants to touch it. It's a 'grave' decision . . . literally."

"But, if her only alternative was to live in constant fear and under constant threat, then killing Bowman would certainly neutralize that, while letting him live would not. So, it boils down to whether or not you believe that she was morally justified in taking the law into her own hands and dispensing justice as she felt necessary, even if that means that Bowman dies."

"In the end, I wouldn't lose any sleep over Bowman getting his chest turned into a funnel. Not a wink. I think he deserved to have his ass kicked, to know what being trapped in a terrifying situation for years felt like. But, I'm feeling a 'stop' in me, just short of saying he *deserved* to die."

Eye for an Eye, However Blind

"Fair enough. And I think I agree with you. It's hard to say that someone deserves to die unless they've knowingly and willingly taken life in unjustifiable circumstances. But, when the legal system turns a blind eye to the punishment of perpetrators of domestic violence, it seems our response—morally as well as legally—is to turn a blind eye also—to the victims of domestic violence 'doing what they have to do'—by not punishing them for their retaliation. And there's a kind of justice in that: an eye for an eye, however blind, still settles the score. So, why do I still *feel* like he deserved it?"

"Bowman's death and Ava's triumph are one and the same. So, it's understandable that your feelings for the one may get confused with your feelings for the other. And so, your reaction to the story about what happened to Bowman wasn't a reaction to Bowman's 'getting what he deserved', much less a feeling of satisfaction in one person killing another. It was, in reality, a reaction to Ava's standing up for herself, in this case in the only way that she could see to really and truly break free of the abusive system. So, you see, you feel proud of Ava for fighting back—even though it means Bowman's death—because she's owning the situation and taking control of her life while at the same time punishing Bowman for years of abuse where the local law has simply failed her."

"I like that. It nicely wraps up both issues—the justification of using extra-legal means and the explanation of the feeling of satisfaction and pride in Ava. On that note, I think we ought to call it a night. This has been really helpful. Thanks for helping me work through it."

"Not a problem. What are you going to do now that we've discussed all of this?"

"I don't know. Maybe I'll write an essay about it. I could call it "I Did What I Had to Do."

He cracked a devilish smile. "Well, *you do what you have to do!*"

9
The Ethical Theories of Raylan and Boyd

GERALD BROWNING

Lawman Raylan Givens is a stark contrast to career criminal Boyd Crowder. The tension between the two men is one of the main reasons why we keep watching *Justified*. Their ways of thinking are diametrically opposite, with Raylan always trying to make sure that justice is dispensed equally and fairly (at least in his own mind) no matter what the costs, and Boyd more concerned with bringing about the best consequences for himself and his loved ones, even if a little lawbreaking occurs in the process.

Duty Bound

Raylan Givens is a good example of a *deontologist*, someone who thinks that the right and moral thing to do is always connected to a rational duty, and that you must "do your duty" no matter what the situation, circumstances, or consequences that result from you doing it.

A married man has a duty to uphold his marriage vow and not have sex with the stripper at his friend's bachelor party, even though everyone else does. George Washington was doing his duty in not telling a lie when asked whether he chopped down a cherry tree, even if it got him a whipping from his old man. Does a cop know he may be killed at any moment? Of course. But he protects people—he does his

111

duty—no matter what may happen to him, even if he gets killed in the process. The first responders who died in the Twin Towers on 9/11 were doing their duty in trying to help people and get them out of the buildings. You get the picture.

Lawmen like sheriffs, deputies, and marshals of the American Old West are often portrayed in movies and stories as deontologists doing their duty, for example, by sticking around town to protect it from outlaws who will be arriving on the noon train when everyone else hightails it outta there. They know they're risking their lives and the lives of their family members but they uphold the law anyway, even if it kills them.

Justified is like a modern-day Western with Raylan as the quintessential lawman bound to do his duty to clean up Harlan County, Kentucky. In the opening scene of the pilot episode ("Fire in the Hole"), we get an idea of Raylan's moral fiber in the interaction with Tommy Bucks. A heinous murder in Nicaragua caused Raylan to track Bucks from South America to Miami to do his duty and "bring him in." Of course, Raylan is no dummy, and he protects himself by being a quicker draw than Bucks, killing him dead. Justice was served, and Raylan fulfilled his duty.

One of the biggest moral concerns that plague the deontologist is how do we weigh one moral duty against another? This is a problem that Givens is confronted with in the initial season. While incarcerated after the shooting at Ava Crowder's house, Boyd learns of Arlo Givens's (Raylan's father) involvement with a serious crime. Raylan, who already has a tenuous relationship with his criminal father, is enticed by potential knowledge that Boyd has about his father's illicit dealings with Boyd's own father (Bo Crowder). "What if I were to tell you, right now, that I found out something about your daddy. Something that you could use to put him away for the rest of his life. What would you say then?" This was a cliffhanger at the end of one episode. This obviously is one of the biggest dilemmas that Raylan has to address. The stress and indecisiveness on which moral duty supersedes the other: his obligation to the law or his obligation to his family?

Throughout the series Raylan's Achilles Heel is women. From his protection of Ava Crowder to trying to reconcile with his ex-wife, Winona, Givens has a hero's complex and rushes to save a damsel in distress. Givens sees this as his duty. However, the dilemma of saving women gets him into trouble. Early in the first season, Raylan sleeps with Ava, thereby putting an inappropriate relationship between a witness and the Marshall into the scenario. This causes Raylan's boss Art Mullen to confront Raylan—which puts their friendship in jeopardy.

One of the most dramatic scenes between Raylan and Art comes in an argument where Art begins to lose faith in his agent and friend. Givens seems compelled to save a woman much in the same way that gunfighters in western cinema seem compelled to save the damsel in distress. This character trait seems to make him very similar to heroes in the Western genre. However, this is where the similarities end. Raylan, unlike many characters in the past genre, does not always make the morally right decision. In many instances, his weakness for women compels him to make several "wrong" choices.

This weakness forces him to place his career on the line because of his ex-wife, Winona. It comes as no surprise when we find out that Raylan still has feelings for his ex (in fact, this is the main sexual tension throughout the beginning of the series). As Winona deals with a con artist for a husband who gambled a major portion of their earnings away, she steals money from a vault after a bank robbery. She turns to Raylan to help her return the money she stole. Both of these incidents have caused Raylan to evaluate the importance of one duty over another.

However, we see that even the main character can make horrible decisions (yet another reason that keeps us watching week after week). This serves to make him a more complex character. In movies starring John Wayne, we see that he makes the right decision nearly every time. However, we see Raylan making different (and even morally wrong) decisions. These decisions serve to move from one plot point to another. Yet, they also serve to add more depth to the character. No, Raylan cannot be trusted to make the "right" choice over and again. It is these decisions that keep him from the life that he has wanted. It is these choices that create complexity in the storylines and authenticity of the character development.

Givens is the traditional gunslinger lawman. He is quick on the draw, has a strong sense of justice and an innate obligation (or duty) to make certain that justice is dispensed equally and fairly. This clearly makes his views of morality a deontological point of view. And one of the most important aspects of morality is addressing the question of how we make the "right" (or just) decision.

Letting Others Choose

One consistent theme in Raylan's moral decision-making process is his need to give choices. He gave Tommy Bucks the option of leaving Miami within twenty-four hours of his being caught, or he would shoot him "on sight." During the tense draw-down scenes (another staple of the television show reminiscent of old westerns), Givens gives his opponents the option of turning away before he inevitably proves that his reflexes are faster. Throughout the series, upon references to Bucks, Raylan speaks with a clear conscience. In Givens's mind, it was Bucks's decision to draw down on him.

In an episode where Ava Crowder (a woman from Raylan's past who needs protection) is held hostage by a rogue sheriff, he asks the sheriff "You really don't see any other way out of this?" This shows that the very choices that his opponents make seem to weigh significantly on Givens. Afterwards, the sheriff takes Givens hostage and forces him to follow the kidnapped Crowder before both turn the tables on their attackers and arrest them. Raylan does this quite often through the series. The importance of choices (and making the right ones) is a device used quite often in *Justified* as well as traditional Western films.

An example of this is the quintessential staple in westerns: the fast draw. "I don't draw my gun unless I intend to kill." This line uttered by Raylan many times is an excellent example of the gunfighter giving the opponent time (and opportunity) to back away. Just like in the old Westerns, *Justified* contains many scenes where an outlaw squares off with Givens. An interesting foil to Givens's fast draw is Fletcher "The Ice Pick" Nix. Nix is a hit man hired by the Dixie Mafia to kill Givens at the beginning of Season Three. In scenes where he uses his quick reflexes to dispatch a target, he "cheats" by moving the gun away from his opponent and towards his hand. Nix exhibits his fast draw, but does it in a dishonest way. Much like Givens, Nix is a deontologist, giving his targets the choice to participate in the kill, yet demonstrates underhandedness. When Raylan and Nix meet, the hit man tries to move the gun, but Givens counters by stabbing Nix through the hand and brutally shooting him.

The choices that the characters make seem to act as a catalyst for their own downfall. One example is the character Dewey Crowe. Dewey acts as the comic relief through much of the series. Dewey is constantly in trouble due to the horrible decisions that he makes. Most of the problems that Dewey incurs seem to come because of the poor decisions that he makes. Watching a heist that occurs on a bus. He decides to steal a shipment of prescription drugs. In addition, to help cover his tracks he places a Stetson on his head and attempts to pass himself off as Marshall Givens, both of which lands him in deep trouble with Givens and the US Marshall's Service.

In Season Two we're introduced to Mags Bennett, the matriarch of the Bennett family, a collection of thieves, killers, and pot growers who try to push their way into a vacuum of power in the Harlan County underworld left vacant by the death of Bo Crowder. Mags's decisions are driven by her desire to increase the power of her family. It seems as if family is the most important thing to Mags. She takes in a little girl named Loretta McCready. She does this after killing her father, a negligent dad who crossed her family one too many times. Mags takes care of Loretta and seems to want to groom her to be a young woman in Mags's own image. Tender scenes with Loretta and Mags act as a stark contrast to the cruel, vicious personality that comes out when she needs to strong-arm those who seek to stop her from making money off marijuana and other illicit vices. Ultimately, Mags's faith in family tends to be her own undoing. Mags is yet another prime example of a person's choices turning into their own undoing.

The choices that the characters make in these episodes can serve to act as their own undoing as well as it can make them who they are. The genius of the show is in its ability to take a character as reprehensible as Boyd Crowder can be and make him seem as if he has a shred of morality to him. In the show, there are no "pure good" or "pure bad". In a character such as Raylan, there is the capacity for evil in Givens, just as there is a capacity for good in Boyd.

Crowder's Consequences

Raylan's foil throughout the series is Boyd Crowder. Whereas Raylan is guided by a sense of justice, Boyd looks to the consequences of his actions. Ethicists would say that while Raylan is a deontologist—following duty regardless of the consequences—Boyd is a consequentialist.

Boyd and Raylan grew up together and worked in the mines as teens. "You watch each other's backs . . . you get to know a man." Boyd Crowder, much like Raylan, is very charming. Beneath the southern drawl and hypnotic rhetoric, lies a career criminal and predator. Raylan is driven by an innate sense of duty. Boyd is motivated by a different moral compass. The consequentialist believes that the morally "right" action is the action that maximizes the good. Much like most complex characters, Boyd Crowder's actions are motivated by a sense of morality.

One of the most interesting examples of Boyd's ethics in action is his very complex relationship with Ava Crowder. In the beginning of the series, their relationship was tenuous, at best. When Boyd found out that Ava killed his brother (her abusive husband), his intentions were to kill her. However, he voiced that he understood why she did it. Yet, in that same episode, his showdown with Raylan resulted in his being shot in the chest by Givens. Afterwards, Boyd seems to have "found his faith" and recites Bible verses while dispensing vigilante justice to meth dealers in Harlan County. Raylan is not quite sure whether Boyd's sincere, but Boyd seems to believe that he's doing the right thing by putting the meth dealers out of business.

It goes without saying that Boyd's actions have serious repercussions. Whether his intentions are "good" or "bad," the results have mostly been negative. When Boyd is released from prison, he forms a "church" populated by former convicts. These convicts acted as vigilantes under the supervision of Crowder. The meth dealers that were driven away helped business for Bo Crowder (a big name in the Harlan underworld). Bo bribed his son to keep business going for him, but when Boyd would not play ball (which resulted in the accidental death of a Confidential Informant), Bo killed the members of Boyd's "congregation." "I set all of this into motion, didn't I?" Boyd asks, as he Raylan and he are driving towards a confrontation with Bo Crowder and his minions. It is obvious (especially in the scene where Boyd stumbles across his followers' bodies) that Boyd is distraught over the deaths of his "flock."

During the confrontation with Bo Crowder, shooters from Miami (gunning for Raylan) kill Bo Crowder before Boyd has a chance to kill him. "They shot my daddy," was Boyd's response to why he wanted to go after the surviving shooter from Miami. When Raylan reminds him of the hypocrisy inherent in that statement, Boyd replies with a curt "But that's different." Boyd's response to the killing of family seems merely retaliatory and has less to do with his positive feelings for his father. Ever the consequentialist, Boyd takes it upon himself to help Raylan take down the killers from Miami. This vendetta continued past the end of the season. Season Two picks up with Boyd in Miami following the shooters, only to be intercepted by Raylan.

The shoot-out which teams Raylan and Boyd together at the end of the first season brings us to a type of ethical theory called contractarianism, which says that two people— two "moral agents"—may act together if the two are working towards a moral "right". With Ava Crowder in jeopardy, Boyd plotting revenge against his father, and gunners from Miami looking to collect Raylan Givens, Givens and Crowder worked together to make certain that an overall perception of justice (Bo Crowder's imprisonment or death) is achieved.

In Season Two of we're exposed to a more complex side of Boyd Crowder. In most of Season One, Boyd is looked at as a suspect and a negative influence on Harlan County. He tried to kill Ava (out of family vengeance), lost a draw-down match with Raylan, and was involved in the death of a confidential informant for the Marshals. However, throughout the course of Season Two we see Boyd atoning for his actions. He moves in with Ava Crowder as a renter and seems to want to stay away on the right side of the law. He even takes a job with Black Pike, a business that wants to mine for coal in Harlan County. Throughout most of the season we see Boyd referring to his family, his past and the crime that is a large part of it. Even though it seems as if Boyd has taken a turn for the better, we can't help but think that it is only a matter of time before he reveals himself to be a criminal (just as Givens suspects).

As the plot advances, it becomes apparent that he is still looking out for his own, independent self-interests. Also there is a slow, yet progressive romantic relationship between Boyd and Ava that starts to blossom. As this relationship begins to solidify, we see Boyd's actions result from him trying to preserve their relationship. When we see this, we see a vulnerable side to Boyd. It is at this point that we see that he cares about something or someone other than himself. Towards the end of Season Two, Ava is wounded during an attack by the Bennett Family. With the consequentialist mentality, Boyd decides to exact revenge. It is this action that, for Boyd, results in his perception of "good."

One result of Boyd being a consequentialist is the fact that in the first two seasons of the series, it can be quite difficult to understand where his loyalties lie. There are many opportunities to see him as a villain, almost as many as opportunities to see him as a hero. For the consequentialist, the truly good (or righteous) action is the action that maximizes the utmost good. However, with a character like Boyd Crowder it's hard to tell whether his actions are for the good of all or whether they're for his own good. Crowder, a calculating and devious individual, poses a very interesting dilemma for the analysis of this consequentialist: whether the consequentialist chooses the right action based on what's good for *all* or what's good for *him*? Once the story progresses and we learn more about Boyd Crowder, we see Boyd (and yes, Ava, too) slowly move into a life of crime. Yet, it seems as if Boyd is out for his (and Ava's by extension) best intentions.

The Perfect Foil

Raylan and Boyd are perfect foils for one another. They are driven by a sense of morality that is in diametric opposition of one another. The deontological moralist and the consequential moralist look at the world around them differently.

Raylan Givens is a lawman who sees the world as black and white. This character is a flawed hero. He attempts to do the right thing and makes good and bad decisions based on a distinctly drawn moral spectrum. He knows the right thing to do and the wrong thing to do, even though sometimes his actions don't reflect this.

Boyd Crowder is a villain whose perceptions of right and wrong best reflect a man who is trying to do the right thing from a perspective that constantly places him at odds with the law. In Givens's case, the law is very close to his perceptions of morality and in most cases; Givens tries to keep within those boundaries. Sometimes he's not successful, however. Boyd Crowder does whatever he can to create the maximum amount of good results for his best interests. Both Crowder and Givens serve a moral compass that forces them (for the most part) to be diametrically opposed to one another. Yet, on a few instances, these two men have worked together for a common interest.

Raylan and Boyd exhibit a southern charm that allows them to manipulate others for their own perceptions of "good". Each character in the series makes a decision that leads them down a road that ultimately creates their own undoing. Raylan's and Boyd's decisions are very much in line with the philosophies of Immanuel Kant (deontology) and John Stuart Mill (consequentialism).

Both Raylan and Boyd are struggling to figure out what is right in an environment mired in ambiguity. In making their moral decisions, they shape themselves into different kinds of persons. Whether we make decisions that ultimately create "good" for others or for ourselves, we're the captains of our own fate. And *Justified* shows that what we do results in who we are.

10
Justified or Just Making Excuses?

ALEXANDER DICK

"He pulled first. I was justified." This is *Justified*'s refrain, at least in Season One. When Raylan Givens shoots Tommy Bucks on a rooftop patio in Miami, he not only sets in motion the plot for the entire series; he also begins an enquiry into the meaning of the word that titles the show. What does it mean to be "justified"? Perhaps it's better to ask: What does it mean to say "I am *justified*?"

Every time that Raylan says "He pulled first; I was justified" he's on trial, either officially by the US Marshall's Service Board of Inquiry, or informally by his boss, Art Mullen, or his ex-wife, Winona Hawkins. In all instances, Raylan says the same thing in the same deliberate matter-of-fact way, as if the force of the statement and the manner in which he performs it will prove its plain moral truth.

But no one's really convinced. Chief Deputy Dan Grant, Raylan's boss in Miami, tells Raylan right after the shooting in the pilot episode that his justification plea will have no bearing. "It's not about who pulled first. Remember that nuthead who pulled a shotgun. That was on page nine. This, this is going on the nightly news."

When Raylan speaks before the Board of Inquiry, he is terse and emphatic: "let's get this over with: he pulled first; I was justified." In other words, let's just go through the formula that will allow us to accept that I committed the act, but also agree that it was not wrong. He makes the same kind of claim to Art Mullen, his boss in Kentucky, and to the federal investigator prosecuting his case.

At the end of the pilot, Raylan himself confesses to Winona that he may have had reasons for shooting Tommy other than self-defense. Raylan and Tommy had both been looking for a money-launderer named Roland Pike in Nicaragua when Tommy caught Raylan and made him watch as Tommy blew another, unnamed man's head off by lighting a stick of dynamite in his mouth. In telling her this story, Raylan explains to Winona that he might have killed Tommy to appease a personal desire for revenge. This would entail that Raylan's motives didn't lie within the realm of legal justification—a situation he can't comprehend. "What troubles me is: what if he hadn't? What if he just sat there let the clock run out. Would I have killed him anyway? I know I wanted to. I guess I just never thought of myself as an angry man." Winona's reply puts the statement into an entirely different register: "Raylan, . . . you do a good job of hiding it but, honestly, you are the angriest man I have ever known."

Denial

So if Raylan can't justify himself, what can he do? In his famous article, "A Plea for Excuses," the twentieth-century philosopher J.L. Austin pointed out that there's a difference between *justifying* an action and *excusing* it. According to Austin, we *justify* an action when we admit that it appears bad but explain that we had legitimate reasons for committing it. We *excuse* an action when we accept that it's bad but explain that we did not intend to commit it. I justify myself when I say that I pushed an innocent person down in order to save him from being hit by a passing bicycle. I excuse myself when I say that I pushed him down because someone else pushed me. "In the one defense," Austin writes, "we accept responsibility by denying that it was bad; in the other we accept that it was bad but don't accept full, or indeed any, responsibility."

Since Austin, many philosophers and legal thinkers have pointed out that excuses and justifications are sometimes not easily distinguished. Take, for instance, the type of justification used by Raylan when he shoots Tommy Bucks: self-defense. Someone is about to commit an act of violence or force against me: I defend myself but in the course of that defense I maim or kill my assailant. "He pulled first; I was justified."

But does self-defense always justify? As in the many cases of the stand-your-ground law in Florida (where the show's opening segment and other important scenes take place), if harm to the defendant is neither inevitable nor immediate, than self-defense can't be a justifiable reason for what is, effectively, homicide. Yet the point of the self-defense claim (and others like it) is that I don't need to justify deathly harm. If I was in a state of fear or disturbance (all claims that have been used in Florida and other jurisdictions), then I can be acquitted, even though the act in question would otherwise be considered criminal.

These are excuses, not justifications. But to what extent can an excuse really reduce my responsibility in a moral or a legal sense? The point is that in either case any claim requires outside corroboration and independent judgment. Someone needs to validate the excuse in order for it to be valid, strictly speaking. We can justify or excuse our actions, but those assertions can only be proven efficacious if they are acceptable to a legal authority, a judge or jury. *Justified*'s opening segment doesn't give us enough information to establish that verdict clearly. Did Tommy intend to shoot Raylan—as Raylan implies he did—or merely threaten him? Did Raylan plan to shoot Tommy before arriving at the hotel? We know there's more to Raylan's case then the fact that "he pulled first." But what that more is, isn't made clear.

Ava's Crowder's shooting of her husband, Bowman, which takes place before the show begins (we never see Bowman) parallels the moral dilemma underlying Givens's shooting of Tommy Bucks. Recent moves in both American and Canadian law to allow women who kill their abusive husbands to plead self-defense (as Ava does) rather than to plead psychological incapacity (what used to be known as "battered wife syndrome") reflect a general trend in criminal law toward justification rather than excuse in such cases.

Justification implies that a decision to commit a lethal act was made for the purpose of preserving not only the life of an individual in a situation of unspeakable horror but also her dignity in the face of legal proceedings that might incline to bias against her. Indeed, Ava's plea of manslaughter and subsequent parole for killing Bowman suggests that this moral shift is only partially complete in the Kentucky legal system. But it also points to doubts about the kinds of verdicts that all such situations can inspire.

Do Bowman's unquestionably horrendous acts of violence against his wife necessarily justify his murder, essentially making murder "right"? Or do they excuse her actions, lessening her culpability for an act that is still morally and legally wrong? If this is the case, then the broader implications of the justification-excuse problem become apparent: how far can issues like domestic violence be used to excuse what would otherwise be criminal activity? In this respect, Bowman Crowder's death serves to highlight the broader political and social implications for the seemingly a-political murder of Tommy Buck's.

The Hammer

Another character who embodies the complexities within the self-defense claim is Mike "the Hammer" Reardon, an incidental character in much of the show, but critical to the episode in which he first appears ("The Hammer"). Reardon is a hanging judge: he never allows criminal acts to be excused by mitigating social or economic circumstances. At the end of "The Hammer," Reardon is confronted by a former defendant seeking revenge for fifteen years' incarceration for the relatively benign charge of possessing marijuana with intent to sell.

The man's aim was to shoot the judge so that Raylan would shoot him in the mistaken belief that at his death life insurance would go to his estranged wife and child. Reardon shoots but only maims the man, later thanking Raylan for forcing him to miss—though that was not Raylan's intention. It turns out that the tough-talking judge has never actually killed anyone and appears horrified by the very idea. The point is that the judge's commitment to clear distinctions between right (justified) and wrong (criminal acts) fails him when he's involved in a situation that doesn't manifest straightforward distinctions.

Speech and Performance

In his book *How to Do Things with Words* (1962), J.L. Austin pointed out that some statements don't describe matters of fact but make things happen. The statement 'I now pronounce you husband and wife' causes two people to become married (as long as the statement is uttered under the right legal conditions). The statement 'I promise to meet you for lunch tomorrow' causes a promise to come into existence (as long as it is uttered under the right circumstances, for instance, not in a theatrical production). These statements are not truth-statements, either true or false, but what Austin called performatives, made under the right or the wrong conditions.

Sometimes it may not be clear whether a statement is a truth-statement or a performative. In the very first scene of Justified, Raylan's part of his conversation with Tommy Bucks is limited to what appear to be a series of truth-statements, mainly how much time Tommy has left before Raylan will shoot him, delivered in a typical "matter-of-fact" way that Raylan likes to speak. Tommy's responses, though, show that he is more interested in the performative aspect of the statements than Raylan is:

> TOMMY: Have a meal with me. Okay? You hungry? I swear, you pass up, these are the best crab cakes in town, I swear to God. Much better than that crap we were eating in Nicaragua. . . .

> RAYLAN: I didn't mind it. They had some pork dish I quite liked. One minute.

TOMMY: About a second ago you said it was two minutes. What's going on here?

RAYLAN: Time flies, huh?

TOMMY: You, you're a character. I was telling my friends this morning how yesterday you was coming to me . . . 'If you don't get outa here in twenty-four hours I'm gonna shoot you on sight'. C'mon, what is that? They thought it was a joke? They started laughing.

At first glance, this scene seems to dramatize the difference between Raylan's commitment to "truth" (which is also at the bottom of his sense of justification) and Tommy's more social sense of the way what we say is founded on our performance of certain roles and conventions: invitations to share a meal, for instance. Tommy even calls Raylan a "character" as if to open the scene to its dramatic quality.

In Tommy's reckoning, the success of statements depends on their uptake by the person with whom we are dealing or the standards of social decorum that condition them. This uptake is in turn what guarantees the legitimacy of actions. Raylan, by contrast, is making statements of truth about the food and the time, but these seeming matters-of-fact (the quality of pork, the duration of a minute) are actually premised on *his* exclusive authority, which, in Tommy's mind, has impeded on the equilibrium of their relationship.

His decision not to kill Raylan in Nicaragua implicitly means to Tommy that Raylan is bound never to kill him; their mutual preservation at any point of contact is determined in large part by the way they remain tied to rules of practice or decorum. Raylan, by contrast, is making promises that he clearly has no authority to make or to keep (either by criminal law or by criminal custom) such that they sound like "a joke." In Tommy's inimitable phrase, Raylan's statements are "supreme bullshit."

The situation is somewhat different in the pilot's climactic scene: when Raylan goes to Ava's house to confront Boyd Crowder, finding him eating fried chicken and nursing a .44 magnum. Boyd asks Raylan a series of factual questions:

"When you shot that gun thing in Miami, was there food on the table?" "You had your gun. What kind of gun was it?" Boyd also repeats some of Tommy's own mannerisms, inviting Raylan to eat and declaring "bullshit" when Raylan says his gun was indeed holstered. Boyd then rehearses Raylan's ultimatum to Tommy Bucks and even changes the time as Raylan himself had done. Boyd, in other words, is creating the conditions that will "justify" murdering Raylan by reiterating what he takes to be the successful set-up that Raylan himself had maintained. It's when Ava enters, to repeat her own killing of Bowman, that the episode really reverts to a repetition of Raylan's shooting of Tommy Bucks. But neither Raylan nor Ava can kill Boyd. Both guns "misfire"—a word that Austin adopts for situations in which peformatives don't work because of insincerity or lack of uptake.

Fire in the Hole!

Boyd doesn't die as Tommy Bucks did. He lives. In his own phrase, he's "reborn." And he credits God for this miracle:

> I have this belief, this conviction, that it wasn't just an accident . . . last night I woke up and knew why you didn't kill me. I was laying here, in pain, in awful pain. But I didn't hit the pump because I knew it wasn't just pain from a gunshot womb. It was something deeper, a pain from my very soul. I realized that I couldn't any more blame you for my situation here than a farmer could blame his neighbor for a hailstorm. . . . God was acting through you, Raylan, through your gun to get my attention, to set me on a new course. Now I know not yet what his will for me is, but I have faith, I have faith, that the path will be illuminated before me as I need it to be. For even through this searing pain, I am at peace. For I am born again in the eyes in the Lord. And I wanted to thank you for playing your part.

God Made Me Do It

In the final episode of the season, after Boyd and his disciples destroy a meth-lab, not knowing that an undercover police officer was inside, Art practically throws the Bible at him, yelling, "Show me one statement in here that justifies the taking of innocent lives!" Although he's a Christian, Art knows the difference between justification in a legal setting and faith in a Biblical one. The former has to be conditioned by evidence and logic: the latter merely by personal conviction.

Boyd's appeal to the word of God is, in Art's more rational Christianity, an appeal to a printed book, a collection of metaphors and aphorisms that, while they might help to soothe the soul, can't in any direct way determine actions or, in this particular case, justify murder. Boyd did not know that a police informant was inside the trailer when he blew it up. But that only serves to make his constant appeals to divine will all the more troubling. To say "God made me do it" amounts in the rational perspective pretty much to saying "I didn't know he was in there." Both, in other words, are simply excuses.

What's a stake then is more than just the sincerity of Boyd's conversion—though that is certainly a matter of some importance. Like Raylan, Boyd believes in the power of his own convictions and in the uptake of those who, for instance, witness his own declarations of faith and conversion. In order to be "justified" Boyd must fulfill all the criteria of justification. But in a performative world, justification is an impossible standard. There are, to put the issue another way, too many fathers for Boyd to invoke—and the failure of fatherhood is one of the running themes of the season and the show. So Bo Crowder tells Boyd: "I'll send Johnny to tell you where the hand of God is going to strike next." Bo refers to his own threats to Boyd as "Crowder gospel."

In an early episode, "Long in the Tooth," Raylan finally finds and almost recaptures Roland Pike, the very fugitive that he and Tommy Bucks were searching for in Nicaragua. Still on the run from the Marshall's service, Pike has resettled in California as a dentist to the poor even accepting gifts in kind instead of cash for his services. This is a man who believes in the innate justice of human exchange. Whether or not a dish of tamales is worth the price of repaired teeth is beside the point. Like any gift, the goodness of the gesture itself outweighs the value of the object and thus demands some kind of thanks or recompense. But when another customer jeopardizes this system by insulting the receptionist when she reveals that his insurance will not cover his procedure (the system failing in general), Pike snaps, threatening to pull out all of the man's teeth if he doesn't behave. Pike, in other words, believes that the value of acts, especially acts of speech, is determined very much by the general good of the system to which they belong. Kindness demands kindness. Injustice demands retribution. There's no divine authority. Only the authority of the social good.

Yet for any system to remain intact to this extent, the desires and wishes of any individual within it have to be compromised. After fleeing with his secretary-girlfriend Mindy to the Mexican border, Pike admits that when he was working for the mob be believed that he was "not a bad guy"; he was "just working for bad people." These are, clearly, excuses by which Pike in his own mind exempts himself from the criminality of the social system to which he belonged. But although he comes to realize that he is "capable" of theft and murder, and thus seems to assume responsibility for his actions, he still clings to the idea that he can be redeemed by the sanction of others. He claims that it was God who wanted him to be a dentist. But as he stands in the desert, knowing that any second he will be shot by a sniper, he declares: "I love you, Mindy"—searching for the reciprocity of his own faithful congregation. Like Boyd, Roland Pike clings to the idea that someone will validate him and his actions so that he will not have to. The alternative, as he somewhat mysteriously says to Raylan, is "nothing."

A Thin Line

Justified presents the line between justification and excuse as blurred and uncertain. Neither claiming full responsibility for our actions on the assumption of their moral integrity nor deferring responsibility onto accidents, emotions, injustice, or the authority of other powers is in itself sufficient to comprise the basis for moral or legal judgments as to people's culpability.

"He pulled first" is never an adequate claim, but neither is any excuse since all excuses seek to escape responsibility for our actions. *Justified*, like Austin's philosophy, helps us understand the complexity and fragility of our judgments about personal responsibility.

IV

Harlan's
Feminine Side

11
We Are Not Your Savages

JOANNA CROSBY

Justified, like many programs in the era of TV that begins with *The Sopranos*, is full of complex and compelling male characters. But like *The Sopranos*, and *Oz, The Wire, Deadwood, The Shield, Breaking Bad, Mad Men, Boardwalk Empire,* and *Sons of Anarchy*, women are, at best, supporting characters.

Raylan Givens and Boyd Crowder set the center on *Justified*, with Winona and Ava orbiting them as the planets circle the sun. While they may be more developed than many, and we may get an episode or two exploring their backstory, it's not like *Justified*'s narrative is driven by anyone but Raylan.

Two of seventeen directors credited on IMDB are men. Of seventeen writers, IMDB credits three women. Is it a surprise the show is male-centric?

Season Two of *Justified,* though, did present a surprise. That season introduced the character of Mags Bennett, single mother, convenience store manager, and Harlan County's queen of weed. A mixture of Ma Kettle and Lucrezia Borgia, Mags's homemade 'apple pie' will make the room swim, if it doesn't kill you. She'll switch gears faster than a moonshiner being chased by the feds, humble hostess one moment and pissed off badger the next. A character so fabulous, Margo Martindale, who brought Mags to life, won an Emmy award for her portrayal.

Mags is strong, she's fierce, but is she a feminist? Certainly, one would not associate smashing Coover's knuckles with practicing care ethics, although, it's just as unlikely that one would accuse her of being lady-like. Neither Gloria Steinem nor Ann Coulter are likely to consider Mags an ally. So, where does she fit? How do we evaluate her actions? Is Mags just a bad person?

There's something in Mags akin to what, in post-colonial theory, is called the 'subaltern.' This is originally a logical term, indicating a claim implied by another, but that does not reciprocate the implication. For example, the claim 'all of Boyd's dialogue is wordy' implies that 'some of Boyd's dialogue is wordy.' However, the second claim can be true when the first is false. Yeah, logic. That's why you slept through it.

Between a Rock and a Much Harder Rock

'Subaltern' in post-colonial theory, though, isn't about logical relationships but power relationships. If the colonizer is at the center of a power structure, those in subaltern positions have been pushed to the margins. They either don't participate in the reigning governing structure, or their participation is strictly limited.

While we don't usually think of the Appalachian South as "colonized," the land and its people have been exploited and marginalized in ways similar to resource-rich, underdeveloped countries. Consider the Bloody Harlan massacres of the 1930s. Unionizers and mine workers attempted to strike for better wages and working conditions to the opposition of law enforcement and mine owners. The latter resorted to violence including bombing and murder to discourage unionization.

Consider Barbara Kopple's movie *Harlan County, USA* documenting the Brookside Strike against Duke Power in the mid-1970s. Kopple shows us miners living in squalid company-provided housing with limited access to electricity and no running water. In the same year that Duke's profits increased 170 percent, the miners received a 4 percent raise.

This didn't do much to offset the 7 percent increase in cost of living recorded that year.

Consider Darrell Scott's song "You'll Never Leave Harlan Alive." In its bleak view of options for residents of coal country, you'll begin to sense the depths of the trouble. There's really only one good employment opportunity, and no matter how hard you try to escape, it pulls you back in. And that's just one county in Eastern Kentucky. There are mining towns in Pennsylvania, West Virginia, Tennessee, and North Carolina similarly situated.

Do we have sufficient reason, are we *justified* in thinking of an area within the continental United States as colonized and suffering under imperial rule from outside? Doesn't seem likely.

Making You Do What You Do

Edward Said (that's pronounced sa-eed) was a mighty smart Palestinian-American who pointed out something about the folks from European countries engaged in colonization and exploitation from the seventeenth century on. He showed how they produced a heap of scholarly work explaining just how different, even savage, those people and cultures were in the areas that the European folks wanted to colonize. If, for example, science could show that the people, language, culture, science, and art of India weren't up to, say, European achievements, then it was perfectly acceptable for the colonizers to replace them. Those poor people *needed* Western intervention. It was rational, if not simply polite, and demanded by God, to bring civilization to those suffering without it.

A whole scholarly field grew up, called Orientalism, based on the separation of the world into the Occident (the west) and the Orient (the east). The Occident was civilized, rational, organized, and moral, while the Orient was its opposite: exotic, chaotic, inscrutable, and amoral. Think of it like comparing the safety of civilized, urban Lexington to the untamed wilds of Harlan.

Let's just say, there's no song proclaiming you won't leave Lexington alive.

If, while bringing the joys of civilization to the wilds of the Orient, you were also able to, say, exploit the natural resources and, thus, bring enterprise and industry to those suffering from its lack, why, wouldn't that, too, fulfill one's duty as a Christian and a capitalist?

This looks a little different, however, from the 'Oriental's' point of view. As Boyd Crowder says to a Detroit mafia representative, "Your a lucky man, Mr. Quarles. You get to come down here, a place you got no right being, you get to eat our food, you get to drink our whiskey, and you get to look at our women, as you try to take it all for yourself. Well, you know what you are? You're a conquistador!

"Only, we are not your savages." ("Guy Walks into a Bar")

Orientalism, according to Said, is the construction of people and cultures as other and subordinate to one's own. Its strength is that it presents itself as objective knowledge, providing large, abstract categories to explain 'those people' who are different enough to be considered beneath us. Whether we then choose to save, civilize, or exploit those others, well, that depends upon which actions we want to justify; and if you're really good, you can accomplish all three. In any case, Orientalism provides us with the necessary knowledge for that justification.

Of course, *Justified* takes place not in India, China, Iran, or any other area known as 'Oriental.' *Justified* takes place in Eastern Kentucky, the heart of Appalachia. What we have isn't Orientalism, but 'Appalachianism'.

Coal Keeps the Lights On

We see Appalachia not for itself but through a frame established by popular culture and the archetype of the hillbilly and the redneck. Whether in Pennsylvania, West Virginia, Kentucky, or Georgia, our expectations of the people who live there will, we expect, refer to these archetypes. Appalachianism shows us things about the mountains and the people who inhabit them that they, themselves, with their humble origins and ignorance about the ways of the world, cannot see. Things that only 'objective experts' can see.

Said exposed the representation, or misrepresentation, of the Orient in western science, showing how it was used to justify colonial exploitation of land, labor, and resources. However, today, we don't need science when we have images. The Image is a much more powerful representation of what is obviously true than anything science might prove.

We rely not so much on science for our understanding of Appalachia, but popular culture, and not even fiction, like the sodomy and incest in *Deliverance,* but reality TV. *Here Comes Honey Boo Boo, Appalachian Outlaws, Moonshiners, Mountain Monsters,* and *Kentucky Justice;* even *Duck Dynasty* and *Swamp Men*: all presentations of The Other that do nothing to challenge the archetype, rather they reinforce our prejudices while showing us urban folk how we are so much more civilized than 'those people'.

I will simply mark the coincidence of growing criticism of King Coal and the popularity of these programs. Of course, the fact that the *Duck Dynasty* guys used to be a bunch of clean cut, golf-playing, preppy-looking, rich boys before Hollywood backed up a truck full of money at the warehouse and started shoveling it out we should all just ignore. Colonization cannot work without collaborators.

You're Playing Harlan Roulette, Dumbshit

It's easy to distance ourselves from the plight of Appalachia. Most of us are so different from 'those people:' Dewey Crowe, Dickey and Coover Bennet, Helen and Arlo Givens. However, what would happen if oil, coal, or natural gas was found under your home? Don't think that the corporate interests would refrain from presenting an unattractive image of you in order to justify taking control of those resources. Just look at what has been said of people who have lost their drinking water to fracking.

Appalachianism, if it is to follow Orientalism, would portray stereotypes of Appalachian people rather than present them as three-dimensional, complicated people capable of good and bad. Orientalism criticizes the assumption that 'Orientals' actually long to live the civilized life of the Occident, to replace their poorly developed culture for the rich treasures of European culture. While no one will deny that a few modern conveniences, like, say, clean running water, and dependable supplies of electricity are things that would raise the living conditions of those without them, this does not imply a desire to abandon your culture and traditions for all things Western.

When we think of the hillbilly and the redneck, the typical inhabitants of Appalachia (if we are to believe either reality TV or most portrayals of those folk), what sort of characteristics spring to mind? Ignorant, backward, simple, and insular, to name a few. Avaricious, illiterate, and even incestuous, if you want to get mean about it. Why aren't these stereotypes questioned?

Unfortunately, the past few seasons of *Justified* have had more of these kind of characters than not. But in Season Two, we get a few hints that, not only do some people in Appalachia not fit this sketch, some are even capable of complexity. I'm thinking specifically of when Boyd barely watches the video Carol Johnson shows him of a man protesting mountain top removal killed by a boulder rolled over the edge of a mining site. Carol asks whether Boyd would like to watch the video again. Boyd, who looks like he's going to be sick, states unequivocally that he would not.

This is Boyd Crowder, no stranger to the death of other human beings, touched by what we might call the death of an innocent.

No Bridge to Cross

Appalachianism hides the contest for coal beneath our archetypes of the hillbilly and the redneck. The wholesale exploitation of people and place in the pursuit of coal is justified by our knowing hillbillies and rednecks as people less equal than others. Let's not underestimate the power of the coal industry, the railroad industry that transports it, or the power companies that burns it to create electricity. Carol Johnson is not wrong when she says coal keeps the lights on; half of the electricity in the US still comes from burning coal. According to the documentary *The Last Mountain*, we burn sixteen pounds for each of three hundred and eighty million people every day. There are many powerful vested interests in making sure that we keep doing exactly that.

The mining companies have convinced some of the folks, particularly those to whom they provide a livelihood, that mining jobs are their only option. And they are pretty much right in counties where coal is dug. In "The Spoil," Carol Johnson puts Raylan on the spot during her public meeting, asking him how much he makes as a federal marshal, pointing out that an employee of Black Pike would receive similar compensation. While $60,000 a year sounds great, particularly in a depressed economy, we have to remember that it only lasts until the coal runs out. The coal company takes the coal and its profits out of Appalachia, leaving very little besides fast food restaurants and broken dreams. Because coal companies broke the unions in the 1980s, that sixty grand does not come with benefits or security. One coal executive explained that it is much harder to replace equipment than workers. You can always just go hire more workers, and there are always people who will take the jobs.

The mining companies, and the politicians in their pockets, have made sure of that. Digging coal, of course, is hard manual labor. Honest labor, and some find it rewarding. Blowing the tops off of mountains, though, is mostly mechanical in nature. And while the coal industry may bring jobs, over the last thirty years in West Virginia, while the industry has increased production by 140 percent, they have eliminated 40,000 jobs (*The Last Mountain*). However, the loss of those jobs cannot be laid at the doorstep of environmentalists, but rather industry cutting costs, mechanizing, and, of course, doing more with less.

Coal may be the only employer in coal country, but throughout Kentucky, West Virginia, Pennsylvania, and Georgia, the counties without coal have tourism, viable main streets, and diversified economies. Coal companies actively discourage manufacturing or other industries coming to Appalachia as that would create competition for workers and push up labor costs. Companies have broken the unions, impoverished communities, and have lobbyists in state capitals and Washington to help them pass favorable legislation.

In his book *Coal River*, Michael Shnayerson says:

> This could never happen in rural Connecticut, Maine, northern California, Washington State, or other places where such devastation would stir outcry, and people with money and power would stop it. But Appalachia is a land unto itself, cut off by its mountains from the east and Midwest. Its people are for the most part too poor and too cowed after a century of harsh treatment by King Coal to think they can stop their world from being blasted away.

The people of Appalachia can be exploited because they are poor, and in the US, we still think poverty is a character flaw as much as it is an economic condition.

Now Sit Your Bony Ass Down

Where's Mags Bennett come into all of this? Well, Mags stands in for hundreds, if not thousands, of strong Appalachian women who have fought for their families, for their cultures, and against the exploitation of mining companies, railroads, and politicians that can be traced back to the discovery of coal in the late eighteenth century. That fight is not pretty, it is not always fought fair, and survival has taken priority over ethics and principle more than once. But while the energy of their men have been spent in the mine, the women of Harlan County have demonstrated strength portrayed by Mags at regular intervals.

Mags speaks in the voice of The Other during the big community meeting with Carol Johnson, representative of Black

Pike Mining, come to Bennett to secure land rights, opening the way to taking the top off of Green Mountain. "Take it from me," Mags says, "story's always been the same":

> Big money men come in, take the timber, and the coal, and the strength of our people and what do they leave behind? 'Poundments full of poison slurry and valleys full of toxic trash. You know what happens when five hundred million gallons of slurry breaks loose? The gates of hell open! . . . And all that runs down through the hollows and poison the water and the land and everything it touches. ("The Spoil")

We all know about the January 2014 chemical spills in West Virginia's Elk River sending 7,000 gallons of chemicals used to wash coal into the drinking water of 300,000 citizens around the state capital of Charleston, and another 100,000 gallons of chemical slurry into the Kanawha river, of which the Elk is a tributary. The companies involved? Freedom Industries and Patriot Coal. Talk about your doublethink.

One of the best things about the timing of the disaster was that the West Virginia legislature was in session. All sorts of important and powerful people and their families were in Charleston and were exposed to the drinking water containing toxic chemicals.

Slurry in the impoundments are only a possible danger; as long as the earthen barriers hold, there is little problem. In mountain top removal, however, the parts of the mountain that are not coal must be blasted off and pushed aside to get to the coal. This is called the 'overburden.' It is not trucked away, but rather is pushed over the side of the mountain, into the hollows and valleys below. This fills streams and destroys habitats. "Mining company has a word for those leavings, dunnit?" says Mags. "The Spoil. The Spoil! And that is what our lives will be if Black Pike has its way with our mountain." Residents beyond Harlan, particularly those is certain parts of West Virginia, just might agree with Mags after this past January.

Joanna Crosby

Bluegrass, Baseball, and Apple Pie

Mags reminds us of the human side of the hillbilly, explaining to Carol, who, as a West Virginia native, should know better, that Appalachia has a culture its people value highly:

> It ain't an easy life here. No ma'am. To an outsider, it's probably hard to understand why we're not all just lining up and saying 'Where do we sign?' But we got our own kinda food, our own music, our own 'likkah'. We got our own way of courting, and raising children, and our own way of living and dying. And to protect all that, we have to say 'No thank you' to Ms. Carol Johnson and Black Pike Mining. Sometimes we need to stop and remember just what it is we got to lose. (Mags, "The Spoil")

Yes, there is something to lose, something most of us don't know how to see, let alone attribute worth: Appalachian cultures. Yes, cultures, because not everyone who lives in the hollows are exactly the same. Music, food, distilled products, and everything else undergoes subtle changes north to south, east to west, just as it does up and down the I-95 corridor, running parallel to the Appalachian mountains from New York to Georgia. Just as Atlantic City is different than Savannah, so too is Scranton and Harlan, or Matewan and Patton Junction.

Mags does more than just talk, she throws a party to remind folks of all the good parts of Appalachian life. There's bluegrass music, dancing, food, and the famous apple cider. We see folk warming themselves around the still, enjoying each others' company. During the scene, I kinda felt like I coulda shown up, thrown some wood on the still declaring my peaceful intentions as Raylan suggested, and felt welcome. Ava even made it okay to be a white girl with no clue how to dance.

Shitkicker-on-Shitkicker Crime

Appalachia is more than what we see on reality TV. When we demean the area and its people, we are complicit in

142

Appalachianism, treating its the residents as less-than-human, dismissing their culture as a poor example of civilization, if you recognize it at all, and the wholesale exploitation of people and their land in order to take the coal in the mountains for our electricity.

Mags Bennett is no angel, however, she plays the hand she's dealt. If she didn't make bad choices, she wouldn't be a dramatic character. She may not win mother of the year, but I wouldn't want to raise three boys in Kentucky coal country as a single mother. Before we judge her too harshly, remember she knows exactly what the coal companies want to do to her and her way of life. She sells it all out, but in an attempt to get her grandchildren out of Harlan. Maybe she should have listened to the song one more time.

12
Boys Will Be Boys

CYNTHIA JONES, SANDRA HANSMANN,
ANNE STACHURA, AND LINDA ENGLISH

One unmistakable aspect of *Justified* is the presence of tons of violence in every episode. Whether it's Raylan's justified shootings of people who just needed killing, the inevitable smacking around of the working girls at Audrey's, or the perpetual need of everyone to beat up petty criminals (or Raylan), there sure is a lot of violence in rural Kentucky.

Lots of interesting philosophical issues surround the rampant violence in *Justified*, especially when it comes to the violence that seems gender-specific, like domestic violence and violence against prostitutes. This is not to say that there isn't ample violence against men in the show. *Justified* has tons of examples of bad boys shooting each other and shooting officers of the law and vice versa. And of course who could forget the super-creepy Robert Quarles from Detroit who likes to tie up and beat up young men?

While all of this violence is striking, let's take a look at the violence perpetrated by men and against women.

Violence Against Women

While violence runs rampant in rural Kentucky, the gendered violence in particular stands out. The first episode of *Justified* has Ava Crowder shooting her husband Bowman in a kind of self-defense after she has spent years as a victim of brutal domestic violence that no one in the family attempts to address. Ava feels her only option is to shoot Bowman, which she does at the dinner table one night while he's eating his favorite meal ("Ham and yams and cream-styled corn and leftover okra fixed with tomatoes," Ava tells Raylan). The powers-that-be in the legal system seem to agree that she had little choice as she avoids jail time after pleading to manslaughter, much to the dismay of Bowman's kin.

Considering what we know about domestic violence in the US, Ava's violent home life with Bowman is not that unusual. Statistics show that the leading cause of injury for women in the US is domestic or intimate partner violence. Although there is currently a greater awareness of domestic violence as a problem in the US than there was in previous generations, domestic and intimate partner violence are amazingly underreported, even more so in particular communities where people feel it is a "family matter" that shouldn't concern outsiders. Research shows that only about 20 to 25 percent of physical and sexual assaults on women are ever reported. Domestic violence is clearly a family affair in some ways, however, as men who grow up witnessing abuse are much more likely to be abusive partners and parents.

Some feminist theorists argue that the underreporting of domestic violence and sexual assault shouldn't be surprising given the patriarchal society in which we live and the huge power discrepancy between men and women. For example, theorists like Catharine MacKinnon argue the inequity of power in most male-female relationships, coupled with entrenched gender stereotypes that encourage violence in men and submission in women, can offer some explanation for the prevalence of domestic violence and sexual assault and the reluctance in reporting them. And culture, religion, and a history of childhood violence can all play a role in underreporting, according to research.

Although Ava's violent home life may be much more common than most people realize, the reaction of the legal system in her case is also interesting and downright unusual. No one wanted to intervene in Ava's abuse while Bowman was regularly beating her, yet she seems justified in killing him, both to the audience and to the legal system. Unfortunately, for most victims and survivors of such abuse, the legal system has not historically been on their side. One of the biggest hurdles to appropriately addressing the problems endemic in violence against women in the US is the problem of blame ascription. When a woman is beaten by her partner or sexually assaulted by an acquaintance, many people still wonder: "What did she do to provoke the attack?" It is standard practice for defense attorneys in sexual assault cases to put the victim on trial and question her motives, her behaviors, and her "virtue." They ask questions and raise doubts regarding the victim's clothing, the victim's behaviors, and the number of sexual partners of the rape victim. A similar issue happens in domestic violence and dating violence cases where the "authorities" involved often ask what the victim did to "deserve" such abuse. Even in more extreme cases like Ava's where her husband beat her and kicked her while pregnant, causing a miscarriage, the number of convictions is disturbingly low. Researchers tell us that victim blaming plays a large role in the low number of convictions for sexual assault and domestic and dating violence.

A perhaps even more disturbing aspect of sexual assault and domestic violence cases arises from how such cases have been historically handled by police departments. Psychologists tell us that although a very small number of women file false reports regarding domestic and partner violence or sexual assault (between 2 and 8 percent, depending upon the study), many of those in law enforcement who are the first point of contact for victims of domestic violence or sexual assault believe the number is much higher (at least 41 percent in a frequently-cited study, although other studies have even higher numbers).

If the interviewing police officer or detective on a case questions the motives, the behaviors, or the virtue of a victim, the likelihood of an arrest or a conviction will surely plummet and the likelihood that a victim will be discouraged from filing future reports will surely be greatly diminished.

The all-too-common problem of re-victimization at the hands of law enforcement or the legal system is known to anyone providing direct services to victims and survivors of domestic violence and sexual assault.

Researchers like psychologist Rebecca Campbell suggest that the interrogation tactics employed by police likely play a substantial role in causing investigators to discount victims' accounts. Sexual assault and domestic violence victims display tendencies like lack of eye contact, confusion over details, and changes in their stories. Police are taught that these sorts of behaviors are indicative of lying in suspects. The problem is, according to Campbell, that these sorts of behaviors are also indicative of trauma and so are to be expected in victims of sexual assault and domestic violence.

Is there a clear solution to problems like Ava's that doesn't involve killing the abuser or perpetrator? Do women need "special" protections under the law? Some feminists tell us that viewing all women as potential victims is probably not doing us any favors either. Victims are to be pitied and require protection by men, in accordance with the rules of a patriarchy. The move from "victim" to "survivor" is an important one in this respect. Empowering women (and men) who have survived abuse requires looking at strengths rather than dwelling on them as victims. Just as the victimization of women through sexual assault and domestic violence is surely not empowering to them, neither is the demeaning of women to the category of victims that need special protection. As many advocates of equal rights policies tell us, "equal" rights for women are not "special" rights, they are rights of equal access and opportunity.

Prostitutes, Whores, and Ladies of the Night

When Ava and Boyd Crowder finally hook up ("Full Commitment"), Ava tells Boyd that she doesn't want him involved with "whores" or in prostitution. In the following season, Ava kills evil and manipulative Delroy Baker, the pimp in charge of Audrey's, who keeps the girls strung out on meth and oxy and uses them to rob a money store while he waits in the van ("Loose Ends"). After dumping the body of Crystal (one of the working girls who is killed in the botched armed robbery) in the coal slag, Delroy kills one of the two remaining accomplices and then tries to kill Ellen May, the third and final accomplice. Ellen May runs off to Boyd's bar and finds Ava, who is determined to protect her despite taunting from Cousin Johnny.

After Ava offs Delroy, shooting him squarely in the chest with a shotgun, she asks Boyd to let her run Audrey's, which is a significant change from her attitude in the previous season. The reason Ava offers Boyd is that someone needs to look after and protect the women employed at Audrey's to "keep them girls from getting swallowed up from some other animal." Perhaps Ava's history of abuse played a role in her decision as she wants to protect the prostitutes at the whorehouse. We expect that Ava will be less violent with and abusive of the prostitutes in her charge and she is, but the working girls at Audrey's still seem to get smacked around in pretty much every episode that features a scene at the whorehouse.

Not all prostitutes are women, although most are. We find out in the episode "Guy Walks into a Bar" that Robert Quarles was prostituted by his own heroin-addicted father at a young age to pay for his father's drug habit. (Quarles's first kill, he tells his compatriot Wynn Duffy and a young man who is pointing a gun at them, was at age fourteen when Detroit crime boss Theo Tonin gave Quarles a chance at revenge for the years of prostituted abuse by enabling Quarles to kill his father.) Some research puts the percentage of male prostitutes in the US as high as 20, although the numbers usually reported are a bit lower. But all of the prostitutes at Audrey's are female, even though we know there are male prostitutes somewhere in the general area, as Robert Quarles clearly demonstrates in the third season by picking up a few. There are some striking differences between males and females who become prostitutes, particularly regarding their feelings of powerlessness and the length of time they spend as prostitutes. Unlike their male counterparts, female prostitutes stick with the "profession" far longer and are much more likely to express helplessness in attempting to leave prostitution.

Prostitution raises two important moral questions. The first is whether prostitution can be good for the female prostitutes and the second is whether prostitution in general, historically and currently, is good for women.

To consider the question of whether prostitution can be a good thing for those involved, we need to think about the motivations and causes for prostitution as well as the relevant debate amongst feminists about whether prostitution can be okay if it empowers the women involved or if it always involves demeaning or subservience. Many feminist theorists also address the question of whether a woman can really freely choose to be a prostitute.

In "Get Drew" Cousin Johnny is questioning Teri (his favorite prostitute from Audrey's) about the possible whereabouts of wayward Ellen May. Johnny asks if Ellen May could be with family or friends or someone who could help her out or someone she could count on. Teri responds simply, "If she had somebody she could count on, I guess she wouldn't be sucking hillbilly dicks for money, would she?" This one eloquent line sums up the situation of many young girls and women who turn to prostitution as the only way to survive that they perceive as available to them.

Most research reports that over 80 percent of female prostitutes claim they want to leave prostitution, which fits with Teri's statement. Research also demonstrates that prostitutes are far more likely to be homeless, physically assaulted, sexually assaulted, and murdered than the average woman. All over the world, many female prostitutes come from backgrounds of violence or from families of low socioeconomic status. Given all of these factors, it's clear that most girls or women who become prostitutes probably didn't have much of a choice in the matter. Media stories about the fabulous lives of a handful of high-priced call girls aside, it's difficult to imagine that most girls and women who end up as prostitutes had it as a top career choice.

But there is ample evidence that some educated women do seem to choose prostitution, as several well-publicized cases of young women selling their virginity on eBay seem to attest. And some women report that selling their assets through prostitution empowers them and gives them control over their own sexuality and their bodies, and gives them a sense of power over those who buy them. "Sex-positive" feminists such as Carol Queen claim that outlawing prostitution is not the answer and the legal system should instead legalize the role of the prostitute or "sex worker." But despite the possibility of some (likely a very small number of) women being empowered by working as prostitutes, it still could be argued that selling herself, even if it seems to benefit a young woman financially and psychologically, may not actually be in her best interests, as treating oneself or another as an object, or a sexual object in particular, is dehumanizing and problematic.

Returning to the question of whether prostitution can ever be a good thing for the female prostitutes, it seems that it can be, but in rare circumstances where the woman involved is able to weigh the costs and benefits and doesn't labor under undue coercion. Given the undeniable harms involved in prostitution globally, however, it is clear that very few girls and women do actually choose to be prostitutes, in any real sense of free choice. So while it may be possible for prostitution to be beneficial for a very small number of women, it is hard to imagine, given current conditions, that prostitution is a good thing for the women involved or for women in general. The prostitutes at Audrey's certainly don't seem to be leading empowered lives that they freely chose.

Sexism, Gender, and Violence in Harlan County

An important question to ask, given all of the violence in *Justified*, is whether violence is higher in men than in women.

In other words, do men commit more violent acts? In "Thick as Mud" Raylan kills the sexy nurse who, despite flirting with him, decides to yank out his organs for the black market after he gets in her way. Raylan later tells Ava ("Loose Ends") that the nurse was the first woman he ever shot. Raylan doesn't usually chase women professionally, he claims, only because women typically don't commit the kind of crimes that require the services of a US Marshal, so there isn't much opportunity to shoot them.

According to recent statistics from the US Department of Justice, men are three times more likely to commit violent crimes than women. In a comprehensive study of murderers and murder victims from 2002, the Department further notes that while men are most often the victims as well as the perpetrators of violent crimes like murder (71 percent of murder victims were male and 90 percent of murderers were male, in cases where the identity of the perpetrator was known), women were far more likely to be victims of murder at the hands of their husbands (81 percent of spousal murder victims were women) or significant others (71 percent of partner murder victims were women).

Although the reasons for this large discrepancy between genders in the commission of violent acts can be debated— whether it's genetic, hormonal, or a product of environment or culture—it's pretty clear that men in the US are considerably more violent, measuring violence in terms of physical harm to others, than women.

You don't have to consider yourself a feminist to recognize that intimate relationships are far more dangerous for women than for men. While it's obviously the case that men, on average, are larger and stronger than women, on average (Boyd Crowder and Mags Bennett are clearly two exceptions to this generalization), this cannot be the sole reason for this huge violence differential. The reasons suggested thus far, such as victim blaming, misperceptions by police and law enforcement, and tactics of defense attorneys, all play a role in perpetuating violence against women in our society, but undoubtedly there's more involved. It's difficult to imagine that the gender inequities are not symptomatic of some larger power inequities, for which we have rather significant evidence.

Violence, Race, and Stereotypes

We might wonder what role race plays in violence in Harlan County as most of the criminals are most definitely white. However, a quick search of demographics of the real-world Harlan County, Kentucky, reveals that more than 95 percent of the people who live there are white and so we should expect to see far more white criminals. Although the residents of Noble's Holler are involved in their own fair share of crime, manipulation, and violence, *Justified* does indeed do a decent job of eschewing the "all black men are violent thugs" stereotype. There are a few exceptions, like Clinton Moss and the drug dealer whose car Clinton steals in "For Blood or Money." (Clinton is Deputy Marshal Rachel Brooks's brother-in-law who was recently released from jail after killing his wife—Rachel's sister—in a car crash while he was high.) But even Clinton is a sympathetic character in the end as he committed his crime spree on the day in question because he wanted to see his son on his birthday and bring him a present. And Ellstin Limehouse engages in various types of criminal activity, although he still also manages to be a reasonably sympathetic character, seemingly focused on the survival of his extended family and their community in Noble's Holler.

While the pilot episode appears to have a blatant instance of racial violence when Boyd Crowder blows up a church in a black neighborhood, we get the feeling that Boyd isn't at all serious about the white supremacist dribble he is spewing in the episode. And after Boyd is shot in the first episode, his conversion to Christianity ends the pretense of substantial racial hatred.

There are a few amusing scenes that involve racial issues, like in the opening episode when Chief Deputy Mullen sends Deputy Brooks to speak with Pastor Fandi, the leader of a black congregation whose church Boyd Crowder blew up, presumably because Deputy Brooks is black, or when the same pastor chides Raylan for assuming that he likes Peter Tosh because he's black and has a Jamaican accent. And in "Piece of Mind" there is a spirited exchange between Limehouse and the three deputy marshals wherein he refers to Givens and Gutterson as "crackers" and calls Deputy Brooks "Little Sister" while chastising her for working for the man. She responds with appropriate threats and posturing in return, which only seems to make Limehouse more interested in her. But other than the clear separation between the black inhabitants of Noble's Holler and the rest of Harlan County, these scenes do not portray weighty racial tensions.

To its credit, *Justified* does not represent stereotypical views of race in a significant way. Possibly the strongest female character in the show is Deputy Marshal Rachel Brooks. But she's also the only recurring black female character. She is rather distinct from the stereotypes of black women and women in general as she is smart, competent, professional, and reasonably unemotional. We also don't really see women of color working at Audrey's. *Justified* is striking in that it doesn't stereotype women of color or portray them as inferior, although it does demonstrate weakness in women in other ways. Mags Bennett despite embodying a rather fierce matriarch in Season Two, ends her life in a decidedly stereotypical "female" manner, by poisoning herself, after the death of two of her sons. Aunt Helen and Ava Crowder are both shotgun-toting women to be reckoned with, although both are clearly traditional females in their support of their men. And both of their men, Arlo and Boyd, go sideways for revenge when Helen and Ava are shot by Dickie Bennett. We can't help but wonder, however, whether Boyd and Arlo are upset because of the harm to the women themselves or are upset because the use and abuse of their women reflects poorly on them as men.

Many of the theorists involved in what is referred to as "third wave feminism" discuss the interplay of race, poverty, and gender and criticize the feminists who came before them for silencing the voices of women of color and disregarding their experiences. Although sexism and patriarchy are in some ways universal, bell hooks, as a third wave feminist, argues that women of color have been marginalized in the feminist movement, as the oppression of women of color and the oppression of poor women are significantly different than the oppression of the middle class white women who typify the feminist movement in the US.

Oppression is necessarily social and it should not be considered separately from race and class, hooks argues. There seems to be evidence of this in *Justified*. Consider the working girls at Audrey's and the challenges they face. Their choices are significantly restricted by the combination of gender, class, and lack of education. Consider also the situation of the black residents of Harlan County who isolate themselves in Noble's Holler as they are isolated by others.

This isolation, together with the destruction of the black congregation's church in the first episode of the series demonstrate what feminist theorist Peggy McIntosh identifies as one of the invisible privileges of whiteness, the taken-for-granted assumption that wherever a white person moves, she or he can be reasonably sure that their neighbors will be friendly or at least neutral towards her. McIntosh likens the unacknowledged advantages of being in the dominant majority group to carrying around an invisible backpack equipped with everything one needs to feel comfortable at all times while participating in public life. She distinguishes between elements of the backpack that should be available to all—like, for example, the ability to trust that one's neighbors will be friendly or at least neutral (and not blow up your church)—from those that (admittedly unwittingly) empower a specific group to dominate others in society, a condition that is demeaning to every member of said society. While *Justified* mostly manages to avoid problematic racial stereotypes, it also subtly demonstrates the separation bell hooks discusses.

The Moral of the Story

And so in the end, what can we conclude about gender and violence in *Justified*?

Apparently, rural Kentucky is really violent, and not a particularly safe place to be a prostitute.

In addition, despite several strong female characters and the matriarchy of the Bennett clan in Season Two, patriarchy is alive and well in Harlan County, bringing with it the violence and oppression of women we are told to expect from men. But this doesn't mean that the male gender is inherently or necessarily violent (the peaceful nonviolent approaches of men like Martin Luther King, Jr. and Mahatma Gandhi spring to mind) or that the female gender is doomed to subservience and domination.

Deputy U.S. Marshal Rachel Brooks, Ava Crowder, Aunt Helen, and Mags Bennett in particular give us hope, although three of the four of these women are involved in significant nefarious activities in Harlan County, including killing a few men. But then so are pretty much all of the men we root for in *Justified* too.

V

Family Values

13
Failed Patriarchs

PAUL ZINDER

Walter Metz has claimed that since 9/11, Westerns give us "classical representations of morally upright men who both save the social order from de-civilizing forces and simultaneously engineer the maintenance of traditional family values" (in Metz's contribution to *A Family Affair: Cinema Calls Home*, 2008). In other words, classic patriarchs.

Yet *Justified* is just littered with damaged or incomplete fathers who don't amount to regular dads, let alone patriarchs. These fathers falter time and time again, their decisions often harming their own children. Daddy's not much of a savior or guardian in the world of *Justified*.

Both Sides of the Law

Raylan Givens occupies an ambivalent moral ground similar to that of the men he pursues. The estranged biological son of Arlo Givens, a life-long criminal, Raylan is repeatedly drawn back to his hometown of Harlan, Kentucky, to respond to his father's misconduct, although some of Raylan's own malfeasance implies that a criminal mindset may be in part genetic. The relationship between Raylan and Arlo in the early seasons of the series serves as a handy template utilized by the writers of *Justified* to model the show's patriarchal characters on both sides of the law.

In the pilot, Arlo Givens is introduced off-screen as both
Ava Crowder and Boyd Crowder separately query the newly-
arrived Raylan on whether he has yet visited his father, with
Boyd mockingly questioning whether Raylan saw his
"Daddy's face" while shooting Miami drug-thug Tommy
Bucks earlier in the episode. Like so much of the familial dis-
cord in *Justified*, Raylan's difficult relationship with his fa-
ther is public knowledge and ripe for comment.

When Art Mullen, Chief Deputy U.S. Marshal and Raylan's immediate supervisor, informs Raylan in Season One's
"Fixer" that Arlo's been arrested (like Boyd, Art uses the
term "your Daddy" to refer to Raylan's father, the childhood
vernacular a reminder that you can never outgrow a parent), Raylan's casual response, "He kill anybody?" places
Arlo's reputation in historical context. Before Arlo is even
seen on screen, the viewer is informed that he has recently
traded mining equipment for cocaine ("Fire in the Hole")
and been arrested (again) for driving under the influence
("Fixer").

In years past, Arlo physically abused both his wife and
the young Raylan (as revealed in several episodes including
"Blind Spot," "The Devil You Know," and "Restitution"). In his
first appearance on screen in "The Lord of War and Thunder,"
Arlo is arrested for kneeing his tenant in the stomach, and
after he's bailed out of jail for that arrest, he beats the tenant's nephews with a bat in a public diner. In the hospital
following the latter altercation, Arlo asks Raylan if he remembers his grandfather, "a preacher . . . a real old-time religion man," (and the inspiration for the title of this
particular episode) emphasizing that Arlo's childhood home
"was nothing but fear." Arlo would rebel against his father
by choosing a life of crime, but Raylan's rebellion against
Arlo takes on a different guise.

Daddy's a Criminal

In "Restitution," Raylan surmises that he probably became
a marshal to prove something to Arlo. Boyd comes to the

same conclusion much earlier in "Blind Spot" when he remarks that Raylan's helplessness in watching Arlo beat his mother was probably "a big reason why you got your gold star and your gun," as does the malevolent Robert Quarles when he jabs at Raylan in "Guy Walks into a Bar": "That's why you are the way you are, Raylan. 'Cause your daddy's a criminal."

Although Raylan breaks the law himself from time to time in the series to achieve his own agendas (even questioning in "Debts and Accounts" whether he's really "a criminal at heart. Truly my father's son"), he always believes that his activity serves a worthy purpose, even when others might disagree. On a philosophical level, Raylan tries to do the "right" thing but the Arlo in him often gets in his way.

By the end of the first season, Arlo's partnership with another law-breaking paterfamilias, Bo Crowder, leads Raylan to offer his father protection from the Marshals service if Arlo informs on Bo. In "Veterans," after Arlo violently grabs his son's arm, insisting that he won't become a turncoat for the Feds, Raylan informs him that, "I came here as an officer of the law because sometimes we have to make deals with lowlifes because we have our sights set on life-forms even somehow lower on the ladder of lowlifes than they." After Arlo slaps Raylan, the parent-child roles reverse when Raylan responds, "Use your words." Their conflict will only escalate.

Film scholar Janet Walker, in *Westerns: Films Through History* (2001), writes that in "Freudian terms, . . . a boy may very well perceive his own beloved father as being eminently capable of violence against . . . the boy himself." Despite Arlo's sordid, abusive past, Raylan seems stunned by his father's lack of paternal instinct in the first season finale of *Justified*. The deterioration of this father-son relationship reaches an early climax when Arlo sets Raylan up to be killed by Bo's men in a seedy motel in "Bulletville" claiming that "This isn't something I wanted to do, son." Raylan rejects his father, responding, "No, don't call me that," before shooting Arlo in the arm.

A Surrogate Son?

As Arlo's mental faculties begin to fail him in the third season of *Justified*, he mutters complaints to figments of his past, including his deceased wife, Frances, in "The Man Behind the Curtain," expressing his psychological disdain for his biological family. Even in death, Frances fails to escape his wrath. Arlo's fraternization with Boyd Crowder allows him a fresh start, a surrogate fatherhood, as Boyd's mistrust of the law and antagonistic relationship with Raylan suit Arlo's discriminatory nature.

Arlo even tells Boyd, "I'm proud of you, son," to which Boyd responds, "Why thank you, Arlo. That means a lot, comin' from you." In "Coalition," after Boyd prevents Arlo from participating in a bank heist by insisting "I respect your age and the place you hold in my heart," Arlo mistakenly calls Boyd "Raylan," a reminder to the viewer that Boyd is the type of son he always wanted.

Janet Walker states that, "the most potent of threats posed by fathers against sons is to come killing." Such a fitting extrapolation applies to "Slaughterhouse," the stunning Season Three finale of *Justified*. Arlo's "replacement" of Raylan with Boyd ends in heartbreak, when Raylan informs his wife Winona that Arlo's killing of a state trooper was an effort to protect his surrogate son from the man wearing a hat who had a gun pointed in Boyd's direction. Arlo had actually tried to kill Raylan to protect Boyd and misidentified the trooper as his own son, a horrific mistake that feels almost mythical in its emotional weight. After confessing to that murder as well as one perpetrated by Boyd earlier in the series, Arlo dies in prison, estranged from Raylan, the offspring he refused to love.

Crowder Gospel

It's no surprise, really, that Boyd so ardently appreciates Arlo as a father figure. Boyd's own father, Bo Crowder, is as dismissive of his own son as Arlo is of Raylan. Bo, the head of Harlan County's drug trade before the series narrative begins, raised sons that inherited their father's predilection for mayhem. Bo's eldest son Bowman was an abusive husband before being killed by his own wife, Ava Crowder, and Boyd's attempts to fill the hole left by his brother Bowman (both in crime and in loving Ava) never pay adequate dividends.

Bo begins *Justified* as an absent father, locked behind bars for his forays into illegal drugs. After his release from prison, his attempts to regain control of Harlan's narcotics trade clash with Boyd's conversion into a born-again anti-drug crusader. Bo threatens Boyd by insisting that if "You destroy me or my shit, it's the same thing as destroying yourself. That there is Crowder gospel. You mark them damn words, son."

In "Fathers and Sons" Boyd ignores his father's warning, successfully firebombing a multimillion-dollar drug shipment with a rocket launcher. In a truly biblical response, Bo savagely murders Boyd's followers by hanging them from trees, proving that Bo takes his own scripture quite literally.

When Boyd, heart-stricken, explains his loss to Raylan, he speaks like a shattered, betrayed little boy. "I am lost, Raylan . . . My Daddy, he killed all my men . . . He killed all of them." But when Boyd has the opportunity to exact revenge, to murder the father that hurt him so viciously, he hesitates, informing Bo that, "There's more than one way to kill a man. You can kill his physical body, or you can kill his spirit within." Bo, ever the sympathizer, asks, "You gonna pull the trigger or talk me to death?" The bullet that takes Bo's life comes from behind, sparing his son further scorn.

Weak, Stupid, and Scared of His Own Shadow

In *Justified*, surrogate fathers on both sides of the law prove unable to control their chosen "sons," only to eventually abandon them. Theo Tonin, the head of the Dixie Mafia and

surrogate father to Robert Quarles in the third season of the
series, chooses his incompetent biological son Sammy as his
successor, leaving Quarles to rebel in response to his "father's" slight. Quarles should have known better than to rely
on a patriarch. He himself is yet another absent dad, who is
only seen talking to his own young son by phone, and although he claims "I love you, buddy" in "The Gunfighter" his
lack of connection to his own fathers (both biological and surrogate) shapes the way he treats his own child. In "Harlan
Roulette" Quarles thinks nothing of nonchalantly asking his
off-screen son about his latest hockey game over the phone,
telling him, "I think you're gonna love it down here . . ." while
approaching a room where a tied, gagged, and whimpering
male hustler awaits.

In the same episode, Quarles offers the viewer a glimpse
of his own childhood when he notes that his father withheld
kids' shows like *Sesame Street* in favor of *Taxi Driver*, a
movie about a psychotic loner whose obsessions impel him
to shoot up a brothel. This same dad would later pimp out
the teenaged Quarles to feed a heroin addiction. Theo Tonin
assumed the position of male mentor by rescuing Quarles
from the abuse, earning his new "son's" respect and affection,
as noted in the episode "Guy Walks into a Bar." But Theo,
whose power and control intimidate the most hardened criminals over the course of the show's first five seasons, in passing over Quarles as his heir in favor of his biological son
Sammy, crushes his surrogate son's confidence and spirit.

In "The Man Behind the Curtain" Quarles claims to be
the son Theo always wanted, the young man "groomed . . . to
take over someday." Quarles's drug-addled response to Theo's
rejection leads to his own symbolic castration, when he
bleeds out after having his arm chopped off by Ellstin Limehouse in "Slaughterhouse," a gruesome death directly connected to his "father's" rejection. Sammy Tonin, meanwhile,
a man described by Quarles in "The Man Behind the Curtain" as "weak, stupid, scared of his own shadow," proves that
depiction apt, as his own incompetence destroys his father's
business during Season Five of *Justified*.

A Positive Side?

Raylan spends most of his time chasing or in conflict with fathers like Arlo Givens, Bo Crowder, Robert Quarles, and Theo Tonin, but he consistently ignores the guidance and care of his own father figure, Art Mullen, the one male mentor on the series who tries to focus on the positive side of a son whose damaging and resentful behavior would drive virtually anyone away.

From the very beginning of their relationship, Raylan proves himself unable to follow simple orders, putting himself and the Marshals Service at constant risk. While *Justified* is full of ineffectual fathers, Raylan definitely qualifies as an ungrateful, rebellious son.

By midway through the first season, Raylan has already shot two people (Boyd and a hitman sent to kill Raylan) in two separate incidents in Ava's house. The second shooting occurs in the same location because Raylan had begun an affair with Ava against Art's advice. In "Blind Spot" Art angrily reminds him, "I tell you to do one simple thing, refrain from screwing the witness in your own shooting and you can't even do that! You think there's never gonna be any consequences for this?" Those consequences are harsh, in fact, as Assistant US Attorney David Vasquez informs both Raylan and Art that the affair has earned Boyd his freedom from prison, as Raylan's tryst looks suspicious when considering that Boyd was shot shortly after Ava killed her husband Bowman in the same spot.

Later, Boyd blows up a meth trailer with an undercover cop inside, so Raylan's affair with Ava has inadvertently led to the death of an innocent victim. This final incident prompts Art to suggest that Raylan consider quitting the Marshals Service ("Hammer"), a metaphorical rejection of his protégé.

Fathers and Sons

The vernacular utilized by Art throughout the series is patriarchal in tone, though Raylan shows minimal interest in honoring the wishes of this particular "father." In the aptly titled episode "Fathers and Sons," after Arlo refuses Raylan's suggestion to wear a wire to nail Bo Crowder, Art tells off Raylan for drinking in his office before breakfast. "No, that's enough. I'm the chief, this is my office . . . And that's my bottle and I'm not going to let you drink it all just because your daddy didn't hug you much when you were little." Raylan's relationship with Arlo may be tenuous and fraught with conflict, but Raylan's über-stretching of the law implies an unconscious but concrete philosophical alliance with his criminal father that Art cannot abide.

In "Save My Love" Raylan knowingly assists Winona in covering up her theft of thousands of dollars from the Marshals' vault. Art comes upon the couple in the storage room after Raylan assists Winona in returning the money, and his cold stare makes clear that he knows what's just happened. Raylan has once again allowed his love-life to interfere with US Marshal business.

After Raylan questions Art on the state of their own relationship, Art puts him in his place. "I think what you want is to walk in here and have me go, 'Just sit down, son. Tell me, in your emotionally crippled way, just what it is that's troubling your heart so that we can get back what we lost'." When Raylan, like a spoiled teenager, responds, "Forget it," Art demands, "Get back here . . . Now you know that thing that never happened? . . . We're not gonna talk about it . . . I'm stuck with you . . . Nothing I say has ever made a difference." Ultimately, in "Debts and Accounts," Art concludes that Raylan is a "problem that will solve itself."

Even after making such a fatalistic prediction, however, Art can't help but retake his role of mentor and savior in "Bloody Harlan," rescuing Raylan from certain death on the Bennett farm by bringing the Marshal cavalry to the rescue. In the chaotic aftermath, Art asks, "Raylan, you okay?" Raylan's, "It's good to see you Art," replaces the "thanks, Dad" one might expect to hear considering each character's archetypal position in *Justified*.

Their relationship seems repaired during Season Three, with Art working hard to protect Raylan, still recovering from the gunshot wound he received on the Bennett farm. Although Art casually tells a visiting colleague, "I've got one boy . . . who keeps finding himself in the middle of it," in "Cut Ties," he eventually reassures Raylan that new feelings of wanting to change jobs will "pass" ("Thick as Mud"). But perhaps Art's most paternal act of the third season is his parlay with FBI Special Agent Jerry Barkley, which ends the FBI's investigation of Raylan's ties to Boyd. After Raylan thanks Art for his help in "Watching the Detectives" Art responds, "Remember that time I told you I didn't think you were going to make it to retirement? I think it's going to be me . . . Having you in this office is gonna give me a stroke."

This playful banter only lasts so long, however. As the fourth season progresses and the search for Drew Thompson intensifies, Raylan's reckless approach to law enforcement further damages his relationship with this "father," perhaps to the point of no return. Raylan blatantly ignores Art's warning to stay clear of the gangster Nicky Augustine, instead catalyzing the Theo Tonin-led assassination of Augustine, blown away in a flurry of bullets inside a darkened limo in "Ghosts." This Art cannot forgive.

Rekindling Relationships

The fifth season narrative of *Justified* reveals a splintered, seemingly irreparable relationship between the two men. In "Kill the Messenger" Raylan finally confronts Art about their conflict, as the latter sits drinking in a bar (this "meeting" follows Raylan's acknowledgment in "Shot All to Hell" that he knows who was present during the Augustine hit while failing to admit any personal responsibility). Art silently glowers at Raylan before punching him in the face and walking out of the bar.

Raylan, after failing the only man who truly cared, struggles with the aftermath, a reality where Art has given up on him. When Darryl Crowe shoots Art, who was protecting

Raylan's latest ex-lover at the time, Raylan makes it his solemn duty to avenge this action, even admitting to Darryl in "The Toll" that Art is "the one man who makes a difference to me." By the end of the fifth season, however, after Art awakens from a coma, he informs Raylan that a transfer to Miami has been approved. Finally, Art may be freed from the "son" who so often disappoints him. This announcement may function as damnation, but this time, the rejection of the patriarch may be blamed on Raylan himself ("Restitution").

A move to Miami would bring Raylan full circle back to the city he left for Harlan in the show's first episode. More importantly, Winona and Raylan's baby daughter live there, and the possibility of a reunion brings Winona to tears of happiness (and relief) in "Restitution." But as *Justified* proves over its first five seasons, when a father has the opportunity to do the right thing, he almost never does.

While Raylan and Winona are divorced when the series begins, they rekindle their relationship during the first season, and it's fairly clear that Winona is the love of Raylan's life. As their renewed connection develops, Winona claims in "The I of the Storm" that she would divorce her husband, Gary, if she felt there was any way that she and Raylan could be happy, and eventually fantasizes about "lots of little Raylans running around with toy guns" ("Blaze of Glory"). And while it appears for a time that he may be willing to sacrifice his career to make Winona happy, particularly after she tells him that she is expecting their first child, Raylan cannot be counted over the long term as either a dependable partner or a dependable father.

After Winona steals the cash from the Marshal's vault and Raylan helps her hide the act in a cover-up, Raylan concludes that he is not "an outlaw. I helped you because I'm in love with you." His suggestion to Winona in "Debts and Accounts" that he would transfer out of Lexington is the first of many promises Raylan makes to his former wife that he simply refuses to keep. In "Bloody Harlan," after discovering Winona's pregnancy, Raylan claims that if his transfer doesn't go through, "I'll quit," but that doesn't happen either.

Winona eventually leaves him after concluding that "I'm done trying to change who you are" ("Thick as Mud"), an eerily similar sentiment to that expressed by Art on several occasions as well.

Deadbeat Dads

After Winona's move to Miami and his daughter's birth, Raylan communicates with Winona primarily by Skype, the electronic communication a regular reminder of how (literally and figuratively) distant he is from his own progeny, even though he promises that "I'm going to be here for you and the baby" ("The Bird Has Flown"). In "A Murder of Crowes," although he has the occasion to visit Winona and his new child since he's been flown to Florida on Marshal business, Raylan decides to rush back to Kentucky instead.

He never explains why he chooses to miss an opportunity to bond with his new child, but fear of being an unfit father feels like logical reasoning for such cowardice. And while for a moment in the Season Five finale it appears that the couple may finally reunite in Florida after Art informs Raylan that his transfer has been approved, the conclusion of "Restitution" insinuates that the opportunity to finally nail Boyd in the show's sixth and final season will most likely relegate Raylan to the role of deadbeat dad for the foreseeable future. He's a man who refuses to prioritize his own parental responsibility, much like the other fathers in *Justified*, making Raylan both a broken father and a damaged son.

In *A Family Affair*, Metz argues that "the end result of the American Western narrative will remain stable, culminating in the noble and happy production of the normative family unit." *Justified* challenges such utopian notions of familial harmony by presenting fathers and father-figures who ignore, mistreat, battle, or abandon their children. The major male characters in the series are emotionally ruined men who find themselves unable or unwilling to be loving fathers.

Throughout the series, the patriarchal leader fails to fulfill the duties of the role, suggesting that traditional Western definitions of masculinity and familial structures are open to question in the show's narrative construction, making *Justified* a postmodern, baroque comment on fatherhood in the Western.

14
Motherhood and Apple Pie

Peter S. Fosl

Here in Kentucky, we love our families, and we're devoted to them . . . most of the time. Season Two of *Justified* (the whole series, really) presents an extended meditation on family, though the kinds of families it portrays aren't exactly what you would call ideal.

The season's narrative begins ("Moonshine War") with a father's failed attempt to protect his daughter, when Walt McCready makes the fatal error of calling the police to keep convicted child molester James Earl Dean away from Loretta (though, come to think of it, that phone call is what ultimately saves her from Dean).

The second episode ("The Life Inside") tells the story of parents selling their child for cash and liberty. We get to know Rachel's family and its history of violence in "For Blood or Money," when her brother in-law (who was responsible for her sister's death) demonstrates in rather vivid ways what's wrong with the principle that you should do everything you can for your children. At the end of that episode, Rachel, Tim, and Raylan, sit down to share a bottle of Kentucky bourbon along with stories about how messed up each of their families is. (Art presides from outside their circle. He is in a sense the father of their little, substitute marshal family, perhaps the only family any of them have at the moment.)

"Blaze of Glory" shows us, in Frank Reasoner—great name—an old bank robber prepared to desert his loving wife for a last score—a man, that is, who puts money before family. "The Spoil" explores the downside of families exacting their own brand of justice, when the relatives of a man killed by illegally dumped "spoil" seek retribution against the government and the companies that treat them as spoil, too. Each of these episodes, you've probably also noticed, prefigure wrongs the Bennett family will commit and suffer.

This Sho' Ain't *The Cosby Show*

At the center of it all in Season Two is the Bennett clan—Mags, Doyle, Dickie, and Coover—ensconced in fictional Bennett, Kentucky, somewhere in Harlan County, not too far from real-world Evarts, where Raylan played baseball for the high school team. Mags is that kind of strong woman we encounter in our commonwealth, if not exactly a steel magnolia, still not one to be underestimated, smart enough to lead her family alone after the men wander off or die, and strong enough to handle steel, when necessary, as it too often seems to be in *Justified*'s Harlan County. (I love Doyle's response to Raylan telling him that Loretta's got a gun; Doyle says in reply, "Who dun't?")

In the wake of her husband's death, Mags has become the family matriarchal monarch, raising her sons, providing for their future, serving up her homemade apple pie—sometimes, on special occasions, even in her fancy killer glassware. At the end of the day, however, she screws it all up.

Mags falls into irredeemable despair, rightly so, when she learns from Raylan that Doyle's been killed in the Season Two finale ("Bloody Harlan"). But, really, the blow had already been struck when upon confronting the depth of Loretta's anger and grief, Mags confesses that she and no one else is to blame for Walt's death, that she—not Coover the brute and not hobbled Dickie—is the one who set the whole sorry train in motion that ends up extinguishing her vain dream of family enrichment and liberation from the travails of criminal life. It took a strong Kentucky woman in the making, more than US Marshall Tim Gutterson's sharp shooting, to undo Mags Bennett.

The series is, in fact, littered with dysfunctional families. To be honest, families seem so often associated with criminality and dysfunction in *Justified* that I've come to think the show is advancing some kind of symbolic criticism of family *per se*. There's the once-and-perhaps-again mighty Crowders, lords of Kentucky weed, petty crime, and white supremacy. There's the Limehouse clan, hunkered down and bristling with guns like Switzerland under siege in its mountain holler, the kind of ancient homeplace that's so important to Kentucky families. There's the ill-fated St. Cyr siblings, too, wanderers and seekers among Appalachia's lost, longing, and hustling faithful, holding on—barely—through the cunning realism of another steely woman, Cassie St. Cyr. There's the Crowes, poison to all they touch, without a bottom to how low they'll sink, though still willing to honor obligations and emotional bonds of family.

Then there's the Givens bunch. It's almost too much to call them a family, which Raylan seems to understand in his refusal to call Arlo by any paternal form of address. Raylan says it pretty well in "For Blood or Money": "I never bore any illusions that my family was the Cosbys." Ties do certainly bind the Givenses, however, and they're all drawn back through a shared family history to the beautiful old homestead, to the family cemetery, and to the many family feuds and wounds that alternatively weave them together and tear them apart, despite anyone's better judgment. As Raylan's Aunt Helen knowingly declaims ("The Life Inside") with the type of dry sarcasm that makes the show (and real life Kentucky) so fun: "That would be a neat trick, escapin' the past."

I'm a Business Woman, Mr. Augustine

Let's start with Friedrich Engels (1820–1895). He argues that the earliest families were matrilineal, meaning that people identified the family to which they belonged according to who their mother was, possibly because of the biological fact that it's easier to identify a mother's children in conjunction with the social fact that society's material resources were in ancient times shared communally.

The establishment of private property changed things. Fathers wished to know to whom they were passing on the property they had acquired so that it only went to their own offspring: and therefore they needed to control sexual relationships. There are, as I'm sure you've already considered, some downsides to this strategy, especially for women. "Mother-right," says Engels, was overthrown in favor of "father right"; and monogamy was established, at least for females. For reason of coerced monogamy alone, relationships came to be no longer entirely free. It's not only the institution of monogamy that undermines freedom, however. More fundamentally it's the relationship to wealth underwriting monogamy that's the culprit, according to Engels.

Under the property-based system, whether to enter, maintain, or end a relationship comes to include calculations concerned with how the decision will affect individuals' access to wealth and ability to transfer it to their offspring. Not only do matrimonial and other family relationships become infected by economic interest, but pseudo-personal relationships that are essentially just economic—such as prostitution—also develop. In brief, money (or, anyway, private property) messes up a good thing. Ending private property might, therefore, Engels speculates, reverse the pathology, making it possible to reconstitute sexual and family relationships as matters of free choice and affection alone—perhaps even ending monogamy. Engels writes in *The Origin of the Family, Private Property, and the State* (1884):

> We are now approaching a social revolution, in which the old economic foundations of monogamy will disappear just as surely as those of its complement, prostitution. Monogamy arose through the concentration of considerable wealth in one hand—a man's hand—and from the endeavor to bequeath this wealth to the children of this man to the exclusion of all others. This necessitated monogamy on

the woman's, but not on the man's part. Hence this monogamy of women in no way hindered open or secret polygamy of men. Now, the impending social revolution will reduce this whole care of inheritance to a minimum by changing at least the overwhelming part of permanent and inheritable wealth—the means of production—into social property. Since monogamy was caused by economic conditions, will it disappear when these causes are abolished?

Mags is no man, but she's stepped into and performs the patriarch's role of acquiring and bequeathing wealth as the central purpose of family life for her and for the younger males she is grooming. Mags wants the Black Pike deal to go through not simply for her own gain but so she can pass on the wealth to Doyle and her grandchildren through him. The name 'Black Pike' is an amalgamation of Black Mountain, which runs through Harlan County and at 4,145 feet is the highest mountain in Kentucky, and Pike County, north of Harlan. There are companies that wish to mine Black Mountain by mountaintop removal, effectively destroying Kentucky's highest peak. So far, environmental regulations related to the impact of doing so on watercourses have prevented it.

Coover is a lost cause to Mags, and she just doesn't seem to like Dickie very much. She cuts him off ("Debts and Accounts") after Coover's death because in her mind he's betrayed the family by giving up to Raylan Coover's location after he abducted Loretta: "You went against the family," she says, "and not for the first time." "You shoulda taken it!" she screams at Dickie when he tries to excuse himself by invoking Raylan's torturing him as an excuse. (Frankly, though, I think she would have cut him off anyway.) Nevertheless, despite the betrayal, the weakness, and the general disdain, Mags does make sure Dickie will have a steady and ample stream of income from Harlan's pot industry. She may hate "those damn boys" ("The Life Inside"); she may physically and emotionally abuse them; she may control them and subordinate them. But she won't leave them without wealth. Dickie's inheritance ain't the Black Pike money, sure, but it does amount to a whole lotta productive capital that he can control and exploit.

Indeed, marijuana production in Kentucky really is an industry. Many have estimated pot to be Kentucky's largest cash crop—bigger than tobacco, corn, or soy. For example, in Francis X. Clines's 2001 report titled "Kentucky Journal: Fighting Appalachia's Top Cash Crop, Marijuana" in the *New York Times,* he notes that "Winter is easing in the rolling hills and hamlet hollows, and all the prespring indications are that marijuana will have another big year and remain this state's No. 1 cash crop, just as it continues prime in West Virginia and Tennessee." Marijuana is "Bigger than tobacco," says Roy E. Sturgill, director of the Appalachia High Intensity Drug Trafficking Area, "the only one of the nation's thirty-one federal antidrug regions focused on marijuana." The estimated value of the crop in 2001 was over $4 billion; and it's a sustainable resource to boot. Maybe Dickie actually got the better deal.

As for the rest, Ellstin Limehouse seems to be amassing capital, too, in order to pass it on to his offspring and his larger family's offspring. He's not only apart and neutral like Switzerland; he's loaded like a Swiss bank. It's one of the many markers of Arlo's failure as a parent, at least within the modern matrix of private property, that he shows no signs of storing up wealth to pass on to Raylan. Yes, Raylan might accidentally inherit the homestead along with any other money Arlo's squirreled away, but there's never any talk about it, even when Black Pike moves to purchase rights to the family property, or after Arlo and Helen's deaths. The depth of contempt between Raylan and Arlo suggests that that's just not gonna happen. Like Bo Crowder, Arlo inverts the business of patriarchy by willing to see his son harmed and even killed before sacrificing his own wealth—if he has any wealth.

Johnny, Hurt My Son

Yet even the putrid human patriarchs of the Crowder and Givens clans are not without moral conflict when it comes to sacrificing their sons. Bo signals as much when, in a scene that really cracks me up, he says to Boyd just before running him off and annihilating his followers: "Who am I kiddin'? I can't hurt my own son. . . . Johnny, hurt my son." And, to be honest, we must acknowledge that both Boyd and Raylan do bite the hand that would feed them through lines of patriarchal inheritance.

Boyd places his duties to God and others above his obligations to the patriarchal property-accumulation project. He even goes so far as to repudiate his father publicly in the diatribe he delivers before the congregation during Sunday church services when he declares:

> We must take the high road of righteousness, even if it means walking, walking and leaving our own flesh and blood behind. Because there is no greater piety, brothers and sisters, than the love of God. (Congregation: Amen.) Amen to that! He is my one true father. There is no other. There is no other, Preacher. There's no other.

Raylan more or less does the same by repeatedly making it very clear that his allegiance to the law supersedes any lingering loyalty to Arlo. If I were to psychoanalyze Raylan, I'd be tempted to say, in fact, that his devotion to the law is so deep because his flesh and blood father has failed him so profoundly. For Raylan, the law (and Art Mullens) substitutes for his natural father. The law is for Raylan the Big Father, the good father—not only the father he occasionally defies, resists, and sneaks around, as if he were a rebellious son, but also the father he forever wishes to please.

This explains in part why Raylan is so relentless and determined to capture and put down criminals. Every criminal he kills or locks up behind bars is simultaneously a representative of his natural father and an offering to his substitute father, Big Daddy Law, the father who might love him because his biological father never loved him enough. That much is confirmed when Arlo asks Raylan, "How long have you known?" after Raylan reveals he's onto Arlo's scheme to turn him over to Bo in the finale of Season One, and Raylan responds as if Arlo's remark were a different, more global question about their relationship: "Truthfully Arlo, I guess I've always known" ("Bulletville"). The screwed-up son of an unloving, screwed-up father, Raylan both loves and hates the law, both tries to please and affront it, both lives outside of it and under it.

If my analysis of Raylan's character and family is right, then Raylan really isn't justified in much of his conduct. His capturing and killing criminals is motivated by his personal family demons, even his desires. Social worker girlfriend Alison Brander from Penhook, Virginia, near Roanoke, has got it right when she wryly observes about Raylan: "You are a hero, Raylan. . . . I can tell you're a man that would run into a burning building without blinkin' an eye. Thing is I . . . I think you're the one setting the fire" ("Kill the Messenger").

Alison herself suffers through a complicated relationship with families. Her very job involves using the power of the state to intervene coercively in dysfunctional families, in a sense to protect them from themselves and to help them do as well as possible in family life. What she's seen in that work, however, has left her with a rather dim view of the institution, part of which she reveals in recounting the story of a man who threatened her with a tire iron when she stepped in to save his abused son from him. He would have likely killed her, had it not been for the police, and in the midst of the attack he was, in Alison's words, "saying there's no way I'm gonna break up his family. . . . All 'cause of this boy he had chained to a radiator. Worse than you'd treat your worst enemy. . . . Family" ("Over the Mountain").

Boyd has family issues, too, especially daddy issues. For the Boyd of Season One (as you know, Boyd is protean), a loving and just God substitutes for an unloving and unjust human father. The death of Bo and the loss of Boyd's flock at Bo's hands (well, his henchmen's hands), however, mark the killing of both fathers for Boyd. He becomes afterwards, fatherless and self-reliant, ready and willing, unlike Raylan, to become a father himself, even placing himself in his own father's role by assuming Bo's work of defending the Harlan drug trade against the interference of religious do-gooders (the St. Cyr's) and the police.

In another curious repetition of criminal family dynamics, Boyd's experience mirrors Mags's downfall when his aspiration to accumulate ill-gotten wealth for his own family and get out of crime is disrupted by the law (motivated by Lee Paxton's scheming) with Ava's arrest. Boyd's Engels-like revenge appropriately finds satisfaction not only in killing Lee and Sherriff Mooney but also by using Lee's mortuary business, his wealth engine, perversely to destroy his stature and patriarchal legacy; Boyd even uses his own family wealth to undermine the familial bonds between Lee and his wife, Mara.

As if following Engels's template, the wealth Boyd uses to destroy the corrupt Paxton family and to free his wife Ava (almost) from Big Daddy Law serves to advance the economic-patriarchal order of Hayes Workman's apparently more deserving family. Workman, whom Boyd bribes to kill Mooney, "has the black lung and ain't long for this world, won't even see a trial. But in six months' time his wife and his boys will have enough money to give them a leg up in this life" ("Over the Mountain").

Engels wouldn't at all be surprised that wife-figure Eva becomes entwined, as if symbolically, in the sex trade; she is "a businesswoman, Mr. Augustine," I suppose, but of a rather distinctive kind ("Decoy"). Although the show has become fascinated with the drama of her love affair with Boyd, readers of Engels will remember that her decision to abandon the anti-crime principles she had insisted upon when Boyd moved in with her and instead join Boyd in a life of crime comes at precisely the same moment Boyd secures and offers her the capital (from the mine robbery) to pay down her mortgage ("Cottonmouth")—a moment bordering on prostitution itself.

Winona's relationship with Gary, yes, *quelle surprise!*, falls apart when he mortgages their largest and most symbolic asset (their home) to speculate on a riskier asset (a thoroughbred racehorse). Just like the failed real estate scheme that ruined their relationship in Season One, it's a risk he's willing to take in order to acquire even more capital ("Save My Love"). Arlo's plan to get hold of capital by robbing Dickie with Boyd leads to the end of his marriage, too—and in the worst possible way. Helen, uncorrupted by money, dies in an act of virtue, protecting Arlo from a man seeking retribution for the disruption of his own capacity to accumulate wealth.

The manner of Helen's death, like Bo's reluctance to hurt Boyd, reminds us that even in the worst of families, not everything is about money. In a plot line that parallels and contrasts Boyd and Ava, Raylan and Winona put back the money, the capital, that Winona takes from the evidence storeroom, even though it could have secured Winona's own vulnerable mortgage. On the other hand, perhaps, in addition to Raylan's failure to balance the civil against the familial, their unwillingness to secure capital is in part why, in the show's logic, Raylan and Winona can't establish a family of their own. In a capitalist society, Engels tells us, families need capital, but capital messes families up.

Hegel: What if Mama Found Out?

Engels, like his philosophical partner Karl Marx, studied Hegel, and the basis of Engels's interpretation of the family is not only, as the full title of his book indicates, Lewis H. Morgan's *Ancient Society* (1877) but also Hegel's *Elements of the Philosophy of Right* (1820).

Hegel does not object to private property, but he agrees that family should not exist for the sake of property. Property is an instrument to serve moral purposes, and at the family's core should be love not financial interest. "The family, as the *immediate substantiality* of spirit, has as its determination the spirit's *feeling* of its own unity, which is *love*" (§158).

Hegel argues that the family exists for the formation of its members, in particular children, to raise and educate them as free, self-sufficient, rational, and moral beings. Family is a rather strange institution in this, because its success paradoxically entails its self-destruction (§181). Once the children are successfully raised, they leave the family and go on to start new families of their own. The very word "family," in fact, derives from a Latin word that means "dependents," but properly raised children should not be living in their parents' basements very far into adulthood. When things run properly, they cease to be dependents and leave the nest.

The ethical dissolution of the family consists in the fact that the children are brought up to become free personalities and, when they have *come of age*, are recognized as legal persons and as capable both of holding free property of their own and of founding their own families.

The Bennetts fail on both counts—love and independence. I don't know about you, but while I think parents deserve ongoing respect and in many ways deference, those Bennett boys seem a bit too old to be living so thoroughly under their mother's thumb. It may be proper to submit quietly, even as an adult, to a tongue lashing from a parent, but a ball-peen hammer hand smashing of the sort to which Coover gives himself over seems more than just a little too far. On the one hand (oops!), Dickie and Coover live like teenagers, like college students languishing in a filthy crash pad, getting high on weed, playing video games, messing around with exotic pets like "Charlie" (I love Coover's reaction when Ava puts Charlie down—"The Spoil"). But, on the other hand, you know very well that Mags orchestrated things that way, that she wants it that way. Yeah, Doyle is a bit more of a big boy, with his job and family and all; but he never shows much independence either, really, as if like his brothers he's never formed an entirely autonomous self.

Then there's the lousy moral development all the Bennett children exhibit. Not only has the Bennett family failed to form independent beings. It has also failed to cultivate their moral characters. Coover's a violent brute. Dickie's a vengeful sadist. But it's no wonder. I doubt Coover's hearing his mother run him down while he stands outside the room where she fawns over Loretta was the first time he'd suffered something like that.

Mags loves her fantasy of a daughter—a daughter she thought she could simply take in the same way she takes money and power and consumer goods—more than her own sons; and I'm sure they know it. Doyle seems utterly lawless and, in fact, seems to find his happiest moments among those actually opposed to lawfulness. I pick that up (don't you?) in the scene where Doyle for a moment thinks he's learned that Raylan is a dirty cop, too, after Dewey Crowe impersonates him to steal the oxy ("I of the Storm"). It's clear in any case, where the Bennett boys got those traits—their parents.

Mags suffers from all of her sons' moral shortcomings herself, though not from their rank stupidity—she can be as lawless, cruel, and vindictive as any of them. It's chilling to see her go from pleading, distraught mother of a dead son when she asks Raylan to see Coover's corpse ("Brother's Keeper") to cold, hard, mean crime boss after he says no. In these distortions of motherhood and moral virtue, she generally seems to have almost perfectly realized Engels's and Hegel's nightmare family.

Now, what about Raylan? Raylan didn't acquire his moral compass from his father (except maybe negatively), though he probably did gain something from his family, anyway, through his mother and through Aunt Helen—contrasting maternal figures to Mags. US nineteenth-century political ideology crafted the concept of "republican motherhood," echoing not only the Hegelian idea that the function of families is to reproduce moral beings but also, frankly, the nineteenth century's wish to segregate women into the separate sphere of female domesticity. Republican mothers were to raise citizens, not only free rational beings but also political participants ready to take on the civic responsibilities of citizenship; and republican mothers were to do that only from inside the domestic sphere of the household. It may be a good thing that Mags refused the segregating objective of republican motherhood, but it's not a good thing that she failed to raise citizens devoted to more than their own family's wealth and power.

Issues with the Law

That families are vehicles for ethical development and that they dissolve (both when they've completed their work and also when the free beings that compose them just decide to split) points to the reason it's important that there be some- thing beyond families to hold society together. The Bennett-Givens feud demonstrates pretty well why a stronger and more rational third party is needed to manage conflict among families; and the failure of both Walt McCready and Mags Bennett to protect Loretta from the predations of James Earl Dean illustrates why families need support of the sort law enforcement provides in protecting their chil- dren (it takes government in the form of Rachel and Raylan, as well as a foster home, to save Loretta). With apologies to home schoolers, even that both Raylan and Dickie attended public high schools signals that families often need support in the business of educating their children, too.

Aristotle understood this in the famous argument he sets out in Book I of the *Politics*, where he argues that in a sense the state (or anyway, the *polis* or Greek city state) is "prior" to the family—that the political is prior to the familial. Aris- totle understood that the state is not prior in a historical sense. He knew full well that historically speaking families developed from older human forms of association—male-fe- male sex and pair bonding and, perhaps troublingly, master-slave relationships. But the political is prior to families in the sense that it's logically prior or, let's say, necessary for their completeness and well-being. That's because human be- ings can't fully develop, for Aristotle, in the context of fami- lies alone and because families are themselves dependent upon the state or society for both security and for the re- sources they need to flourish. Human mental capacities re- quire intellectual, artistic, scientific, and legal goods of the sort only found in the wider social order to realize them- selves most fully; and because of the contingencies to which family is subject in its self-destruction and fragility, families require something more stable, rational and self-sufficient to secure those goods—that something is civil society and the state.

This establishes a sometimes conflicting set of duties for people. Unabomber Ted Kaczynski was turned over to the authorities by his brother, David. David Kaczynski understood that no matter how much he loved his brother and would hate to see him locked up, he had duties to others and to the larger civil society, too—duties the Bennetts don't recognize. Raylan, on the other hand, won't stay with Winona or quit his job in service to the civil order, no matter what damage it does to his relationship to her, to their child, or to Arlo and Hellen.

Acknowledging this conflict between families and the larger social order and taking note of the way people too often conduct themselves like the Bennetts in relation to other people and civil society has led thinkers such as Michèle Barrett and Mary McIntosh to conclude in their 1999 work titled *The Anti-Social Family* that the family is at least in our historical moment an anti-social institution. Excessive focus on the family can dilute our wider social duties, and the ideology that everything from education to health care should be performed principally by families weakens our commitment to providing those services through the civic order. That's why people who favor home schooling often support cutting social services generally.

Plato argued that the state has responsibility to educate and care for children, but he also understood that family can be a threat to the state, that familial interests often stand in opposition to state and civil society's interests. Family conflict leads to faction, and family often entices officials to use the state to enrich themselves privately. Family members, unrestrained, are liable to give preferential appointments to other family members rather than to those most qualified to hold office.

So, Plato has Socrates in the *Republic* argue that in the ideal society the rulers should not have personal families. Among the philosopher kings and queens that are to run Plato's ideal society, sexual unions are arranged for the sake of eugenics, children are to be raised in common, not knowing whom their biological parents are, and children will call all adults of their ruling class "mother" and "father." It's not so much in this ideal society, as people often say about Plato, that the rulers have no family or that Plato abolishes the family; it's that the family and the political community become for the rulers the same. In a way, that's how it is for Raylan.

People like Doyle and Mags are just the opposite of Plato. They reject the claims and interests of the civil society—or at least they subordinate them to the claims and interests of their own family—and they use the state (Doyle as county chief of police) for their own gain. That's part of the inversion of the proper Platonic and Aristotelian relationship of the family to the state the show presents and criticizes. It's an inversion symbolized by the twisted implications of moonshine (illegal and deadly) apple pie (nurturing domesticity).

Not only do the Bennetts break the law by engaging in murder, threats, assault, fraud, and illegal drug sales to advance their power and wealth. Mags morally violates her membership in the larger civic community in the run up to her Black Pike deal, putting on a helluva deceptive performance at the community meeting where people assemble to discuss the project (as well as at the party the next day), a performance that silenced even the remarkable Carol Johnson, a woman of considerable persuasive powers of her own and in her smooth-talking sexuality a symbol of corporate money as an almost irresistible object of desire.

Nut Jobs Living in Caves and Tree Houses

But hold on a moment here. I hope you'll forgive me if, as a Kentuckian, I make a number of observations about the way the Black Pike deal is portrayed by the Yankee story editor Benjamin Cavell and, I suppose, the many other non-Kentucky writers and producers associated with the show. (Benjamin Cavell, by the way, is the son of the fine Harvard philosopher Stanley Cavell, which may in part explain the many interesting philosophical dimensions of the show. Now, Stanley Cavell was raised in the south—in Atlanta. But I'm suspecting, though I could be wrong, that Benjamin has spent very little time in Harlan County.)

I remember having dinner with Christopher Hitchens in Lexington (not Massachusetts) at a French restaurant when he came to Transylvania University in 2005 to lecture and teach. Hitchens was, as you may know, a rather devoted smoker. Now, Lexington enjoys a smoking ban in restaurants; but soon after we sat down and Hitchens was of course recognized, a small, elegant ashtray appeared beside him on the white linen-draped table. Hitchens incredulously asked the waiter how this was possible, exclaiming that people in Washington DC, where he lived, would never tolerate such an offensive flouting of the law. The knowing young man, decked out smartly in classic Parisian waiter garb, casually responded in a beautiful Kentucky accent: "Well, I guess, Mr. Hitchens, we here in Kentucky just have a different relationship with the law." (Hitchens also loved about Kentucky that drug stores commonly—and legally—devote an entire aisle of shelves to whiskey and other spirits. They are drugs, after all.)

It's true that Kentuckians' relationship with the law can be complex. That complexity suggests some Kentucky fried qualifications are in order to Plato, Aristotle, Hegel, and Engels's ideas. Philosophical inversions of the relationship between family and state of the sort we witness in the Bennetts are not unknown in Kentucky. Guns and proclamations of gun rights, in defense of family, are ubiquitous (Google "Knob Creek Machine Gun Shoot" if you don't believe me). Gay marriage is prohibited to all (except in federal matters) on the basis of the perceived threat it poses to some forms of family. One hears from elected officials in state and federal government, such as US Senators Mitch McConnell and Rand Paul, all kinds of anti-government clichés, clichés repeated by many of those whose families nevertheless depend upon government assistance or government supported jobs, like those at and around Fort Campbell and Fort Knox or in agriculture.

Kentuckians, however, have not had an entirely positive history at the hands of government (it's the law, after all, that would rape Ava and keeps her locked up), and they know perfectly well the smug contempt borne against them by outsiders, coasters mostly, who refer to them with terms like: hillbillies, inbreds, shoeless, pellagra-infected, backward, white trash stuck in a flyover state. (I've heard all of these spoken, and they find their way into characters in the show from Detroit, Canada, and elsewhere—even from the upper classes of Kentucky.)

Many poor eastern Kentuckians derive from Scottish and Irish ancestry. They were driven from their ancestral lands during the Clearances of the seventeenth, eighteenth, and early nineteenth centuries by wealthy absentee lords, factors, and others with attitudes similar to those of the contemptuous on the scene today—looking to make a buck off sheep and "improved" agriculture at the expense of their lives. After they crossed the woods (*trans-sylvania*) with Daniel Boone into Ken-tuck-ee, they of course turned it into the "dark and bloody ground" through murder and clearances of their own, stealing Cherokee and other Native American lands as they pressed westward. Hounded and burned out of their homes, they resettled in the new highlands of North America's east coast, cheap land where they thought they could be left alone.

Some of those lands in Western West Virginia and Eastern Kentucky became the site of resistance to additional mistreatment at the hands of a new class of powerful, often better educated trouble during the early twentieth century's mine wars—including the Harlan County War of the early 1930s and the Battle of Blair Mountain in 1921, the bloodiest armed insurrection in the US since the Civil War. One of the significant early uses of the phrase "redneck" dates from this period, apparently from the red bandanas members of the multi-racial miners' army wore as its miner-soldiers fought for better pay, safer working conditions, and the right to organize unions.

The practice of wearing red around the neck, in fact, fits well with the history of the region's people, as it seems to have been used back in eastern Kentuckians' ancestral Scotland, too, by Covenanters in the Bishops' Wars of 1639 and 1640, where once again they struggled against upper class and episcopal rule in religious and other affairs. (So, with this proud history, why is "redneck" a derogatory term?) The government (the Big Law) as usual took the side of the companies in most of the mine wars, with the US Army Air Corps flying recon for the company forces who actually bombed the Blair Mountain rebels from the air. US Army troops were dispatched to suppress Appalachia's restive poor. Until the 2011 bombings of Abdulrahman al-Awlaki and Anwar al-Awlaki, this was perhaps the only time the federal government has intentionally played a role in bombing its own citizens, and it remains the only time the US government participated in the bombing of its own citizens on US territory—though perhaps you might count the City of Philadelphia bombing the MOVE house in 1985.

A bit more recently, although the 1989 Exxon Valdez spill garnered sustained national attention, to no one's surprise relative indifference prevailed in the wake of the 2000 Martin County Coal Slurry Spill, a disaster thirty times larger than its Alaskan predecessor, even though it happened just a few hundred miles from Washington DC. At the time, the Martin County spill was the biggest environmental disaster east of the Mississippi, affecting some of the world's richest woodlands as well as thousands of people along hundreds of miles of river in the Ohio Valley watershed. The federal government first fined the subsidaries of multi-billion dollar Massey Energy, a measly $110,000 for the release, possibly through the influence of another Kentucky family, Senator Mitch McConnell's. The penalty was later reduced in the government's administrative courts to just $5,600.

Justified seems to acknowledge this sorry alignment between government and those who would exploit the families of Harlan County when Raylan, like so many government agents before him, is assigned to protect Black Pike Coal Company's Carol Johnson and pantless Judge Mike Reardon. Alternatively, neither Raylan nor any other government official does anything to help the dead environmentalist's family, a Kentucky family for whom no one on the show has a kind word but whom the script has Judge Reardon call "nut jobs."

I wonder what names were hurled at Dennis and Cindy Davidson when they sought legal redress after their three-year-old son Jeremy was crushed to death in 2005 under "fly rock" that smashed through the wall of his bedroom at 2:30 A.M. near the Kentucky-Virginia border. A&G Coal was fined by the government $15,000 for the transgression—about, I suppose, what in many people's minds killing poor mountain people (nut job families) warrants. The Davidsons have sued for over $20 million. Let's hope they don't get Judge Reardon, but US marshals will protect whomever they get, though probably not marshals as good looking as Raylan Givens. Judge Reardon's courtroom portrays, I think, one of the truest moments in the series, truer I suspect than the show's makers understand. So, you might forgive or take just a bit of pause before you criticize Kentuckians for their backward anti-government attitudes and hostility to outsiders.

Justifying Families

I have stood on the ridge of Black Mountain near the town of Lynch in Harlan County and peered into Virginia from a place quite different from MLK's "mountaintop" towards the Davidson home. I've watched there mining companies blow the "overburden" off the tops of mountains nearby; and I've pondered some of the issues raised about Kentucky and its families by the big corporate television show, *Justified*.

People know about Jeremy Davidson, and the Martin County disaster; they know about the deadly 1972 Buffalo Creek flood and scores of other, smaller incidents like it. Fewer of the people in Eastern Kentucky are, however, as opposed to the mining operations as the liberal fantasy of a community meeting portrayed in *Justified* ("The Spoil") might lead one to believe. People need jobs to support their families; they live amidst an enthusiastic and well-funded public relations campaign aimed at linking their local identities to coal mining; and many hold fast to belief in the beneficence of coal.

I've walked up Pine Mountain, too, through Harlan's near-virgin Blanton Forest, among its ghostly sandstone caves (suitable, Judge Reardon, in a pinch for habitation), cascading streams, mountaintop bogs, and a diversity of flora and fauna that exceeds the Amazon's (the river basin, not the web site).

I've walked among the wreckage of the village of Dayhoit, in Harlan County near White Star Hollow, and its Super-fund site, where PCBs, trichloroethylene, volatile organic compounds, and grease were poured into the ground water adjacent to the Cumberland River. I pondered all the while there what happened in that forsaken place to "nut job" activist Teri Blanton's family—an intimidating coal company truck ripping up her yard by driving circles around her house for a full day after she appealed to the government to protect her children from the pollution to which they were being exposed.

I think, too, about the Givenses, the Crowders, the Lime-houses, and Bennetts. They remind me that the very idea of family presents a challenge to moral and political philosophy, because living in families means privileging family members above others and approaching the rest of society sometimes in an ambiguous, cautious way. That's because the interests of families aren't always congruent with those of the larger society or civil society, and the rest of society often fails families. We devote more care, time, and money to our own children than to others—even when we know other children may deserve or need it more—and few of us think it would be a good idea to do otherwise. By the way, that unequal treatment of persons by families is warranted is argued persuasively through the thought experiment of a society called "Equim," where everyone is treated absolutely equally (family members treated the same as acquaintances and strangers) in the book edited by Diane Tietjen Meyers, Kenneth Kipnis, and Cornelius Murphy, *Kindred Matters: Rethinking the Philosophy of the Family*.

But family obligations sometimes do supersede duties to the larger, embedding society. The ambiguity in our duties is difficult to navigate, especially when historical experience teaches us that rather than protecting us, promoting our general welfare, and nourishing us so that can we develop our human potential, the larger social order (especially its commercial and political institutions) often works against us in league with those who would carelessly exploit and demean us.

Justified reminds us of what Hegel understood, that families and the unequal treatment they require are crucial for the formation of human selves, for creating and reproducing free, rational, and morally sound people. *Justified* also illustrates Plato and Aristotle's insight that the state and the larger social order are necessary in relation to families and that sometimes duties to the civil order trump obligations to family.

But part of the genius of *Justified* is that it also understands something these venerable philosophers seem to have missed but that Kentuckians have long experienced. *Justified* also understands that those wider duties to the civil order become destabilized and sometimes lose their binding force when the economic and civil institutions of society fail people.

Families are not enough; but in a corrupt and incompetent world populated by oppressive and exploitive institutions sometimes family seems like all you've got, the best you've got. The social-political challenge with which, then, *Justified* presents us is to figure out whether it's still possible for families to flourish in cooperation with the civil and commercial dimensions of our society—and do so within the law.

The moral challenge of the show is, therefore, still a bit deeper. *Justified* challenges us to consider whether, in the circumstances in which we live today, families—corrupted and exploited by the demands of wealth and treated as spoil even by the political order that should be helping them—can flourish at all, in any morally justifiable way.

15
Family Matters in Harlan County

GERALD BROWNING

Raylan Givens's estranged relationship with his father, Boyd Crowder trying to preserve the much-sullied Crowder name following his father's death, and Mags Bennett attempting to sustain a criminal business under the guise of strengthening the bonds of family—all the most complicated and compelling relationships in *Justified* are those forged by blood and kin.

A major storyline is Raylan's relationship with his father, Arlo Givens. In the beginning of the series, whenever there is a reference to Arlo, Raylan seems to roll his eyes and is quick with a negative quip to display his animosity towards his father.

Sigmund Freud's theory of the Oedipus Complex says that sons see their fathers as rivals for the mother's affections. The very first time we see Raylan and Arlo on camera together, Raylan is bailing his father out of jail. He is quick to admit that the only reason that he is doing it is because his step-mother, Helen Givens, asked him to do so.

Helen and Raylan seem to have a more amicable relationship than Raylan and his father. Raylan credits Helen with raising him after his mother passed away. Helen is one of the few amicable characters in the story who doesn't have much of a negative side. Other than turning a "blind" eye to Arlo's dealings (and aiding him at times with his criminal activity),

Helen is viewed through a mostly sympathetic lens. There seems to be nothing but warmth and love for the Givens men on her part. On many occasions, she is pitted between the warring Givens men and tries to placate both of them.

When Helen is killed by Dickie, both Raylan and Arlo set their sights on Dickie. Whereas Arlo means to kill him in retribution, Raylan forces himself to stop short of doing so. He points a gun at the back of Dickie's skull in the middle of the wilderness in the dead of night. With Dickie shivering and crying for his life, Raylan arrests him. There seems to be a theme throughout many of the relationships that blood is very important, but there are some times which bind deeper than blood (or at the very least are cherished more than just blood relationship).

As the story unfolds we see that Arlo is still involved with organized crime in Harlan County. He is actually collecting protection money for Bo Crowder, who comes looking for Arlo when he gets out of prison. Arlo, being unapologetic about his criminal behavior, finds himself in protective custody under the watchful eye of his son, who is investigating the Crowder family. Throughout the first season (and it has become a theme for each of the seasons), we observe a metaphorical chess game played between father and son to see which can manipulate the other to get what they want.

Boyd and Bo

We can easily see the same relationship (but on a much more vicious level) between Boyd and his father, Bo. When Boyd and Bo meet in prison, it's plain to see that Bo is part of the reason why Boyd has been able to survive in prison. With his recent "conversion" to religion, he has not made many friends in the underworld of Harlan County. So, when some thugs attempt to exact revenge on Boyd, his father steps in to protect his son. Later Boyd is released on a technicality and moves out into the wilderness of Harlan with ex-cons and creates a church (which turns into a front for vigilante justice enforced by Crowder).

When Bo gets out of prison, he finds that due to Boyd's actions against local drug dealers and meth cookers, a lot of the competition has been destroyed or driven out of the county. In a tense scene where Bo attempts to bribe Boyd into controlling who he attacked, Boyd confronts his father and tells him that his "services" are not for sale. Yet, as we watch this unfold, we can't help wondering whether Boyd has a motive other than the "righteous" cause that he communicates to his congregation. The tenuous relationship between the Crowder men indirectly leads to Boyd attempting to kill his father.

The Crowder-Givens relationship seems to be murkier throughout the series. In the third season, we see Boyd and Arlo bonding. Arlo goes to work for Boyd's criminal enterprise. Ava and Boyd take care of Arlo as his memory seems to deteriorate. He's having visions of Helen, who acts as his conscience (something she did many times when she was alive). Throughout the third season, Arlo seems to be succumbing to Alzheimer's disease. It is Ava and Boyd who see to it that he takes his medication. The closer Arlo is to the Crowder gang, the farther he is drifting from his biological son.

This seems to become an even bigger issue towards the end, when Quarles, a mobster from Detroit, moves to Harlan (or rather is exiled to Harlan) to influence the underworld (due to Mags Bennett's passing and the gap in the drug trade that has occurred). Quarles is at odds with Boyd (who also wants to dominate the Harlan underworld) and revels in revealing to Raylan that it was Arlo who killed a friend of Raylan's, Trooper Tom Bergen.

When Raylan confronts his father, he admits to shooting the trooper because he was aiming at Boyd. However, upon reflection Raylan realizes that a confused and disoriented Arlo shot a lawman wearing a Stetson hat, which causes Givens to wonder (due in no small part to his own trademark Stetson) exactly *who* Arlo was trying to shoot. Could it have been that Arlo Givens was trying to kill his son? This reflection ends Season Three, leaving Raylan with a sense of unease.

The Godmother

Boyd and Raylan aside, the most pronounced source to show the Achilles Heel of family would have to be the exploits of Mags Bennett. Mags is one of the biggest underworld masterminds within Harlan County. Mags has owned the marijuana business in Harlan County for a long time. Her family has a rich history which goes back to Prohibition. Her main focus for all that she does is her family. Her attitude towards the "family business" is not unlike that of mafia crime families as dramatized in movies.

Much like Don Corleone in *The Godfather*, family is the most important thing to Mags Bennett. She has three sons Dickie, Coover, and Doyle Bennett (much like Vito Corleone's sons Michael, Fredo, and Sonny). She also "adopted" a child, Loretta McCready. Vito Corleone adopted Tom Hagen. Whereas Tom was an orphan on the streets whom Vito took in, Loretta's father crossed Mags one too many times and she had him killed. While he died, she took it upon herself to inform him that she would take care of Loretta as her own kin.

It seems rather ironic that even though Mags Bennett is quick to talk about the importance of family, she notices that each of her sons acted incompetently and directs her affections and love onto Loretta McCready, much to the envy and chagrin of Coover (the simpleton of the sons), who is ridiculed and debased on a regular basis by Mags.

Coover is brutalized by Mags when she takes a hammer to his hand to teach him a lesson. The Oedipus Complex seems to apply strongly to the relationship that Coover has with Mags. Coover is the most submissive of the three sons in his relationship with Mags. "Yes, Mamma" seems to be his most often used line in his stint on the show. In the scene where Mags destroys his hand with a hammer, he cries while being cradled in the arms of Mags. "I'm sorry, Mamma," he whimpers over and again. With Coover's strong and constant need for Mags's approval, coupled with his ability to ruin plans and reveal secrets, we can surmise the reason for Mags's disdain for him. Coover's one strength seems to be his ability to grow and cultivate marijuana. "He had a gift" Mags sighed over hearing of Coover's death. It seemed to be the one positive thing she could say about him.

If Coover is the oafish member of the Bennett family, Dickie is obviously the hothead of the clan. Dickie and Raylan have a lot of history together. During a baseball game in high school, Raylan gave Dickie the limp that he has throughout his tenure on the show. Much like Coover, Dickie is very intent on making "Mama" happy. However, his motives are much more subversive. Dickie, highly involved in the distribution and selling of the illicit marijuana that they have cultivated, wants to inherit the family business after Mags passes away. As such, he does whatever he can to strengthen the family business.

Dickie's impetuousness that gets him into trouble on many occasions. Dickie tries to strike out to make a name for himself. This motive is purely self-aggrandizing. It's easy to see that he wants money, fame, and power. However, in most cases this results in him meeting with Raylan and regretting his choices. In an altercation with Helen Givens, Dickie is the one who kills her, prompting Raylan to seek revenge.

The third member of the Bennett clan is Doyle Bennett. Doyle, who happens to be a sheriff in a small town in Harlan County, seems to be the smartest of Mags's offspring (which isn't saying much). Being a sheriff, Doyle has perfect (and multiple) opportunities to cover up for his mother's misdeeds, which he does time and again. However, he spends most of the series covering up for what his brothers have done to endanger their family business.

Life Is Suffering

Yet the most telling family relationship in *Justified* seems to be between Raylan and Winona Hawkins, the mother of Raylan's daughter. In the second season, we find out that Winona is pregnant with Raylan's child. During the pregnancy, Winona and Raylan discuss the idea of raising a child in such a violent environment as Harlan County. This evokes Arthur

Schopenhauer's pessimistic view of life. The nineteenth-century German philosopher expounded a quasi-Buddhist philosophy in which life is suffering.

This pessimistic outlook forces Winona to leave Harlan County to move to Louisville to live with her sister, Gayle. Winona turning her back on her life in Lexington demonstrates her pessimism. With an ex-husband who was involved in organized crime, which led to his demise, plus being involved with missing money, it is easy to see her opinion of life as suffering in Kentucky. Schopenhauer's belief that life is suffering is merely a premise to his notion that because life is suffering, to bring a child into this type of world would be a negative action.

Winona seems to be detached from Harlan County. She lived in Lexington and only seems connected to Harlan through Raylan. Raylan, however, grew up in Harlan and has roots there. Winona seems to wonder about the ethics of raising a child in such an environment (her musings might lead us to wonder if she is even contemplating not having the child); whereas Raylan has no doubt in his mind as to raising the child and taking care of her.

Try as he might (especially in the beginning of the series) Raylan seems to want to distance himself from Harlan County, traveling so far away from his home town of Harlan (all the way to Miami) to be a "big city . . . federal lawman". This very action shows that Raylan Givens is just like the people of Harlan County, which would not come as a shock to anyone who sees Raylan interact with anyone within that county.

Schopenhauer's perception of Harlan County would be one where procreation would not be moral. Who would want to raise a child in an environment like this? Schopenhauer would see irony in Mags Bennett's rhetoric of parenting and looking out for the best interests of Harlan County, all the while establishing an empire based on drugs and murder. In *On the Vanity of Existence*, Schopenhauer writes that due to the fact that life is suffering there seems to be no real significance or value to life. As such, humans create value or purpose (vanity) by using religion. Inherent in this is a type of selfishness. If we bring a child into a world where there is suffering and chaos, then we must be doing it merely for self-ish reasons rather than to make the world a better place.

Mags Bennett is using her sons for selfish motives. Her interactions with her children are mostly connected to her criminal empire. The only person with whom her motives are "pure" (if anything Mags does could be construed as pure), would be her relationship with Loretta McCready. However, Schopenhauer would most likely note that even though Loretta is treated with more love and devotion by Mags than her sons, the effect of Mags's apparent benevolence toward Loretta is to expose her to violence and corruption.

Where the Greed and Selfishness Come From

What is it that parents stand to gain from having children in such an unpromising environment? Where is the greed coming from? Some would argue that a potential reason for the desire for procreation would be due to the fact that the parents could see this as a way to make their memory last (even after their death). This could be a way to become immortal, and this is the "vanity" that Schopenhauer writes about.

Mags's constant mention of the importance of family reinforces this. Family is a major theme for all the characters in the show. In many cases, the family members create a sense of duty for the characters, which leads them into many of the situations that they find themselves in. Harlan County seems to have a long memory. Throughout the series, there have been many instances in which two or more members of a family mention how their family has helped (or hurt) another family, which created a feud. With the lineage of the family as being an important backdrop to the storylines, we can see that the concept of "immortality" can be a useful metaphor in understanding just how valuable family can be. On the other hand, it is also easy to see just how selfish a motive this is.

What motivates this selfishness? Schopenhauer writes that the strongest will that man has is the will to live. It seems to be a driving force in a lot that mankind does. If it is impossible to live forever, then the next best thing is to ensure that your family name survives. This would explain the importance of lineage and heredity in Harlan County. If you can't be immortal in the purest sense of the word, you want to be immortal in that you're not forgotten and your name will live on long after you have passed away.

The Will to Live

Ironically, one of the seemingly "purer" relationships in this sordid story is the one between Boyd, Ava, and Arlo Givens. When Arlo is wracked with dementia, it is Boyd and Ava who take care of him. Even though they're trying to keep an eye on him and don't trust him not to spill the secrets of their fledgling criminal enterprise, Boyd and Ava seem to care for him as if he were a blood relative. They make certain that Arlo takes his medication and they live in the same house (or hideout) together. Apparently there's no need to preserve a family name or ensure a lineage. They're just people who seem genuinely interested in taking care of him (even though, he is a member of their crew and a weak one at that).

The characters in *Justified* are driven by very complex agendas and motives. However, beneath the surface of their tough exteriors are souls who are very cognizant of their own mortality. Being in a kill-or-be-killed lifestyle may cause them to reflect on what will happen to their name once they have passed away, or been executed. This vulnerability forces the family members to emphasize their family history and the continuation of that history.

A lot of what these characters do is fueled by the fear of their own mortality. This is what makes them so authentic and what makes their stories so believable. There most powerful motivation is the will to live.

VI

Quite the Characters

16
Pleasure Über Alles

ROD CARVETH

When we're introduced to Ava Crowder in the Season One opener, "Fire in the Hole," she has just shot and killed her abusive husband Bowman with a deer rifle, while he was enjoying the dinner she had prepared for him. She had finally tired of him getting drunk and beating her. When Raylan Givens hears the news, he remembers that Ava lived down the street from him, and agrees to talk to her.

Pursue Your Pleasure

When Ava sees Raylan, she welcomes him with a passionate kiss and asks if he's still married. She then admits she has had a crush on him since he had been twelve years old. Normally, someone who has just killed a spouse is not likely to go after another man so quickly. But it's clear that Ava operates according to a form of utilitarianism, one that focuses on hedonism—the pursuit of pleasure as the over-riding goal.

It's not clear if Ava was always a hedonist, or that the shooting of her husband allowed her to feel it was okay for her to want what she wanted. Regardless, from the first episode through the rest of the series, Ava always sought what was pleasurable for Ava. And, Ava is not taking "No" for an answer, if the recommended course of action is not to pursue her pleasure.

When Boyd kidnaps Ava, and attempts to shoot Raylan, Raylan's boss Art warns Raylan that he should not get involved with Ava as she is a witness. So, even though Raylan knows full well that it goes against proper protocol for a Deputy Marshal to socialize with the defendant in an active murder investigation, he nevertheless finds himself unable to resist Ava's persistent advances.

Ava wants what Ava wants. Ava's apparent irresistibility soon results in an ongoing sexual relationship. When she mentions to Raylan that she derives comfort from knowing that the "A-number-one gunfighter in the whole US Marshals Service is watching her back," he reminds Ava that he continues to watch every part of her. It turns out that Art's warning was correct—because of Ava's affair with Raylan, Boyd Crowder ends up being released from prison early because both of them have been compromised as witnesses.

When confronted with a choice, Ava pursues the one that maximizes her pleasure, and minimizes her pain. This pattern of behavior is best shown by her behavior in Season Five, a season that begins with her entering jail and ends up with her getting ready to betray her former fiancé, Boyd.

Hedonism

"Hedonism" comes from the Greek word for pleasure. Aristippus (who died in 366 B.C.E.), a student of Socrates, founded this ethical philosophy. Aristippus believed that people should "act to maximize pleasure now and not worry about the future." Aristippus, however, was referring to the pleasures of the mind—intellectual pleasures—not pleasures of the body. Aristippus proposed that individuals should devote their time to intellectual pursuits, while, at the same time, exhibiting restraint in acting out their physical relationships.

This phrase by Aristippus probably best describes the hedonist philosophy: "I possess; I am not possessed." Despite his emphasis on pleasures of the mind, in the twentieth century, hedonism became more associated with such expressions as "Don't worry, be happy" or "YOLO" (You Only Live

Once). As these slogans suggest, if a belief or behavior is based on a purely personal motivation (such as the acquisition of wealth, fame, or sexual partners), then the underlying philosophy governing such actions is hedonism.

English philosopher Jeremy Bentham (1748–1832) is considered to be one of the founders of utilitarianism. The Oxford-educated lawyer and philosopher was a prolific writer, though his most acclaimed work was his *Introduction to the Principles of Morals and Legislation* (1789). His vision of utilitarianism held that the greatest happiness for the greatest number of people is the fundamental and self-evident principle of morality. Bentham identified happiness with pleasure and devised a moral arithmetic for judging the value of a pleasure or a pain. He argued that self-interests, properly understood, are harmonious and that the general welfare is bound up with personal happiness.

Enunciation

Bentham distinguished between the "enunciative principle" (that each person's sole ultimate motive is the maximization of their own happiness) and the "censorial principle" (that it is the effects on the happiness of all affected which determines what they ought to do). In other words, society works best when the people pursuing their own personal pleasure are doing so in a community that rewards behavior consistent with the benefit of the whole community and punishes behavior that is inconsistent with best interests of that community.

Bentham employed a quantitative approach—or "hedonistic calculus"—to discussing the principle of hedonism underlying his form of utilitarianism. He proposed that there were seven dimensions of pleasure (and, conversely, pain):

1. Intensity, that is, how pleasant at each moment the pleasure is or how painful the pain.

2. Duration, that is, how long the pleasure (or pain) lasts.

3. Its certainty or uncertainty, that is the probability that the pleasure or pain will occur.

4. Its propinquity or remoteness, or how close the source of pleasure or pain is.

5. Its chance of its being followed by further pleasure if a pleasure, or further pain if a pain.

6. Its purity, or the chance of its not being followed by further sensations of the opposite kind.

7. Its extent, that is, the number of people who will experience it.

Bentham recognized that the hedonistic calculus was only an ideal, and there may be many cases where there's just no way to determine how many times more pleasant or painful one experience is than another, or how pains and pleasures compare.

The enunciative principle is based on a psychological theory of human behavior. By contrast, the censorial principle is an ethical one. There is a tension between the two principles as it assumes society functions best when the two principles operate in concert with one another. And, according to Bentham, that would be the ideal. But, what happens when a person seeking pleasure does not care about the socially agreed upon norms of a community? What if an individual insists on following a path that only focuses on the enunciative principle, and disregards the censorial one?

Orange Is Definitely Not the New Black

It is not surprising that throughout the series, Ava Crowder would pursue a path of maximizing her pleasure. She's from Harlan County, and possesses a certain toughness that many of its residents display. Ava endured a marriage to Bowman Crowder that at times was so bad that she took refuge at the "holler" under the protection of Ellstin Limehouse. One of the beatings that she received from Crowder resulted in her suffering a miscarriage. It's not surprising that, for Ava, enough was enough and she shot her husband. Given how abusive Crowder was, when Ava pleaded guilty to man-slaughter, she was only sentenced to parole.

After such a prolonged period of time being subjected to pain, it would not be surprising that Ava would want to enjoy pleasure. So, throughout the series, her decisions appear to be governed by her maximization of pleasure. Even though it is not in society's best interests to threaten the integrity of a case against Boyd, she pursues an affair with Raylan. When Raylan decides he still loves Winona, Ava pursues an affair with Boyd—enjoying not only the physical comfort of Boyd, but the psychological pleasure of having a relationship with Raylan's nemesis.

When Ava sees an opportunity, she takes over the local prostitution business. Though prostitution is not something that is in society's best interest, the position and economic rewards Ava receives gives her great pleasure. When Ellen May poses a potential threat to Ava and Boyd because she knows Ava shot and killed Delroy, Ava agrees to have Ellen May eliminated. Agreeing to the murder of an individual is not beneficial to society, but it's in Ava's best interests.

That Darn Body

It is that shooting of Delroy that will land Ava in a great deal of trouble. In the last episode of Season Four, "Ghosts," Ava and Boyd are afraid authorities will find the body of Delroy where they left it—in a mineshaft. So, they concoct a plan to get Delroy's body from the mine and move it. When they get there, though, they find that law enforcement has already beaten them there thanks to an anonymous tip. Boyd then comes up with a plan to use his connection with Lee Paxton, who owns the funeral home that Delroy's body has gone to, to switch Delroy's body with a corpse from the cemetery. They are successful in making the swap. Unfortunately, Ava is arrested while attempting to dispose of Delroy's body that night. The charges against her are evidence tampering, obstructing justice, and desecrating a body. As Season Five opens, Ava is in jail, and relying on Boyd to get her released.

While during the first four seasons of *Justified* Ava made decisions to maximize her pleasure, during Season Five Ava makes decisions to minimize her pain. Though Boyd assures her he will get her released from custody, by the third episode of the season ("Good Intentions"), Ava doubts that Boyd is concentrating on getting her out.

Sent to State

Boyd turns out not to be Ava's only problem. While in the county jail, corrections officer Albert Fekus tries to molest her. His attempt is thwarted by the arrival of fellow officer Susan Crane, who warns Fekus to stay away from Ava. In "Shot to Hell," it appears that things are looking up for Ava when she learns from her lawyer that the judge is dropping the now-crumbling case against Ava. Later that night, however, as she is talking to fellow inmate Sally, Fekus comes into the cell under the ruse of doing a bed search and plants a shiv up under the mattress. He then pretends he has discovered an illegal weapon. Though Ava knows Fekus is setting her up, before she can do anything, Fekus stabs himself and cuts his forearm. He charges that Ava attacked him, and Sally plays along. Fekus then leaves the state, and, with no proof that she didn't stab Fekus (the security cameras were turned off) Ava is sent to state prison.

At state prison, Ava is moved into the general population and bunks with an inmate named Nikki. She is soon befriended by a prisoner named Penny Cole, who fills Ava in about how to survive in the prison. As Ava is adjusting to prison, Boyd is working on her protection, making a deal with a neo-Nazi whose sister, Gretchen, is in the same prison as Ava. Ava meets Gretchen and Gretchen tells her that she was paid to protect Ava. Instead of protecting her, Gretchen punches her in the face, saying she despises Boyd for being a "race traitor" (Boyd had allowed African Americans into his church). One of Gretchen's crew cuts Ava's hair. It is after this experience that Ava decides, in order to minimize her pain, that, no matter what she needs to do, she has to put herself first.

In the episode "Raw Deal," Ava will get her chance. Fellow prisoner Judith leads a religious congregation inside of the prison. Judith agrees to protect Ava, but only if Ava helps her smuggle heroin inside for the congregation. Ava will be taking the place of Penny in the operation. Ava, looking for protection to minimize her pain, agrees.

Not Servicing Milam . . .

In a prison shower room, Penny fills Ava in on the drug-smuggling operation. Penny introduces Ava to a plumber named Rhymer, who brings in the heroin, and Milam, a prison guard who provides cover. In return, Milam gets "serviced" by Penny. Ava realizes that in the future, she will be the one "servicing" Milam. Ava then gets the idea to plant some of the dope in the plumber's equipment bag. When he leaves, he gets busted, thus shutting down the drug smuggling.

Later, Judith tells Ava that things could get bad for them if the other inmates learn that Judith and her congregation can no longer supply them with heroin. Ava, hoping to avoid having to be involved in any operation that involves her having sex with a guard, volunteers she can provide a new connection to heroin. Judith wonders out loud if it is just a coincidence that Rhymer got caught with heroin the day he is introduced to Ava. Judith warns Ava, "I hope to God Almighty you didn't risk all of our lives to keep from having to screw a guard." Penny later tells Ava that if she truly has a connection, Penny might know how to get it into the prison.

Killing Judith

To get the heroin into the prison, Ava will need the co-operation of Rowena, a nurse at the prison. To connect with Rowena, Ava needs to go to the infirmary. Faced with choosing between the pain of suffering an injury to get into the infirmary versus the possibility of Judith hurting her, Ava has Penny dislocate her arm. Rowena eventually agrees to help Ava on two conditions: Ava can't let Judith know she is the source of getting the heroin in to the prison, and Ava has to get Boyd do a favor for Rowena. Ava gets Boyd to agree. Rowena reveals to Boyd that her favor is for Boyd to help Rowena "get me my retribution" against a man who murdered her prison partner, Vernon, by burning her house down with her in it. Boyd locates the man, and kills him. So, to protect herself from enduring pain from Judith, Ava is—indirectly at least—responsible for a man's death.

Before the heroin smuggling operation can resume, an inmate named Lara attempts to shank Ava because she believed that Ava caused the disruption in the dope supply. Judith comes to Ava's rescue. Later, Ava meets with Rowena who adds a third condition to resuming the drug smuggling—she needs to kill Judith.

Ava follows Judith into the bathroom armed with a shiv, intending to kill Judith. Penny interrupts, though, as it is time for bed checks. Penny tells Ava that she knows Ava was preparing to kill Judith and that she is all for it. It turns out that Judith forced Penny to have abortions when she was impregnated by having sex with the guards to keep the drugs flowing. Penny even provides Ava with a shiv, and tells her Judith goes to chapel each night to pray.

When Ava arrives at the chapel, Judith reveals she knows that Ava is there to kill her. She attacks Ava with a steel chair, and starts choking her; however, Ava manages to stab Judith to death.

Source of Pain

In the episode "Weight," Boyd visits Ava and is excited that he has a lead on finding Fekus. Ava, however, has news for Boyd—she's breaking off their engagement. Ava tells Boyd that she will always love him, but that she might never get out of prison. It's also likely that the reason she's breaking it off with Boyd is that he is no longer providing pleasure for her. She is in prison in part due to Boyd's actions, and he has not come through with his promise to get her released quickly. Some moves, such as arranging for Gretchen to get paid off, have backfired. Instead of a source of pleasure, Boyd has become a source of pain for Ava.

Raylan visits Ava in prison, and tries to get her assistance in attempting to get Boyd to help bring down Daryl Crowe. Ava tells Raylan that she and Boyd broke up, but also that she didn't want to help Raylan anyway. Her refusal may have been out of loyalty to Boyd, or out of the pleasure she got from getting a certain measure of revenge against Raylan for his choosing Winona over her. Later, though, the action backfires. After Penny is killed, Ava tells Raylan she's ready to help him. If Raylan can help her get out of prison, then the pleasure she will derive will clearly outweigh any loyalty she has toward Boyd. Raylan tells Ava, however, that Boyd already helped him, and he no longer needs Ava's assistance. Ava asks Raylan what Boyd wanted for his help. Raylan tells Ava that Boyd wanted a clean slate—for himself.

Turn of Events

Just when things look the bleakest for Ava, her lawyer calls saying that Fekus and Sally have both recanted their statements against Ava, and that the case against her has fallen apart. As a result, she is going to be released. When she arrives home, Boyd is there. They talk and then he leaves to conduct some business. While Boyd is away, Ava also goes out. She meets Raylan, who has arranged for her release from prison. She has agreed to help Raylan in developing a RICO case against Boyd.

By the time Ava has gotten home, she has been directly responsible for one death, and indirectly responsible for two others. Causing the deaths of three people while maximizing your own pleasure and minimizing your own pain in not in best interest of society. But, it was personally good for Ava—which, for her, is all that matters.

17
Mags Bennett—Outlaw Mother

JULIA MASON

Mags Bennett, isn't your typical TV mommy. She's the strong, powerful matriarch of the pot-growing, outlaw Bennett clan of rural Kentucky, continually engaged in dangerous, illegal practices.

Mags is well aware that she's outside of mainstream conceptions of the good mother: "I had every intention of living a simple life. Raising my boys, keeping house. Then Purvis got killed and I accepted this role. Did what I had to do for my family" ("Full Commitment").

Mags understands her rejection of traditional motherhood as an intentional strategy necessary to preserve her family. Her role includes violently managing the Bennett clan and its illegal enterprises, and she clearly perceives that her position is more complex than mere single motherhood.

Apple Pie Moonshine

Viewers are introduced to Mags in the first episode of Season Two "The Moonshine War." She asks Raylan if he'd like some apple pie, which turns out to be moonshine. "I make 180 proof, I cut it with apple cider, cinnamon and vanilla. Reach me that glass, would ya, could have done with a pinch more cinnamon, cinnamon really sells the pie." Thus apple pie, the home-baked symbol of motherhood in America, has been subverted by the Kentucky outlaw staple, moonshine. This is just a taste of how Mags Bennett operates, outside the law and outside of conventional motherhood.

As the scene progresses we learn more about Mags. At first she claims to be a simple storeowner providing a valuable community service. "I run a store. Help these poor people from the holler, with food stamps, when's anybody seen me cultivating herb?" After Raylan reminds her that he's not with the DEA, she does admit to being a "reefer farmer." Later in the episode she feeds a poisoned version of her apple pie moonshine to Walt McCready, who had been growing weed without her permission and most egregiously had called the state police to report a sex offender. She tells Walt "you never go outside, you know that." As Walt is dying she explains the nature of the poison she has just feed him: "Mixture is all natural, from up in the hills. All kinds of knowledge up in them hills. I learned it from my grandma, who learned it from her grandma." This scene demonstrates the outlaw code that Mags operates under and reveals her to be a murderer who is connected to previous generations of women and who has a long history in that community.

This Is Gonna Hurt Me More than You . . .

As well as being ruthless to community members who cross her, Mags is also tough on her sons when they step out of line. Mags's deviation from the traditional nurturing role is illustrated in a scene from the episode "Cottonmouth" where she takes a hammer to adult son Coover's hand for betraying her. In the context of outlaw justice and from Mags world-view, Coover needs to be punished. Mags even believes herself to be benevolent for not hurting his dominant hand: "I'm saving your gun hand. Cross me again and I will leave you nothing." She also explains that she isn't physically punishing her other son Dickie because he's already dealing with a physical impairment.

Throughout this exchange, Mags makes it clear that she believes she's only doing what's necessary for the greater good of the family, which in her view, benefits from preserving her power. Coover begs for forgiveness, explaining how sorry he is. Mags responds "Coover, I know you're sorry, that's why it's gonna hurt so much to have to do this." The hurt Mags is referring to is her own hurt, from being forced to break her son's hand.

This scene provides insight into how Mags operates as a mother. She is unforgiving, physically abusive, and willing to put the family business above individual children. Throughout Season Two viewers learn that Mags is universally feared, both in the community and within her family, and that her reputation for violence is well-deserved, as Messer says "Ain't enough money in the world to cross the Bennetts" ("Bloody Harlan").

You Look Real Purdy

Mags's general appearance falls outside what's allowed for the traditional good mother, who is expected to be beautiful and feminine. Feminist television criticism continues to draw upon the influential film theories of Laura Mulvey, who first theorized that visual images encourage viewers to look pleasurably at females through the male gaze. While Mulvey's work has rightly been criticized for not adequately addressing lesbians, many contemporary visual images continue to position women as objects to-be-looked-at while simultaneously denying women's subjectivity and agency.

In contrast, Mags Bennett, is not portrayed as an object nor are viewers encouraged to look at her pleasurably. She's an older woman, who dresses very simply and practically. She doesn't wear make-up and her hair is unkempt. Her clothes are loose-fitting and typically in muted colors. They appear to be inexpensive, old, and quite worn. Her shoes are practical and she often wears a thick, utility-type belt. The overall impression is of a poor country grandmother; however, this image is misleading, as she is a powerful and feared woman, both within her family and in the surrounding county that bears her family name.

While Mags understands that she is neither typically beautiful nor feminine she recognizes the type of power beauty represents. She shares this knowledge with Loretta, the young girl she embraces as her surrogate daughter, who comes into Mags's care after Mags has poisoned her father for going to the law. In a scene from "Brother's Keeper," while combing Loretta's hair in preparation for the whoop-de-do celebration, Mags says: "You look pretty as a picture. Ain't no shame in a woman looking beautiful. My time is past, ain't nothing for it. But you, you've got something, a power you ain't even come to understand."

This statement reinforces a narrow vision of women's power being tied to beauty. However, Mags is clearly powerful in ways that surpass the limited power beauty allows. A further exploration of the contrast between feminine power being linked to beauty and the challenges of a woman embracing masculine power is illustrated in "The Spoil" when Mags tells Ms. Johnson, the representative from Black Pike Mining: "It's not easy being a strong woman, take it from me. But you just keep doing what you're doing, don't let 'em see you sweat." Despite opposing Ms. Johnson and the company she represents, Mags feels a connection with her as a powerful woman in a masculine context.

We've learned a lot from Adrienne Rich's analysis of motherhood in her book, *Of Woman Born*. Rich identified how mainstream beliefs about motherhood served to confine women's options and opportunities. Despite almost forty years of efforts to challenge narrow philosophies of mothering, women with kids are supposed to be the so-called "good mother," which can lead to tremendous pressure.

According to Marie Porter in her 2010 work *Focus on Mothering*: "I do not know a mother who is unaware of the 'shoulds' of motherhood. As the 'shoulds' are an impossible burden, all mothers with whom I have ever spoken have an undercurrent of guilt about their motherwork."

Uninvited Don't Mean Unwelcome

The good mother is a nurturer and provider of sustenance. While Mags typically fails to be nurturing, at least in the traditional sense, she does embrace her responsibility to feed her family and community. In "For Blood or Money" when Raylan shows up at Mags's home during family dinner, she makes him understand both the rules and her role with the statement: "Uninvited don't mean unwelcome." In a show of deference to her hospitality Raylan gives her a store-bought apple pie. Mags lets Raylan know he does not belong but that she will play the hostess nonetheless. She offers to get him a plate and to set aside a jar of her apple pie moonshine when the next batch is ready. As the conversation continues she reminds him that he is intruding by saying: "Yet, you find it acceptable to bust in on my family dinner" and "You gonna sit there on my lumber." She ends the interaction with: "Sure I can't fix you a plate? How 'bout some dessert."

Food and community are central to Mags's identity. Her commitment to feeding her people is illustrated when she invites everyone to a whoop-de-do at her place. This celebration of the unique culture of rural Kentucky is designed for the community to remember what they stand to lose at the hands of Black Pike and also for the community to recognize the power and position of Mags Bennett. Raylan explains the proper way to honor Mags, telling Ms. Johnson: "Get up there and lay a chunk of firewood on her still, shows respect, that you've come here with peaceful intent" ("Brother's Keeper"). Mags's role as matriarch of the Bennett clan appears to extend into the larger community. When she chastised, and ultimately poisoned, Walt McCready, it was for going outside.

In the episode "The Spoil" Mags gives an impassioned speech encouraging the community to rally against Black Pike Coal. She talks about preserving the community's unique food, way of courting, music, and everything that makes them special. This speech seems to be the genuine rallying cry of a maternal folk hero; however, in the following episode "Brother's Keeper" Mags reveals that instead of being a true champion for her community and way of life, she has her own personal endgame. She has bought the properties needed to get the coal off the mountain and will sell for a stake of the company "sufficient to provide for my kin for generations to come." Her earlier concerns about maintaining the unique way of life are sacrificed for financial gain.

A Maternal Side?

Even while conducting herself as a ruthless outlaw, Mags displays a more traditionally maternal side when she interacts with Loretta. Since she never had any daughters Mags views Loretta as a chance to do things over and perhaps give Loretta a different life than was allowed for Mags. In "Brother's Keeper" Mags tells Loretta "You're like a dream come true for this old girl" and "things are going to be different. You are going to be proud of your old Mags."

However, this glimpse at a maternal side doesn't erase viewers' awareness that Mags killed Loretta's father and used a hammer to break her son's hand. As reviewer Tim Surette noted: "Even when she was gently combing out the knots in her adopted daughter Loretta's hair, I thought Mags was just as likely to slit Loretta's throat as she was to plant a kiss on her forehead." While Mags appears to want something different for Loretta, she puts the fourteen-year-old to work weighing weed at the Bennett store.

Loretta learns that her father is dead, not away on Bennett business as she'd been told, and believes that Coover was the killer. In the final episode of Season Two she pulls a gun on Mags, who responds: "Breaks my heart seeing you holding that gun. I wanted to keep you away from this life. I wanted to let you be a child a little longer. Wasn't Coover who did it. It was me." Mags shows no remorse, instead she indicates that she believes that she was acting in Loretta's best interest by telling her "I tried to make it up to you by giving you a better life here." This is Mags's vision of motherhood—violence, murder, and crime are all acceptable if you can eventually get at least some of your family a better life:

"Someday when you have tads of your own you'll understand that you do what you must to protect 'em" ("Bloody Harlan").

Black Pike

From Mags's perspective, selling out to Black Pike was justified. She rationalized that getting out was worth everything she had done as long as she was doing it to get her family a better life. But she could only manage to save some of her family, specifically Doyle, and his sons. Mags explains this to her other son Dickie: "Black Pike is the future. Its proceeds go to your brother and his family. They are the future, not you" ("Debts and Accounts"). She's reconciled to all that she had to do to survive but "I'll be damned if my grandchildren are gonna live it the same way. I got Doyle's boys a path outta this holler. Ain't nothing that's more important to me than that" ("Reckoning").

At first, Mags was planning to get herself out, but she realizes that isn't possible. "I don't know who I was kidding. Can you see your old Mama sitting on some suburb porch cashing dividend checks? This is where I belong" ("Bloody Harlan"). Later in the episode, after she finds out that Doyle was killed, Mags decides to take her own life by drinking apple pie from a poisoned glass: "Put an end to my troubles. Get to see my boys again. Get to know the mystery." While this choice appears consistent with her character, it also represents a loss for the viewer. Mags Bennett presented a complex and multifaceted depiction of an outlaw mother.

Encoding and Decoding

Stuart Hall's hypothesis of encoding and decoding in his 1973 article, "Encoding and Decoding in the Television Discourse" has been helpful in understanding that viewers can engage with a TV show or advertisement on a variety of levels that are more complicated than simple and straightforward communication of information. Hall advanced a four-stage model of communication that takes into account the production, circulation, use, and reproduction of media messages:

- *Production* refers to the first stage where the encoding of a media message takes place, and the producer of the message usually draws upon a particular society's dominant beliefs and values.

- *Circulation* refers to how individuals perceive things, whether it is in visual or written form, and so the manner in which media messages circulate influences how audience members will receive the message and put it use.

- *Use* refers to the decoding stage of the media message where use, consumption, and interpretation of the message occur.

- *Reproduction* refers to the final stage in Hall's hypothesis where audience members have interpreted the message in their own way based on their experiences and beliefs, and will either act or not act on the message.

One important implication of Hall's hypothesis is that the sender of information can never be sure that it will be perceived by the target audience in the way that was intended, because of this four-stage chain of discourse.

Hall's work continues to be used and adapted by feminist TV scholars who analyze the complex process of viewers making meaning of TV messages. Feminist TV scholars have resisted simplified analysis, focusing instead on ways that television can both present problematic images and be a site of empowerment. Mags Bennett illustrates these contradictions. She's a strong, powerful woman, over the age of fifty, who is neither thin nor traditionally beautiful, elements that serve to disrupt stereotypical good mother representations. However, Mags Bennett is not positioned as a character to emulate. She is a violent, ruthless murderer who deals in illegal drugs. While Mags clearly displays elements of the monstrous, she also has sympathetic moments and seems to adhere to a code that is consistent with her worldview.

Challenging Roles

A redefinition of motherhood from a feminist maternal perspective will include subverting and replacing dominant narratives with additional and alternative visions of mothering. Some feminists have promoted the term *outlaw mothering*, primarily a metaphorical revision. According to Andrea O'Riley in her 2010 book *Outlaw Mothering*: outlaw mothers "do not always put their children first; actively question the expectations that are placed on mothers by society; challenge mainstream parenting practices; and challenge the idea that the only emotion mothers ever feel toward their children is love." Mags Bennett not only conforms to Riley's description, but is also *literally* an outlaw.

18
Raylan Learns to Restrain Himself

NATHAN VERBAAN AND ADAM BARKMAN

"But I was justified" is one of the last lines US Marshal Raylan utters at the end of the first episode of TV's *Justified*. However, his actions are continually questioned by many characters, including Boyd Crowder, Art Mullen, Arlo Givens, Tim Gutterson, and Rachel Brooks. Each of these characters looks past some of Raylan's actions because he gets the job done, but they have also criticized Raylan about those same actions.

There comes a point when each of these characters accuses Raylan of lacking self-restraint. Though they may not know it, they make this charge primarily from Aristotle's perspective of what someone lacking self-restraint looks like. As time goes on these accusations do begin to affect Raylan, and he starts to become a more self-restrained person, but it is a long and painful road before he finally gets there.

This is the mindset that the characters of *Justified* have when confronting Raylan concerning his actions and decisions. They challenge him and accuse him from this basis. Some are more subtle, others more direct, but in either case this is the starting point of their confrontation with Raylan.

Art Mullen

Chief Deputy US Marshal Art Mullen is always getting on Raylan's case—not only for Raylan's actions in Miami, but his actions in Harlan as well. Art continually lectures Raylan about what he can and cannot do, to which Raylan seldom listens.

He voices his frustrations almost every episode to Raylan, who mostly ignores him. Eventually Art has had enough and lets Raylan know how he is feeling about Raylan's actions and attitudes. In "Debts and Accounts" Art lays into Raylan telling him:

> I'm stuck with a man who's a lousy marshal, but a good lawman. You are who you are, nothing I say has ever made any difference, no punishment that I can dream up will ever change you. Kinda makes me sad, believe it or not, because I thought at one point that maybe someday you and I could look back on all this and laugh, but shit, I don't think you're going to live that long. You just go on and do what you do and I'll just keep cleaning up after you, and sooner or later this problem's gonna solve itself.

Art is talking to Raylan about his lack of self-restraint. A person with some form of self-restraint would abide by their calculations. Their calculations would take into account the opinions of others, especially the orders of their boss, but Raylan does neither. Art is saying that Raylan does not abide by his calculation as he does not listen to others. He does not value their opinions or their input. Art also makes the point that this will eventually kill Raylan, which it might. In later seasons Raylan's life does indeed come crashing down on him because of his prior decisions, not to mention the many near-death experiences along the way.

Art does disagree with Aristotle in that he does not believe Raylan is in any way curable. He reveals this belief in the episode "Truth and Consequences" while reprimanding Rachel because she put herself into a dangerous situation. Rachel complains that Raylan puts himself into worse situations all of the time and he does not get reprimanded. Art responds, "Oh he's a lost cause; we still have hope for you." Art does not think that Raylan will ever gain self-restraint. He believes Raylan will continually be how he is and never change, whereas Aristotle says that the person lacking self-restraint is curable, if they feel remorse and Raylan, as we shall, does show some remorse.

Arlo Givens

Arlo Givens, Raylan's father, is not impressed with his son. Not because he lacks control, but because he became marshal and did not follow in his footsteps. He believes that he and Raylan have quite a lot in common. After all, although their ends may be different, their means are similar. He makes no secret that he does not care for his son, at one point choosing Boyd over Raylan and shooting him because of it, or so he thinks he did.

In a confrontation between Bo Crowder and Arlo Givens, the two are talking about the current state of their sons and how far removed they are. Each one thinks the other's son is worse off. Neither of them denies that their sons are loose cannons, but Bo claims that he does have Boyd under control whereas Arlo does not have any control over Raylan. Arlo doesn't deny this ("Veterans").

Arlo first confronts Raylan on his lack of self-restraint when he sees Raylan for the first time in the episode "The Lord of War and Thunder." Arlo has heard about the shooting in Miami and thinks himself a more controlled man than Raylan. He begins to compare the two of them, albeit against Raylan's wishes. He culminates in saying, "In all the shit I've pulled I've never shot anyone—not a one." Arlo is pointing out that he has more control over his actions than Raylan does. He's showing Raylan that Raylan isn't using his knowledge and reason wisely. Arlo uses himself as an example to show how things can get done without firing a shot. He's accusing Raylan of not using the knowledge within him before acting, not thinking of another way to go about a situation.

This harkens to an Aristotelian point of view: that "those lacking self-restraint must be said to be in a state similar to [someone who is] mad, asleep, or drunk." The idea is that these people will primarily act without thinking, doing things rashly and without forethought. Arlo believes he knows what he's doing and remains in control because he thinks before he acts, whereas Raylan just acts, usually not taking much time to think. Arlo's telling Raylan that it's necessary to think before acting, and if he had done so in Miami, Raylan would be in a very different situation than he is right now.

Tim Gutterson and Rachel Brooks

U.S. Deputy Marshals Tim Gutterson and Rachel Brooks are always on Raylan's case to get his act together. While they are primarily concerned with their own jobs and cases, they do cross paths frequently with Raylan. Although these two rarely challenge Raylan explicitly, their demeanor towards him speaks when they do not.

There are many points throughout the series where both Tim and Rachel will roll their eyes, or turn away from Raylan, visibly showing their detestation of his actions. This detestation eventually leads Rachel to take a stand. It's more of a passing remark than a direct accusation but her point still holds true. When discussing a case with Raylan in "Long in the Tooth," Rachel remarks that Raylan is "a tall, good-looking white man with a shitload of swagger that can get away with just about anything"—her point being that Raylan could do what he wants, in this case wearing a cowboy hat, and get away with it. Although the cowboy hat is not a major infraction, the point she brings forth is that because of who Raylan is, he can do things that most people would not be allowed to, and these things have few or no consequences for him.

There are occasions where Raylan does have to face consequences, such as giving up his gun and badge, getting suspended, and being forced to take time off. Without fail, Tim, Rachel, or both will be there to make their points. Tim and Rachel's presence primarily reminds the audience that what Raylan does is not strictly permissible, no matter what his results. A "lack of self-restraint is not only to be avoided but is also blameworthy," as Aristotle puts it. Raylan is at fault for what he does, and is culpable for his actions. Tim and Rachel try to remind him of this at every possible chance they get—normally when Raylan is being punished, but it happens on other occasions as well.

Unfortunately Tim and Rachel do tend to let Raylan get away with his actions. They let things slide that they would not let others get away with. They repeatedly help him on cases from which he is suspended. Rachel even admits that she "can deal with" his aloofness. It's annoying, but she can "let it slide" because Raylan "gets the job done" and is "easy on the eyes." They let him do things, or get out of doing things, simply because he's good at what he does.

Aristotle would probably hold Tim and Rachel equally culpable to Raylan because they are allowing him to continue in his ways. By allowing him to remain lacking in self-restraint, it is as if they are lacking in self-restraint themselves, and thus, are morally blameworthy as well.

Boyd Crowder

We might think that Boyd's not the most likely candidate to criticize Raylan for his lack of self-restraint. After all, in the first episode Boyd kills a man and blows up a church. As we would expect, it's during Boyd's brief conversion to Christianity in prison that his criticism of Raylan's lifestyle begins to appear. While in prison Boyd gives not so subtle hints that Raylan's lifestyle is not a very controlled or righteous one. Boyd asks Raylan to "think about his immortal soul," considering he's a violent man and has "left a trail of dead" behind him ("The Collection").

While going through his brief conversion experience, Boyd's accusations and concerns for Raylan are primarily spiritual. He's more concerned with Raylan's past actions than his future ones. Boyd's first big accusation to Raylan comes when Raylan is wondering if one of the Crowder boys ordered a hit against Ava Crowder. Amidst Raylan's frequent interruptions, Boyd begins to dig into Raylan's relationship with Ava and his past. He discusses how hard it must have been for Raylan to see his mother getting beaten by his father, and how that could have been the motivation for Raylan getting his badge. In "Blind Spot" his accusation is that he thinks that what Raylan "might be unaware of, is just how powerful such a motivation can be. Powerful enough to cloud your vision and cloud your judgement." Taking note of what Boyd is doing, Raylan tries to push Boyd past this to get the information he came for regarding the shooting that took place the night before.

Boyd accuses Raylan of acting out of passion rather than reason. He believes Raylan is so bent on finding out who took the shot at Ava that he did not even stop to think. His will to protect Ava, which could be stemming from his past, is blinding him from the truth. This point is very similar to that of Arlo, in that Both Boyd and Arlo say that Raylan is forgoing reason. This is very big sign of a lack of self-restraint for Aristotle.

Boyd continues to talk to Raylan in similar ways for both the duration of his conversion and after he gives up his faith. In one argument between Boyd and Raylan, Boyd turns what Raylan says back against him. Boyd asks Raylan, "What do you tell yourself at night when you lay your head down, that allows you to wake up in the morning pretending that you are not the bad guy?" What is interesting is that Raylan is silent, completely contrary to his usual personality. He offers no response to Boyd ("Ghosts").

In essence, Boyd has just said that Raylan is no different from him, and Boyd does not deny that he lacks self-restraint. This brings to the forefront something that Raylan has denied and ignored for the entire series up until this point—that he does indeed lack self-restraint. Although he has been challenged in this respect, he has never been completely called out. So when Boyd does call him out, he has no response, because he knows it's true. Boyd forces Raylan into a corner in which his only response is to admit that he lacks self-restraint, thus, Raylan does not respond.

Boyd reveals that Raylan—importantly—recognizes that he lacks self-restraint, and has only avoided admitting such until now.

Aristotle points out that the "lack of self-restraint does not escape the notice of those lacking self-restraint." Boyd reveals that Raylan does know that he lacks self-restraint, and has pushed Raylan to the point where he must admit that he does know this.

Raylan Givens

Main characters in the series are constantly challenging Raylan from an Aristotelian perspective. They do so for good reason; he fits the description quite well. While there are many aspects of a person lacking self-restraint, not all are necessary. In addition to those brought up by the characters, Raylan fits three more qualities of a person lacking self-restraint as discussed by Aristotle.

Firstly, the person must act on account of passion. This is evident when Raylan sleeps with Ava, even though she is in the witness protection program and he is specifically told by Art not to get involved with her. Raylan is acting on account of passion and not thinking clearly about what this means for him, her, and the witness protection program. His actions end up destroying the case he has against Boyd Crowder, and Boyd ends up walking free.

Secondly, Raylan is a person who sees a pleasure coming towards him, and does not try to stand against it. This is most evident when Raylan sees his remarried ex-wife, Winona, take off her wedding ring, and he proceeds to make love to her. As soon as her wedding ring came off he saw this pleasure coming, but he did not stand against it even though he knew what he was doing was wrong. He acted out passion even though he knew he was cheating on his current girlfriend and committing adultery with his ex-wife ("Fathers and Sons").

Lastly, Raylan feels regret. There are many situations where Raylan regrets his actions in the line of duty. After

Rachel has shot Flex, a drug runner associated with her brother-in-law, Raylan assures Rachel that she did what had to be done. He also asks if she is having second thoughts; she says no, but Raylan says she will ("For Blood or Money"). He's speaking from personal experience, showing that he does feel regret for doing the things he does in the line of duty.

The most evident sign of regret takes place outside of his work, when Raylan calls Winona after their first encounter to talk in "The Moonshine War." Before long they make love once again, and Raylan's immediate reaction is regret. Winona even comments on how Raylan is regretting what they just did.

All of this regret in Raylan's life means only one thing for Aristotle: Raylan is curable. Contrary to what Art and other characters may think, Raylan is not permanently set in his ways.

Is Raylan Justified?

Aristotle makes a point of discussing the just nature of an individual lacking self-restraint. He says that a person who lacks self-restraint is not an unjust person, but they will commit injustices. Most, if not all of the requirements for an individual to be viewed as lacking self-restraint by Aristotle result in an injustice. Granted, where lacking self-restraint in regards to money may not directly be an injustice, but it can easily lead to an injustice. Raylan clearly thinks he is justified in his actions, especially if he kills someone because they pulled first. Aristotle would say such actions are on account of passion, and thus show a lack of self-restraint.

Raylan normally forces the people he wishes to kill to pull first. In doing so Raylan claims he is justified. In other words, Raylan knows that what he is doing is unjust, he cannot kill a man for the reasons that he has, even though he believes it may be right thing to do. In order to satisfy his own conscience he forces the others to pull first, in his eyes, doing so justifies his actions.

Unselfrestrained by Habit, or by Nature?

Aristotle makes a distinction between habit and nature. If a person lacks self-restraint by habit, they are all the more curable; if by nature, it's more difficult to change.

Raylan lacks self-restraint habitually, not naturally. The distinction is that there are some situations in which we expects Raylan to act in an unselfrestrained manner, and he does not. If it was natural that he lacked self-restraint than he would always act as we would expect him to. An example of this is when Raylan is sitting in the limo with Nick Augustine and doesn't kill him. Rather, he asks Nick to turn himself in, granted he does so in a threatening manner, but he does not kill Nick. This is one example of the many that occur throughout the series. As time goes by Raylan is becoming more and more self-restrained. He is doing things, or rather, not doing things that he would do if he lacked self-restraint to the same extent that he did at the start of the series. This change and growth is possible only because he lacks self-restraint by habit rather than by nature.

Nick Augustine also comments on how Raylan is not lacking self-restraint by nature. In the same scene mentioned before he says that Raylan needs him to pull first so Raylan can have a reason to kill him. Raylan does reply that he already has a reason, namely, Nick has threatened his family. Nick responds to Raylan saying "I take one look at you and I know that you're not the kind of guy that just executes me, it's not who you are" ("Ghosts"). He is saying that although Raylan does lack self-restraint, it's not a defining characteristic of him, it's not part of his nature. Rather it is only by habit that Raylan acts the way he does.

From an Aristotelian perspective Raylan does indeed lack self-restraint, but he is not unjust or wicked, nor does he lack self-restraint by nature. Rather he commits injustices by habit. He thinks about the things he has done and it haunts him. The title of Season Four's "Ghosts" reflects this. Raylan is haunted by his past and the decisions he has made. The longer he continues in his unselfrestrained ways, the longer the list of decisions that haunt him will grow.

Aristotelian Self-Restraint

Aristotle, who lived from 384 to 322 B.C.E., gave a philosophical theory of self-restraint. He believes that a self-restrained person is someone who sticks with the results of their own calculation—a person who follows reason. Someone lacking self-restraint gives up their reason in order to fulfil their desires. This is not to say that people are giving up reason whenever they eat or make love, but that sometimes these appetites need to be kept in check.

Aristotle compares someone lacking self-restraint to someone who is asleep, drunk, or mad. The individual has knowledge, but doesn't fully use the knowledge they have. The person knows what they should do, but they disregard or temporarily forget what that knowledge requires them to do. It may not be intentional, in fact it usually isn't, but in the moment of excitement a person loses contact with the relevant knowledge.

An individual lacking self-restraint will see a pleasure coming before him, and will not try to avoid it. Simply giving in to a pleasure without even trying to leave it be and move on shows a lack of self-restraint. Once again, this does not mean a person enjoying a pleasure is necessarily lacking self-restraint—rather, it's the indulgence of this pleasure when they can see that they should not be indulging in it.

The most important aspect of a person lacking self-restraint is that the individual knows that they lack self-restraint. Thus they feel regret, and while they may commit injustices, they are not unjust. As long as the individual feels regret, it shows that they are curable. Lacking self-restraint is not necessarily permanent but it requires practice and work to develop self-restraint.

For Aristotle, the fact that someone lacking self-restraint is curable helps us to understand why the person is not to be considered unjust even though they may commit injustices. If they are curable, then they are not making a permanent choice. They have not chosen to be unjust; they are merely acting on account of passion and forgetting knowledge and reason in the moment. When the person does not feel any regret, they are choosing to act against knowledge and reason, rather than forgetting it. It is the aspect of choice that determines the justified nature of the individual.

Aristotle would agree that acting in self defense by gunning someone down would be justified, but Raylan's method of forcing such a situation is not justified. It's a perversion of justice, because Raylan is bending justice to his own will, even though he is doing so in pursuit of what he believes to be right. Aristotle thinks that a person who is lacking self-restraint may not be wicked, when the motivation for his choice is decent. Raylan is not acting for pure selfish gain—he does what he does because he believes it is the right thing to do. As a result of that, he is not wicked, but only half wicked as Aristotle describes it.

Raylan-Restraint

Raylan Givens exhibits many of the aspects of the Aristotelian viewpoint of someone who lacks self-restraint. Many of the characters in the series have picked up on this and have challenged him. From giving in to passions to giving up reason he is the complete package.

However, Raylan is curable. When he feels regret, it shows that he cannot fully justify his actions, although he may try. The realization that he can't justify all of his actions is coming to Raylan. When that realization does fully develop, he can change his ways and become a self-restrained man. This can already be seen as aspects of self-restraint are starting to develop in his life. He feels regret more often, chooses not to get involved with women he certainly could, and feels that he needs to settle down in order to raise his child. Other characters have had a huge impact on his life in the short amount of time they have known him, but that time was well spent. As Raylan continues in his career and social life, if others continue to challenge him, it may not be long before his self-restraint develops even further.

Justified Killings?

ROBERT ARP

Raylan Givens puts a bullet in Tommy Bucks on a rooftop patio in Miami, and lots of people who didn't see the exchange question whether Raylan really was justified in shooting the cartel thug.

We the viewers know that Raylan probably was justified in that case because we see that Bucks did in fact "pull first" causing Raylan to quick-draw-McGraw him into the next life. Killing in self-defense when your life truly is threatened seems justified from almost any worldview—except, perhaps, from the pacifist's perspective. (Believe it or not, the great Catholic philosopher and theologian, St. Augustine, was opposed to killing in self-defense because he thought it was self-centered and sinful, remarking that "Private self-defense can only proceed from some degree of inordinate self-love.")

However, there are other times that Raylan shoots people dead, and we have to wonder if he could have arrested them or even put a bullet in a non-vital organ and then arrested them. This "shoot first, ask questions later" mentality likens Raylan to the justice-dispensing vigilante marshals of America's Wild West of the late nineteenth century like Wyatt Earp (1848–1929). Those marshals were judge, jury, and executioner all wrapped up in one. Below are controversial—and, at times, shocking—cases of people who felt they were justified in doing what they did.

You be the judge. You could even be the jury. . . . But please don't be the executioner!

Earp Brothers Justified

This was the headline for a story written by John Clum in the *Tombstone Daily Epitaph* on Thursday, October 27th, 1881, one day after the most famous gunfight in the history of the American Wild (Old) West, the Shootout at the OK Corral.

This was a thirty-second gunfight that took place near the rear entrance to the Old Kindersley horse corral at about 3:00 P.M. on Wednesday, October 26th, in Tombstone, Arizona, between the town's marshal, Virgil Earp—with the assistance of his brothers Morgan and Wyatt, and John Henry "Doc" Holliday—and Billy Claiborne, Ike and Billy Clanton, and Tom and Frank McLaury. Earp and his group had heard that Claiborne and his other outlaw cowboy buddies were secretly packing their Colt .45s in violation of the town ordinance that guns had to be kept in the marshal's office while visiting Tombstone. Plus, the cowboys had been claiming for several days that they were "gonna fill them Earp brothers full 'a lead."

So, the Earps and Holliday confronted the cowboys and . . . Bang! Bang! Bang! Billy Clanton and both McLaurys were killed, while Claiborne and Ike Clanton turned yella and hightailed outta there. Virgil was shot through the calf and Morgan was shot in the back, but both lived—Wyatt and the Doc came through the fight unharmed.

Clum wrote in the *Tombstone Daily Epitaph* that the "feeling among the best class of our citizens is that the Marshal was entirely justified in his efforts to disarm these men, and that being fired upon they had to defend themselves, which they did most bravely," and that's the story that made its way around the States. In popular culture, the Earps have always been the good guys, with Wyatt stealing the spotlight; consider the numerous movies made throughout the years, such as *Frontier Marshal* (1934), *Gunfight at the OK Corral*

(1957), *Tombstone* (1993), and *Wyatt Earp* (1994) where the Earps are portrayed as squeaky-clean, law-abiding, God-fearing, family-oriented folk. But scholars in the past few years who researched the events surrounding the OK Corral—including the dozens of first-hand accounts of towns-folk—probably would sympathize with the epitaph under portraits of the McLaury brothers found on a plaque located at the historic site that reads: "One owes respect to the living; but to the dead, one owes nothing but the truth."

And the truth seems to be that not only has way too much been made of Wyatt Earp's role in Tombstone and at the OK Corral, but also that the only thing really distinguishing the Earps and Doc Holliday from the outlaw cowboys they often confronted was the fact that they wore tin stars on the lapels of their jackets. Take Wyatt, for example: throughout his life he was a killer, arguably a murderer, horse thief, "misappropriator" of funds, pistol-whipper, cold cocker, convict, escaped convict, brothel frequenter, brothel owner, pimp, adulterer, husband of a common-law wife who was convicted of prostitution, saloon keeper, gambler, extorter, bouncer, teamster, miner, and boxing referee, in addition to being a deputized marshal, city policeman, and county sheriff.

On November 30th, 1881 Justice Wells Spicer ruled that the killings at the OK Corral were "a necessary act, done in the discharge of an official duty" and that the Earps and Holliday

> saw at once the dire necessity of giving the first shot to save themselves from certain death. They acted; their shots were effective, and this alone saved all the Earp party from being slain.

There's a continuation to the OK Corral saga, however, that rivals the infamous Hatfield-McCoy feud (1863–1891). When Virgil Earp was partially crippled in a December 1881 assassination attempt, Wyatt took his place as deputy US marshal. After younger brother Morgan's murder in March of 1882 at the hands of relatives and sympathizers of the so-called "bad guys" at the OK Corral, Wyatt went on the notorious "vendetta ride" that resulted in the killings of cowboys Frank Stilwell, Florentino "Indian Charlie" Cruz, "Curly Bill" Brocious, and, some believe, Johnny Ringo. Wyatt was allowed to ride off into the sunset—amazingly(!)—even further west to Los Angeles, where he lived a prosperous and famous life, dying of prostate cancer on January 13th, 1929 at the age of eighty.

Justifiably Standing Your Ground

A person who is not engaged in an unlawful activity and who is attacked in any other place where he or she has a right to be, has no duty to retreat and has the right to stand his or her ground and meet force with force, including deadly force, if he or she reasonably believes it is necessary to do so to prevent death or great bodily harm to himself or herself or another or to prevent the commission of a forcible felony.

The above quotation is the essence of the so-called *stand-your-ground law* from chapter 776 of the 2011 Florida Statutes (776.013: Home protection; use of deadly force; presumption of fear of death or great bodily harm) that Florida and several other US States have adopted. It's a type of self-defense law that gives someone the right to use deadly force to defend herself or himself without any requirement to evade or retreat from a dangerous situation. And, given the "reasonable belief" part of the law, someone can use this deadly force based upon the *perception of* imminent danger—essentially, if I *think* my life is in danger as a result of your actions, I can kill you and legally get away with it.

As you can imagine, it's controversial for at least two reasons. First, if Frank and John get into an altercation with one another, Frank could easily kill John in what Frank claims is "self-defense," but it's really just that Frank is pissed off and wants John dead; thus, Frank has abused the law or manipulated it to his own advantage. Second, and more significantly, the person who has "the other side of the story" in an altercation—in this case, John—can't tell his side to the police or lawyers, since "dead men tell no tales!" If just Frank and John were involved in the altercation, and no one else was around to witness it, who can corroborate Frank's claim that he "reasonably believed" that his life was in danger as a result of John's actions?

In fact, since 2011 self-defense claims in Florida alone have tripled! Fancy that! Before passage of the law, Miami police chief John F. Timoney called the law unnecessary and dangerous: "Whether it's trick-or-treaters, kids playing in the yard of someone who doesn't want them there, or some drunk guy stumbling into the wrong house, you're encouraging people to possibly use deadly physical force where it shouldn't be used." In 2007, the US National District Attorneys Association's American Prosecutors Research Institute published a report echoing Timoney's claim, and an Internet blogger has wisely noted:

> It is important to remember that the US justice system is not set up to pass judgment on thoughts and motivations. . . . Florida's stand-your-ground law may inadvertently protect people who overreact to potentially dangerous situations.

The Curious Case of Curtis Reeves

On a sign in the lobby of the Cobb Grove 16 Theater complex located in Wesley Chapel, Florida (30 miles north of Tampa Bay) it says, "No cell phone use, including texting, in the theater auditorium," and "No weapons allowed." But texting is exactly what forty-three-year-old Chad Oulson was doing before the 1:20 P.M. showing of *Lone Survivor* on January 13th 2014. It would be the final text message of his life. That's because a seventy-one-year-old retired Tampa police officer who was sitting near Oulson, Curtis Reeves, put a bullet from the .380 semi-automatic pistol he was carrying in his pocket straight through Oulson's heart.

Apparently, Reeves didn't read the sign in the lobby either. Reeves was charged with second-degree murder in the shooting of Oulson, who was texting his twenty-two-month-old daughter's babysitter during the previews. Oulson was at the theater with his wife, while Reeves was at the theater with his wife anticipating the arrival of their son, Matthew, who was running late. After Reeves complained to Oulson about his texting, and Oulson replied that he was texting his daughter's babysitter, an irritated Reeves left briefly to complain to the theater management. He returned alone, and the argument continued.

Witnesses said Oulson got up and threw a bag of popcorn at Reeves. In an instant, Pow! Reeves shot Oulson dead with a bullet to the chest that passed through Oulson's wife's finger as she was trying to hold him back from confronting Reeves. Matthew Reeves had just shown up to the darkened theater, actually, seconds before the shooting, heard the shot, went over to Oulson, and tried to save his life by applying pressure to the wound with a t-shirt—all the while not realizing that it was his own father who shot the man. Reeves's lawyers are playing the stand-your-ground card and have argued that he "was in the best position to perceive that the danger to him and his elderly wife was imminent and that deadly force was absolutely necessary to prevent death, great bodily harm, or the commission of a felony/forcible felony."

After all, Reeves claimed that Oulson "scared him shitless"—apparently from the force of the five-ounce bag of popcorn hitting him in the head. Surveillance video from the theater does show Oulson getting up, standing near Reeves, and throwing the popcorn at Reeves, but Reeves had claimed that "Suddenly he's virtually on top of me. . . . I'm either saying 'No, no, no' or 'Whoa, whoa, whoa . . .' He hit me with his fist or something. I assume it was his fist . . ." Other witnesses, including Reeves's wife, say they never saw Oulson strike Reeves. Oulson's wife testified that when Reeves came back after complaining to the management, he taunted her husband: "He said, '*Now* you put it away, are you scared?' 'Oh, so *now* you put the phone away.' And my husband turned around and stood up and said, 'Dude, what is your problem?'"

The judge at Reeves's initial hearing said that "throwing an unknown object does not equal taking out a gun and shooting someone." Several of the twenty-five movie-goers who witnessed the altercation said that Reeves spoke to Oulson first, raised his voice loudly to be heard over the previews, and was "obviously angry," "nasty-sounding," and "angry because the guy was texting." Now here's the kicker: Reeves had used his own phone to send a message to his son, Matthew, moments before the incident, telling Matthew he was already seated inside the theater.

The Killing of Trayvon Martin

"This guy looks like he's up to no good or he's on drugs or something" is what George Zimmerman, the organizer of the Neighborhood Watch program of the Twin Lakes housing community in Sanford, Florida, told the non-emergency police dispatcher at approximately 7:09 P.M. on the evening of February 26th, 2012. Twenty-eight-year-old Zimmerman was following and referring to seventeen-year-old Trayvon Martin, who was returning to his father's home in the community after having been to the local 7-Eleven to purchase Skittles and an AriZona Watermelon Fruit Juice Cocktail.

In his role as neighborhood watchman, Zimmerman had made numerous calls to the Sanford police between 2004 and 2012, reporting thefts, vandalism, people peering into windows, and a loose pit bull, which prompted him to purchase a Kel Tec PF-9 handgun in 2009. This would be the gun that Zimmerman used to shoot Martin dead during an altercation approximately seven minutes after his chat with the non-emergency police dispatcher.

According to Zimmerman's account of the event, the altercation began after Martin confronted Zimmerman. Zimmerman was told by the police dispatcher not to follow Martin, but he did anyway to see where Martin was going so as to give a report to police, who were on their way. As Zimmerman was walking back to his truck between homes in the Twin Lakes community, Martin "came out of nowhere" and asked him, "Why are you following me? You got a fucking problem, homie?" After Zimmerman replied No, apparently

Martin said, "You got a problem now" and proceeded to punch Zimmerman in the face (which broke his nose), knock him to the ground, and pound his head into the concrete walkway. Zimmerman yelled "Help!" numerous times, prompting Martin to say, "Shut the fuck up!" and "You're gonna die tonight, motherfucker!" after which Zimmerman shot Martin in the chest with a bullet that penetrated his heart and left lung, killing him.

Much of what Zimmerman claims seems to have been corroborated by eyewitnesses, recordings of 911 calls, and pictures of Zimmerman shortly after the fight. There's almost universal agreement that Zimmerman exercised bad judgment in not listening to the police dispatcher when she told him not to follow Martin, since, if Zimmerman had not followed Martin, then of course the altercation and subsequent shooting never would have taken place. But, was Zimmerman justified in what one of his lawyers claimed was a "live or die situation in which George exercised classic self-defense"? Given Florida's stand-your-ground law, Zimmerman was not charged with any crime by Sanford police that winter night in 2012. However, after word of the events got out, many Americans—including Reverends Jesse Jackson and Al Sharpton—wondered whether this case really was closed, given the fact that Martin was seventeen, unarmed, and of African-American descent. Was Zimmerman, a mixed-race Hispanic, racially profiling Martin with the intent to kill him? After all, he didn't heed the police dispatcher's request not to follow Martin.

On June 10th, 2013 Zimmerman went on trial in Sanford, and on July 13, 2013 he was found not guilty of second-degree murder as well as not guilty of manslaughter. Before jurors deliberated, the judge did remind them about Florida's stand-your-ground law from chapter 776 of the 2011 Florida Statutes: "Mr. Zimmerman had no duty to retreat and had the right to stand his ground and meet force with force, including deadly force." Zimmerman may have had the right to meet force with force, but it's questionable whether he should have been following Martin in the first place.

Double Trouble

There's an old principle that many of us may not have heard of by name, but still understand well enough called the *principle of double effect*. It's the idea that one can be justified in bringing about some harm or evil result—even killing someone or lots of people—provided that the evil result 1. is not directly intended and 2. isn't greater than the good result that *is* intended. There are two effects, results, or consequences then; one (single) is a great or greater good that's intended, while the second (double) is a lesser evil that isn't intended.

Action	Intended Good (Single) Effect, Result, Consequence	Unintended Bad (Double) Effect, Result, Consequence
Performing a risky medical operation	Remove tumor, or fix disorder, or cure disease	Infection occurs, or heart stops during operation and kills the patient
Worker blows whistle on corrupt business practice	Stopping corrupt business practice	Business actually closes down, hundreds of workers lose their jobs
Bombing a terrorist group's installation to destroy armaments	Getting rid of armaments that have been/will be used to kill innocent people	In bombing process, people in the installation are killed
Sergeant jumps on top of a grenade in his squad's tent	Using your body to shield the squad from the blast so as to save lives	Sergeant is killed by grenade
Hysterectomy to remove cancerous tumors	Removing cancer, saving woman's life	Fallopian tubes are removed, woman had ectopic pregnancy, embryo is killed
Giving large dosage of pain killer to terminal patient	Relieve someone from pain and suffering	Patient dies of overdose

It's a controversial principle because oftentimes we *know* that there's going to be an evil effect that results from one of our actions, even though we don't intend it directly. While talking about self-defense in his famous work, *Summa Theologica*, the great Christian philosopher, St. Thomas Aquinas (1225–1274), formulated a version of the principle that is still utilized by people, governments, judicial systems, and religions all over the world today:

> Nothing hinders one act from having two effects, only one of which is intended, while the other is beside the intention. . . . Accordingly, the act of self-defense may have two effects: one, the saving of one's life; the other, the slaying of the aggressor.

So, as long as Raylan intended to protect his own life by shooting Tommy Bucks, then the double effect of Bucks being killed (which is a great evil done to him, since he loses his life) is justified. Other well-known—some controversial—actions where the principle of double effect is utilized include:

Here are some other cases of self-defense, or what is *claimed* to be self-defense:

Ossian Sweet

On September 8th, 1925, an African-American physician named Ossian Sweet moved into his new house at 2905 Garland with his wife and infant daughter in a modest white neighborhood in Detroit, Michigan. It was difficult to unpack dishes with the crowd of angry white folk outside shouting, "Nigger get out!" and "You better leave, Nigger!" Other blacks in recent years had been driven from their newly purchased homes in all-white neighborhoods, and in one case Detroit Police stood by as people threw rocks at a young couple who were being shown a home by a realtor.

Fearing that blacks would lower house values, whites in Detroit formed the Waterworks Park Improvement Association in the early 1920s to oppose blacks moving into formerly all-white neighborhoods. The coppers reluctantly helped out the Sweets, however, and police officers were stationed around their house the evening after they moved in. Ossian also had invited his two brothers and seven other friends to his home to help with the move and serve as extra protection. On the evening of September 9th, a large mob of nearly a thousand people showed up and began making more racist threats. Rocks were thrown at the house, and when folks stepped on the front steps, shots were fired from the upstairs window, and the bullets ended up killing a man named Leon Breiner and wounding another man in the leg. Everyone in the house but Ossian's daughter was arrested and charged with murder.

The case soon drew the attention of the National Association for the Advancement of Colored People (NAACP) and renowned attorney Clarence Darrow was brought in to join the defense team. The trial took place in front of an all-white jury, but Darrow argued that all of the defendants were in legitimate danger that night and that Ossian was justified in exercising the right to defend himself, his family, and his home by shooting the attackers. The good news: a hung jury, the case thrown out, and the prosecution gave up on an appeal to re-try Ossian. The bad news: Ossian's daughter died a year later, his wife and brother both died of tuberculosis before the age of thirty, Ossian went into debt, became depressed, and eventually put a bullet in his head on March 20th, 1960.

Bernie Goetz "Mugged" on the Subway

Rob Arp went to high school in downtown Chicago, a block away from the John Hancock Building on Michigan Avenue, the main drag where people go to shop when they visit the Windy City. He lived outside of Chicago in Cicero (where Al Capone ran the city in the 1920s and 1930s) and so he took the third-rail-powered El (or L) train everyday to school. It was nicknamed "the El" because at certain points it rode on track that was elevated, as can be seen in pictures of Chicago's downtown Loop area. Literally, hundreds of thousands of people in and around Chicago took the El every Monday through Friday going to work or school, and many more still do today.

On his very first day of school—true story, no bull—he witnessed two robberies: one was a situation where the El doors opened at a stop and a guy ripped a gold chain off of a lady's neck as he was exiting and she let out a faint "Oh!" just before the doors of the train closed and rode away with her stunned and clutching her neck. Then, within twenty minutes, the second robbery was one where a guy ran past Rob as he was switching trains at an underground transfer station, and the guy grabbed the purse of a lady about ten feet in front of Rob and kept running. She screamed "Hey!" and ran after the robber. The train police actually caught that guy, as Rob noticed him handcuffed and surrounded by coppers with the lady giving her statement just before he got on his next train.

That set the tone for what would be (an at times scary) four years of Rob riding the city train operated by the Chicago Transit Authority twice a day, five times a week, with low-life scumbags all too often stealing things, harassing people, swearing at people, fighting, spraying graffiti, throwing gang signs, pissing on things, and intimidating anyone they thought was easy prey. That was late August of 1984. Four months later, just three days before Christmas, Bernhard Hugo Goetz (pronounced like "gets") got on the seventh car of a New York City subway train at the 14th Street station stop where several people—including Barry Allen, Troy Canty, Darrell Cabey (all nineteen years old), and James Ramseur (eighteen years old), all with prior criminal convictions—were riding. Allen, Canty, Cabey, and Ramseur were carrying screwdrivers because they were headed to Manhattan to break open video game machines to steal the change.

Dramatically different from the situation today, in the mid-1980s crime in the Big Apple was at an all-time high in the city's history, and hard-working, law-abiding people were pissed. Remember the Guardian Angels, the dudes with the red berets who rode the New York City subways to deter criminal activities? They were big in the early-to-mid-1980s. Goetz claims he was attacked in 1981 at a NYC subway station while transporting electronic equipment and subsequently purchased a five-shot light-weight .38 Special for protection. He was carrying that .38 Special on the train that fateful day. After the four teenagers surrounded him and one asked him for five dollars, Goetz got up and shot all four of them in a matters of seconds. According to the account given by the New York Court of Appeals:

> The first shot hit Canty in the chest; the second struck Allen in the back; the third went through Ramseur's arm and into his left side; the fourth was fired at Cabey, who apparently was then standing in the corner of the car, but missed, deflecting instead off of a wall of the conductor's cab. After Goetz briefly surveyed the train scene around him, he fired another shot at Cabey, who then was sitting on the end bench of the car. The bullet entered the rear of Cabey's side and severed his spinal cord.

All four of the youths lived, but Cabey was left paralyzed from the waist down. Goetz fled and later turned himself in, was tried, and claimed he was merely defending his life. While Goetz was on the lam the media, not knowing who exactly fired the shots, referred to the shooter as the "subway vigilante." A Manhattan jury eventually found Goetz innocent of attempted murder, assault, and reckless endangerment, but guilty of carrying an unlicensed firearm in the city.

Now, several factors make this case controversial. First, the youths never brandished the screwdrivers and had merely asked Goetz for the five dollars, so this makes Goetz's self-defense claim suspect. Second, Goetz claimed in his videotaped statement to police that "My intention was to murder them, to hurt them, to make them suffer as much as possible. . . . If I had more bullets, I would have shot them all again and again. My problem was I ran out of bullets." Third, Goetz mentions that after firing the first four shots, he walked up to Cabey (who was cowering in one of the train seats) and thought to himself, "You don't look so bad, here's another" just before firing the last shot of his .38 Special into Cabey, which was the shot that paralyzed him. Fourth, Goetz was white, while all of the youths were black, which effectively divided the nation all throughout the duration of this case and for as long as it was mentioned in the media.

Some have argued that this was a clear-cut case of Goetz being angry and intending to murder the youth; after all, Goetz has claimed as much! Others have argued that Goetz had to shoot the youths for fear of his own life and was intending to defend himself in the process. Interestingly enough, in a November 1985 interview, Cabey stated that the other members of the group planned to frighten and rob Goetz because he "looked like easy bait." And Canty told the first police officer on the scene, Peter Smith, "We were gonna rob him, but the white guy shot us first."

In May of 1985, Ramseur held a gun while his friend raped, sodomized, and robbed a pregnant eighteen-year-old woman on the rooftop of a Bronx building. He was caught, served thirteen years in the New York State Department of Corrections system, was released in 2010, and found dead in a Bronx motel room due to a drug overdose. Coincidentally, Ramseur was found on December 22nd, 2011, which was the twenty-seventh anniversary of the Goetz shooting. Allen committed two robberies in 1986 and 1991 (one was chain-snatching just like what Rob witnessed his first day of school on the El), and was sent to jail for four years. Canty was arrested many more times, entered a drug-treatment program, and was charged with assault, robbery, and resisting arrest in an altercation with his common-law wife in August 1996.

In 1996 Goetz was found guilty of reckless behavior for shooting Cabey and was ordered to pay $43 million to the paralyzed man; Goetz filed for bankruptcy soon after. In November of 2013, Goetz was caught trying to sell marijuana to an undercover cop. We'll leave you with the musings of a blogger from 2009:

> If Goetz had been wise, he wouldn't have fired right away. He should have pulled the gun and backed away; if any of those guys

made a move after that, THEN he should have fired. Seriously, I don't think a bunch of hoodlums would risk death just for a few bucks. This would have saved him the headache of a criminal trial, but still symbolized the whole "subway vigilante" thing.

If It Had Been Your Child, You Would Have Done the Same Thing Too

Google "Leon Gary Plauche video" and you'll be directed to a YouTube video from Court TV showing a decent-looking, unshaven handcuffed man in his mid-twenties wearing a burnt orange sweatshirt being escorted by two plainclothes officers in handcuffs past a line of payphones in what appears to be an airport. As the handcuffed man gets about halfway down the row of payphones, another man wearing a baseball cap, sunglasses, and light jacket who had been pretending to be making a phone call pulls a gun from his boot and shoots the handcuffed man in the side of the head. You can see the hair on the handcuffed man's head fly up in the air from the gun blast just before he falls flat on his face dead. The two plainclothes officers then subdue the shooter by pushing him up against the payphone, raising his arm, and grabbing the gun from his hand.

The shooter in the video is Leon Gary Plauche. The handcuffed man he shot dead was Jeff Doucet, who had just been extradited from California and was back in Baton Rouge, Louisiana to face charges that he had kidnapped and sexually assaulted Plauche's eleven-year-old son three weeks earlier sometime in February of 1984. The local TV station was at Baton Rouge's airport to film Doucet's arrival and caught the shooting on tape.

When asked "Why, Gary? Why did you do it?" by one of the officers at the airport, Plauche responded simply, "If it had been your child, you would have done the same thing too." Apparently, throughout most of 1983 Plauche's son, Jody, was taking karate lessons from Doucet and Doucet was fondling and molesting the boy. Plauche was charged with second-degree murder. In court, one of the psychologists who examined Plauche claimed that a "voice inside his head was telling him that he had to kill Doucet or else he would continue to abuse and harm his son." This defense worked, and Plauche was sentenced to five years probation and 300 hours of community service work, which he completed in 1989.

Some were outraged at the verdict claiming that Plauche straightforwardly murdered Doucet. Others, mostly parents, note that Plauche was completely justified in his actions claiming, "It's a basic law of nature to protect your own, no matter what." Plauche claims to this day that he did the right thing, and his son now travels around the US giving talks to people about sexual violence and abuse.

Justifiably Killing the Pedophile

Part of the 911 call went like this: "This guy's going to die! He's going to fucking die! The ambulance needs to get here! Come on!" The guy being referred to was Jesus Mora Flores. Apparently, Flores was a pedophile, and he did in fact die. Flores died because a twenty-three-year-old father discovered him in the act of raping his five-year-old daughter in the chicken coop on his ranch in Shiner, Texas (about 100 miles east of San Antonio), and beat Flores to a pulp. After the beating, the father realized that Flores was in bad shape and called 911.

The man had sent his son and daughter out to feed the chickens on the ranch in the late afternoon of Saturday, June 9th, 2013. The son came running into the house telling his dad that his sister had been abducted by Flores, a family acquaintance. The father could hear the girl's screams outside of the coop, and when he went inside found Flores and his daughter naked from the waist down with Flores on top of the girl. At the local hospital later that day, it was confirmed that the girl was sexually assaulted. A grand jury ultimately declined to indict the father for any crime, finding that he was justified in using deadly force to protect his daughter. In Texas, you can use deadly force in order to stop an aggravated sexual assault or sexual assault. "Flores got what he deserved, big time," said one Shiner native, while another noted, "I would probably have done worse."

However, some have wondered whether such use of deadly force is in fact justified. Indeed, in such a horrific and unimaginable moment, it's easy to believe that many parents would have reacted similarly. How could you control yourself from not beating this guy to death? But one or two or three blows probably would have been sufficient to separate Flores from the girl, while the dad pummeled him into unconsciousness, then death. That degree of force seemed unnecessary, many would claim. When all's said and done, there aren't any winners in this situation: a man is dead, a father killed someone, and a five-year-old is old enough to remember what happened to her for a very, very long time.

About Our Authors

CALEB ACTON, MA is an adjunct professor at Hope International University. His interests include process philosophy and ecology.

This is what Caleb did one time that was controversial (and some people didn't like it), but he felt justified and did it anyway:

> Closing a book by Simon Weil with the word "journey" on his mind, Caleb decided it was time to take a trek across the US without planned transportation. Ridding himself of cell phone, credit card, and everything but some books, water, and $50, he left the East Coast, flying westward. Detractors said it was too dangerous, it would take too long, and it was pointless if he had the means to fly, but Caleb felt justified by his innate desire for experience and adventure. Plus, he figured that if he died he'd at least get out of his student loans.

ROBERT ARP, PHD works as a researcher for the US Government. He has written and edited numerous books and articles in philosophy, ontology in the information-science sense, and other areas.

This is what Rob did one time that was controversial (and some people didn't like it), but he felt justified and did it anyway:

> There have been times when someone knowingly leaves their cart at the register, or their plates on a table of a restaurant where you're supposed to bus your own table—like a fast food place or a Panera's—

and Rob is present and has made a comment to the person along the lines of, "Oh, I think you forgot something" as they're getting ready to leave. They then get red faced and complete the task appropriately. He feels justified in doing this because it's like, "What the heck? Put stuff back where you found it, or clean up after yourself, gosh darn it!" It just so happens that Rob has done this kind of thing in front of his wife, and she doesn't like it, as it makes her feel a little embarrassed. She told me that she's embarrassed because the person gets embarrassed. "Who made you the morality police?" she asks. To which Rob always responds, "As a follower of Kant, I recognize the moral law as self-legislated by rational minds—of which I am a part—so the answer to your question is that I made myself the morality police, that's who." She smirks and says, "Uh huh. Okay, Dr. PHD . . . Piled Higher and Deeper." (She's actually more legalistic about things than I am. She's a wonderful person, and I love her to pieces.)

ADAM BARKMAN, PHD is Associate Professor of Philosophy and Chair of the Philosophy Department at Redeemer University College. He has authored and edited more than half a dozen books, most recently *The Culture and Philosophy of Ridley Scott.*

This is what Adam does sometimes that is controversial (and some people don't like it), but he feels justified and does it anyway:

Having four young kids at home, Barkman feels justified having the occasional drink before noon (especially when doing Play-Doh).

GERALD BROWNING is the Program Director of English at Baker College of Muskegon. He has written and published several short stories and his first novel, *Demon in My Head*, was published two years ago. He regularly keeps two blogs, writes comic book non-fiction, and writes essays. He's working towards finishing his PhD while training in three separate martial arts systems.

This is what Gerald did one time that was controversial (and some people didn't like it), but he felt justified and did it anyway:

Gerald is not a controversial person. He seeks to stay in the crowd and draw very little attention to himself. However, he found that in graduate work the genres of mystery and detective fiction were marginalized by his peers and at a cocktail party for the English faculty, he defended the scholastic merits of Dashiell Hammett and Raymond Chandler. His last words at the party were "If you'd take your head out of your ass long enough, you would see the social constructivism in Mickey Spillane rather than go to the obvious authors that you can find! Dumb ass!" To this day, he's still getting email regarding that "social faux pas."

ROD CARVETH, PHD is Graduate Program Director in the School of Global Journalism and Communication at Morgan State University in Baltimore.

This is what Rod did one time that was controversial (and some people didn't like it), but he felt justified and did it anyway:

One night, Rod talked a friend of his into going rowing with him. The problem was that the rowboat was on top of a seafood restaurant in his hometown (which was noted for its fishing). Though Rod and his friend had a great time, the owners were not pleased. Neither were the police, who felt compelled to have him and his friend visit their place of business for several hours. A firm believer in carpe diem, Rod felt justified.

CHRISTIAN COTTON, PHD teaches courses in philosophy and religion at Piedmont College in Northeast Georgia. His interests lie mainly in moral philosophy and moral psychology, especially the role of emotions in moral action.

What Christian did one time that was controversial (and some people didn't like it), but he felt justified and did it anyway:

Once, he was driving along a busy section of Interstate 20 through Louisiana, having a good time, listening to tunes, cruising along, when behind him he saw this car approaching . . . fast! The driver could easily have gotten over in the other lane, but no! He came barreling up on Christian's ass . . . so, he let him get right up on Christian, then Christian slammed on the brakes real quick and made the guy get over in the other lane. The guy shot by Christian cursing and flipped him off, but dammit, he felt good about it! Serves that guy right!

JON COTTON, MA works as a duck captain at Boston Duck Tours. He entertains and educates people about Boston by land and on the Charles River.

This is what Jon did one time that was controversial (but everyone liked it), but he felt justified and did it anyway:

> Once when Jon was giving a trolley tour to a tour group, a young lady was talking very loudly on the phone making it difficult for people to hear and focus on Jon's narrative. Jon politely asked if the lady might be willing to speak a little more quietly, and she shook her head "No" and smiled. Jon then politely inquired about location at which she might be disembarking, and she told him. Jon then cut the route short and drove directly to her stop and with utmost courtesy informed the young lady that this was her stop. Shocked, the young lady said "It can't be! Already?" And Jon with utmost courtesy referred her to the brochure and pointed out the window to corroborate, indeed, that this was the very location she had specified. The woman arose, confused, and Jon thanked her sincerely and spoke gracious words to her, then headed back to the right place in the schedule to restore order. And everyone enjoyed themselves, and no one told his boss.

JOANNA CROSBY, PHD is Associate Professor of Philosophy and Religious Studies at Morgan State University. Her areas of specialization include Critical Social Thought, Issues of Gender, Race, and Class, Michel Foucault, and Confucian Philosophy.

This is what Joanna did one time that was controversial (and some people didn't like it), but she felt justified and did it anyway:

> Joanna and her husband Michael had gone to see a movie at an old movie palace in walking distance from their house. The Senator Theatre is a fabulous place to see a film, if you are ever in Baltimore. Gorgeous architecture. Big, cushy seats that recline. Cup holders on both arms. Michael, who used to own a snobby video rental store, thought of the movie theatre as a sacred space. Nothing pissed him off more or faster than someone talking in a theatre. Even if the movie was Con Air. A few minutes into the movie, a gentleman in the row behind them and a few seats off to the right, asked his wife, several times, about what was going on in the movie. Again, Con Air—not a difficult plot to follow. Joanna could feel the waves of anger coming off of Michael, and was not surprised when leaned back in his seat and asked the couple to be quiet. Of course, Michael's opening salvo was "Shut the fuck up." Yes, Joanna married a diplomat. At the end of the movie, the couple in question at the end of the isle waiting for Michael and Joanna. The man with the hearing problem and Michael begin arguing with one another. Joanna

inserted herself between the two men, not taking seriously the escalating tension, and the woman said to Joanna, "Don't you touch my husband, missy!" Joanna responded, "That's Dr. Missy to you!" The woman snorted. "Doctor of what?" she asked, incredulously. Proud as punch, Joanna declared "Doctor of Philosophy!" Shortly thereafter, both couples were encouraged to leave the theater by different exits. Walking home, Joanna knew she had been justified.

ALEXANDER DICK, PHD is Associate Professor of English at the University of British Columbia in Vancouver. His latest book is *Romanticism and the Gold Standard: Money, Literature, and Economic Debate in Britain 1790–1830* (2013). He has also published several articles on literature, philosophy, and political economy.

This is what Alex did one time that was controversial (and some people didn't like it), but he felt justified and did it anyway:

Alex used to be a rock drummer and played in lots of bands—some good, some not so much. One time he was playing in a pretty big club with one of the not-so-good bands and interrupted a song to play an awesome fifteen-minute drum solo. The rest of the band was annoyed but he got a standing ovation anyway. The band broke up soon after.

LINDA ENGLISH, PHD is Associate Professor of History at the University of Texas–Pan American and an American historian who focuses on region, gender, race, and class in her research and publications.

See Cynthia Jones's bio below.

JOHN FITZPATRICK, PHD is a lecturer in philosophy at the University of Tennessee, Chattanooga. He's the author of *John Stuart Mill's Political Philosophy: Balancing Freedom and the Collective Good* (2006), and *Starting with Mill* (2010). He's also a contributor to several Popular Culture and Philosophy books.

This is what John does sometimes that is controversial (and some people don't like it), but he feels justified and does it anyway:

The conventional wisdom is that you should never give cash to homeless people, because they will spend it on drugs or alcohol; buy them some food instead. But John routinely violates this principle, reasoning as follows: If I'm willing to help, I see no reason not to supply cash money. First, there is some fairly reliable empirical evidence that people in these situations (where they are reduced to begging) normally tell the truth about what they need. Secondly, if one has the general skepticism about Ronald Reagan's Cadillac driving welfare queens, and find the distinction between deserving and undeserving poor often unhelpful, then the idea that some poor people enjoy getting intoxicated and might want to do so is less than shocking. And since I find myself now and then in the situation where I have nothing better to do than knock back a few cold beers, why should I not think poor people find themselves in similar situations? If anything, it would seem easier to argue that someone in my situation could almost always find something more productive to do.

PETER S. FOSL, PhD is a Kentucky Colonel (HOKC), Professor of Philosophy at Transylvania University in Lexington, Kentucky, and a David Hume Fellow with the IASH at the University of Edinburgh. Co-author of *The Philosopher's Toolkit* and editor of *The Big Lebowski and Philosophy*, Fosl's interests include skepticism and bourbon. See: www.PeterFosl.us.

What Peter did one time that was controversial (and some people didn't like it), but he felt justified and did it anyway:

When Peter was a kid he saw a boy from up the block named Todd steal the batteries from the enormous, laser-sound-emitting, ribbon-streaming headlight he had mounted on the handlebars of his pride and joy—his banana-seated-sissy-bar-sporting bicycle. Peter chased Todd home and marched up to the front door, demanding from Todd's mother that the batteries be returned, posthaste. Todd's mom responded with the indignant rebuke that her "little angel" would never have done such a thing. After the screen door slammed shut, Peter, mouth gaping, stomped off. But rather than return home, Peter took the law into his own hands and found a baseball bat in Todd's garage—fatefully, a Louisville, Kentucky, Slugger. That Slugger became Peter's favorite bat. Todd didn't much like it, but the Slugger swung with gusto every time Peter played ball against Todd's team.

SANDRA HANSMANN, PhD is Associate Professor in Rehabilitation and the Director of International Programs at the University of Texas-Pan American.

See Cynthia Jones's bio below.

About Our Authors

MICHAEL JAWORSKI, PhD is a lecturer in the Philosophy Department at the University of Texas–Pan American. Current research projects include studies of animal morality and God of the Gaps reasoning.

What Mike did one time that was controversial (and some people didn't like it), but he felt justified and did it anyway:

> Mike was asked to write a brief account for a book he was contributing to about something controversial he had done, but then he looked at a stack of 250 final essays waiting to be graded, and felt totally justified in sending back a really short, smart-ass response that referred to itself as the example.

CYNTHIA JONES, PhD is Associate Professor of Philosophy and the Director of the Ethics Center and the Campus Violence Prevention Project at the University of Texas–Pan American.

Cynthia, Sandy, Linda, and Anne were asked to write a brief account of a controversial action they had taken, but disobligingly they decided not to do it. They felt justified in not writing the recollections because they had already co-authored several pieces for the Popular Culture and Philosophy series, and Cynthia had even contributed two chapters to the present volume! Although some disagreed with their actions, most especially one of the editors, who continued to send them emails all summer, they remained resolute in their decision. For more biographical information about these professors, come on down to the pool, and bring a damn margarita.

CLINT JONES, PhD is currently Visiting Professor of Philosophy at the University of Wisconsin–Stevens Point. He has published several articles on popular culture and philosophy and his second book is being published soon on the individual and utopia.

This is what Clint did one time that was controversial (and some people didn't like it), but he felt justified and did it anyway:

> As an undergrad, Clint found himself displeased by the academic environment fostered by the administration, so he decided to make his graduation a platform for criticism and protest. His friends and family, and some of his professors, were whole-heartedly supportive of his actions, but many weren't, especially because it was graduation. But

Clint felt justified because something needed to be done to draw attention to the waning academic climate.

JULIA M. MASON, PHD is Associate Professor of Women and Gender Studies at Grand Valley State University in Allendale, Michigan. She has written articles and chapters about the representation of women in popular culture.

What Julia did one time that was controversial (and some people didn't like it), but she felt justified and did it anyway:

Julia was the co-narrator for the GVSU production of The Vagina Monologues. The play is controversial for its use of language and bold discussion of women's sexuality (and some people didn't like it), but Julia feels justified because the V-Day movement is about ending gender-based violence.

ANTHONY PALAZZO is a licensed professional counselor/renegade mystic/freelance malcontent/adventurer in private practice. His interests are primarily in the realm of folklore, myth, primordial spiritual traditions, alternative psychotherapies, wilderness wandering, maintaining a state of preparedness for catastrophic social collapses, and anarcho-primitivism. He currently lives on the forested and rugged coast of Maine.

What Anthony did one time that was controversial (and some people didn't like it), but he felt justified and did it anyway:

While still an intern, Anthony had a client, a thirteen year-old girl in foster care. A good girl, but naive and reckless. She was one of the first clients he forged a real therapeutic bond with. She allowed some shady thirty-year-old man from Texas to talk her into "running away with him" to get married. She slipped away from her foster mother's home late one night, and was kidnapped, taken down to the Mexico-Texas border. In the multi-department and multi-agency panic that followed, Anthony was instructed to take no action, and let "the other authorities" handle the situation. Feeling that perhaps other important persons (and their agencies) were not willing to risk getting in trouble over this girl, especially since it seemed likely she'd be found floating face-down in the Rio Grande, Anthony researched her Facebook contacts until he discovered the man that seemed like a likely candidate to be her husband—and he was right. Contacting him through a number he had left on his wall for another friend, Anthony began a long text conversation—seven hours long—with him and her. In the end, Anthony convinced him to come out of hiding and surrender himself and her to the police down on the border. She's seventeen and happy now; he's in jail for a long time yet.

ROBERTO SIRVENT, PHD is Associate Professor of Political and Social Ethics at Hope International University. His interests include political theory, existentialist thought, and philosophy of religion.

This is what Roberto did one time that was controversial (and some people didn't like it), but he felt justified and did it anyway:

One day in college he was playing Scattergories with a large group of friends. Halfway through the game, the letter B was rolled so everyone was expected to name an object within five different categories beginning with that letter. One of these categories was "State." While everyone failed miserably because they couldn't think of a state in our country that began with B, Roberto and his genius teammate (and fellow Kierkegaard admirer) Tony went another route. They wrote down the word "boredom." After reading their answer proudly, Roberto was shocked to see the entire group reject this answer and vote not to award him any points! No matter how hard he tried, Roberto couldn't stop his elitist and condescending side from coming out. "Are you serious??" he yelled. "What the hell did we do wrong? Isn't the whole point of the game to be this creative and this brilliant??" Roberto quit playing that night. And he vowed never to play that game ever again.

ANNE MARIE STACHURA, PHD is Assistant Professor of Spanish and the Interim Director of Medical Spanish at the University of Texas-Pan American.

See Cynthia Jones's bio above.

NATHAN VERBAAN is currently pursuing a graduate degree in philosophy with an interest in logic and metaphysics.

This is what Nathan has done that is controversial (and some people don't like it), but he feels justified and does it anyway:

Nathan feels himself justified performing a number of controversial activities, but few he savors more than preventing cross-country runners who cheat from placing.

About Our Authors

PAUL ZINDER is Senior Lecturer in Film Production at the University of Gloucestershire. He is co-editor of the anthology *The Multiple Worlds of* Fringe: *Essays on the J.J. Abrams Science Fiction Series* (2014), and his writing on genre and cult television appears in the volumes *Contemporary Westerns: Film and Television Since 1990* (2013), *The Last Western:* Deadwood *and the End of American Empire* (2012), *Investigating* Veronica Mars: *Essays on the Teen Detective Series* (2011), and *Investigating* Alias: *Secrets and Spies* (2007). He's also an award-winning filmmaker whose work can be seen at www.paulzinder.com.

This is what Paul did one time that was controversial (and some people didn't like it), but he felt justified and did it anyway:

When the gorgeous new administrator arrived at Paul's former institution, he was immediately enamored with her. Although he quickly learned that she was unavailable, he regularly visited her office to flirt and hang around. When the university announced her resignation due to her impending relocation to another country, Paul reasoned that it was time to tell her how he felt, inviting her out under the guise of a "thank you" drink. Nine happy years and two beautiful children later, Paul feels like she was justified in her decision to leave that guy.

Index